EARTHQUAKE
RESURRECTION

Supernatural Catalyst for the Coming Global Catastrophe

su·per·nat·u·ral (soo'per-natch'er-ul) adj. Of or relating to the immediate exercise of divine power; miraculous.

cat·a·lyst (kat'a list) n. Something that precipitates a process or event, especially without being involved in or changed by the consequences.

ca·tas·tro·phe (ka'tas tro-fee) n. A sudden violent change in the earth's surface; a cataclysm.

EARTHQUAKE RESURRECTION

Supernatural Catalyst for the Coming
Global Catastrophe

David W. Lowe

- TABLE OF CONTENTS -

This book is dedicated in loving memory of my mother and father, Janice and Jerry.

Special thanks to my wife Vivienne for encouragement during this project. I love you very much.

I thank Tony B. for your stimulating input in this work and your willingness to discuss ideas; Peter G. for your book <u>Red Moon Rising</u> and your web site, which got me started on this work; Terrence T. for your sharing of ideas and for your encouragement; Sharon B. for the email telling me to boldly state my points rather than suggest them, and for your prayers and your input on chapter 6; and Mike S. for helping me to avoid the mistake of delving into Greek and Roman mythology; and finally, Cory F. for your words of encouragement, and your amazing work on my cover and the web site. All of your help and influence was instrumental in bringing this work to fruition.

Finally, to my Creator and Savior Jesus Christ, thank you for your unprecedented courage and humility in the face of unimaginable suffering. You alone are worthy of all my praise.

- FOREWORD -

Reverend Gail B. Ott

* * *

It is with joy and a sense of justifiable pride that I write the Foreword for David Lowe's new book, <u>Earthquake Resurrection</u>.

As a born-again Christian, minister of the gospel, and avid student of the Word of God for over 50 years, I have always had a keen interest in Bible prophecy. It is interesting, fascinating, and enlightening. In a very real sense, it is "the story of the future"–history written in advance! Anyone can guess, imagine, or speculate–a work of fiction does this; but God alone can accurately tell what will happen in the future. He possesses an Eternal Plan and has revealed it to us through Bible prophecy. In Isaiah 41:22-23 the Lord God challenges false gods saying, "Let them bring forth and show what will happen . . ." But while walking the earth, the Lord Jesus Christ stated in John 14:29, "And now I have told you *before it come to pass*, that when it is come to pass, you might believe."

In this book, David Lowe has brilliantly woven together a clear, concise, and comprehensive teaching from the inspired writers of both the Old and New Testaments concerning end-time events leading up to the glorious appearing of our Lord Jesus Christ! As you read and study its contents, this author will introduce you to a wealth of scriptural truths. His profound insight into the prophetic scriptures and superb writing skills will lift you to a new level of understanding.

There are many books to choose from dealing with the subject of Bible prophecy that are good. This work is excellent! In it, the author has provided a volume of sacred truths that are sure to abide unto the dawning of that great and notable day of the Lord. It is unquestionably, a rare masterpiece!

I would caution the reader not to peruse this book as you might read a novel or a newspaper. The nuggets of truth uncovered in this volume are both sacred and binding–much too precious and powerful to be considered lightly. As you read and study the truths presented on every page, let it build encouragement and understanding into your daily walk with Christ.

What you hold in your hand is a precious jewel for every serious believer in the Lord Jesus Christ who hunger and thirst for enlightenment and understanding concerning God's Eternal Plan for His redeemed ones. It is sure to bless and stir the hearts of all who are earnestly contending for the faith once delivered unto the saints. I wholeheartedly recommend <u>Earthquake Resurrection</u> to anyone sincerely interested in a deeper, more clear understanding of the prophetic scriptures.

Sincerely in Christ,

Rev. Gail B. Ott
(Uncle of the author)

- INTRODUCTION -

There are several different styles of Bible prophecy interpretation, including preterism, spiritualism, historicism, and futurism. The style used in this book would be best described as a hybrid of the historical and futuristic style, which will become clear throughout the book. What follows are the rules of scripture interpretation that were used in development of this prophetic model.

Rules of Scripture Interpretation

<u>Rule 1</u>. When a prophetic verse or portion of prophetic scripture clearly makes logical sense with a literal interpretation, one should seek no other sense, but interpret it literally.

This is a very important undertaking, because, if the Holy Spirit is attempting to convey a message using literal language, but the reader attempts to symbolize it, the reader has missed the message. This is also true if the Holy Spirit is attempting to convey a message using symbolism, and the reader attempts to take the symbols in a literal fashion. Using the first and second rules, the reader can better understand when a passage should be taken literally or symbolically.

The first rule can be exercised when attempting to interpret the meaning of the 144,000 sealed individuals who mysteriously appear in Revelation chapter 7. Many authors have expounded on their identity. Some believe they are representative of Christians throughout history, sealed symbolically with God's name on their foreheads. Others view them as representing a Jewish remnant on the earth during the beginning of the Daniel's 70th week.

This rule requires that a passage should be interpreted literally when it makes logical sense to do so. Therefore, when the scripture indicates that the 144,000 are made up of 12,000 men from each of twelve tribes of Israel, that is how the passage should be interpreted:

Rev 7:4 Now I heard the number of those who were marked with a seal, one hundred and forty-four thousand, **sealed from all the tribes of the people of Israel**:

The verses that follow further elaborate on what verse four means, as twelve different tribes of Israel from which 12,000 different men are chosen are listed by name. Therefore, it makes the most logical sense to interpret this passage literally rather than symbolically: that 144,000 men will receive a literal seal on their foreheads which will be the name of God, and that those men will be 12,000 in number from each of twelve tribes of Israel.

Rule 2. When a prophetic verse or portion of prophetic scripture clearly makes sense only with a symbolic interpretation, one should interpret it symbolically.

To understand what certain symbols used throughout the Bible were meant to represent, the whole of scripture must be surveyed. The exercise of this rule produces a most desirable result: scripture interprets scripture. A good example is the following passage from Revelation chapter 13:

> Rev 13:1 Then I saw a **beast** coming up out of the sea. It had **ten horns** and seven heads, and on its horns were ten diadem crowns, and on its heads a blasphemous name.
> Rev 13:2 Now the **beast** that I saw was **like a leopard**, but its feet were **like a bear**'s, and its mouth was **like a lion**'s mouth. The **dragon** gave the **beast** his power, his throne, and great authority to rule.

The most logical interpretation is that the beast, horns, heads, and dragon in this passage are symbolic rather than literal. The beast with ten horns that came out of the sea is further associated in verse two with a leopard, a bear, and a lion. A passage in Daniel, written hundreds of years before Revelation, includes information about the symbols of the beast being like a leopard, a bear, and a lion:

> Dan 7:4 "The first one was **like a lion** with eagles' wings. As I watched, its wings were pulled off and it was lifted up from the ground. It was made to stand on two feet like a human being and a human mind was given to it.
> Dan 7:5 Then a second beast appeared, **like a bear**. It was raised up on one side, and there were three ribs in its mouth between its teeth. It was told, 'Get up and devour much flesh!'
> Dan 7:6 After these things, as I was watching, another beast **like a leopard** appeared, with four bird-like wings on its back. This beast had four heads, and ruling authority was given to it.

The two passages, when studied together, reveal that the writer of Revelation intended his readers to go back to the prophecies in Daniel in order to understand what the symbols of the lion, bear, and leopard represent.

Rule 3. The Lord uses patterns and parallels to establish truth throughout the Word. Prophetic scripture should be examined in light of their prophetic patterns and parallels.

Much time could be spent to show the myriad of examples of prophetic patterns and parallels in the Bible. Those examples include Abraham's near sacrifice of Isaac on Mount Moriah and the many parallels to the Father and Jesus Christ. The patterns in the temple plans given to Moses which point to the coming of Christ and his fulfillment of them. The parallels of the ashes of the red heifer to the crucifixion of Jesus Christ. The seven major feasts of Israel and how Jesus Christ's birth, life, death, burial, and resurrection were all fulfilled within the activities of the feasts. However, a passage in Colossians sums it up well:

Col 2:16 Therefore do not let anyone judge you with respect to food or drink, or in the matter of a feast, new moon, or Sabbath days—

Col 2:17 these are only the **shadow of the things to come**, but the reality is Christ!

The reality of the feasts and Sabbath celebrations set up by the Lord in the past is Jesus Christ. An extension of this rule is the awareness that to understand the future by reading the scriptures of prophecy, one must go back and look at the past. This is a tenet established by the Lord himself in the book of Ecclesiasties:

Ecc 1:9 What exists now is what will be, and **what has been done is what will be done**; there is nothing truly new on earth.

Ecc 3:15 Whatever exists now has already been, and whatever will be has already been; for **God will seek to do again what has occurred in the past**.

Patterns and parallels within scripture provide important clues for the student of prophecy, and this rule was paramount both in the discovery and the development of the information in this book.

Rule 4. The original Hebrew and Greek manuscripts, penned by the original authors, are the inspired Word of God, not any translation of them.

Unfortunately, none of the original full-length manuscripts written by the original authors are still in existence. What exists are early copies of those originals, or copies of copies, and with some books there are hundreds of copies. The King James Version (KJV) of the Bible is the most popular English translation of the Greek and Hebrew manuscripts. The history of the KJV, and the manuscripts on which it is based, is a topic that has been covered by literally thousands of authors. Therefore the long and interesting history of the KJV will be only briefly explored below.

The 1611 King James Version was based principally upon Theodore de Beza's 1588, 1589, and 1598 editions of the Greek New Testament, which themselves differed little from the printed Greek editions of Desiderius Erasmus of 1527 and 1535 and those of Robert Stephanus published between 1546 and 1551. The self-proclaimed "Textus Receptus," published by the Elzevir printing family in their 1633 edition of the Greek New Testament, was based primarily on de Beza's 1565 edition. The KJV itself was published in 1611, before the Textus Receptus in 1633. Both, however, were based upon the earlier editions of Erasmus, Stephanus, and de Beza.

These were all noble efforts of their day, but they did not have access to the wealth of additional manuscripts that have been found since that time. In fact, as older Greek manuscripts were discovered during these years of publication, these editions were corrected in several places to conform to the earliest and most reliable manuscripts. Over the years scholars have noted many editorial errors in the Erasmus editions, including typological errors as well as readings that were based upon the Latin Vulgate rather than any known Greek manuscripts. Some of these errors were even reproduced and found their way into later editions, upon which the KJV was ultimately based. These errors included several words in Revelation and 1 John which do not appear in any other ancient manuscript or papyri preserved to this day.[1]

Despite these perceived limitations, the KJV is a worthy translation into the English language, and was instrumental in the preparation of this book. However, a new translation that also exhibits solid scholarship and textual criticism is the New English Translation, or NET. This translation is used almost exclusively in the scripture passages quoted in this book.

Rule 5. It is not only beneficial, but a necessity, to understand the meaning of the underlying Hebrew and Greek words, and to study where key words and phrases are cross-referenced.

Many times, the Greek and Hebrew languages do not easily or coherently translate into English. Some words and phrases simply do not have a good, clear English counterpart. Therefore, proper understanding of the meaning of scripture is almost always enhanced by study of the meaning of the original Hebrew and Greek words. An example of studying the different Greek words compared to their English counterparts follows:

King James Version:
I Cor 1:7 So that ye come behind in no gift; waiting for **the coming [apokalupsin] of our Lord Jesus Christ**:

II The 2:1 Now we beseech you, brethren, by **the coming [parousias] of our Lord Jesus Christ**, and by our gathering together unto him,

The same author, the apostle Paul, wrote identical phrases to the Corinthians and the Thessalonians: "the coming of our Lord Jesus Christ". As seen above, the KJV uses the word "coming" in both cases, yet in the Greek, two different Greek words are used: *parousia* and *apokalupsis*.

A casual reading of these passages might result in skipping by these verses without giving any thought about whether the underlying word for "coming" is the

---

[1] For a thorough discussion of the origin of the Textus Receptus and King James Version, see Bruce M. Metzger, *The Text of the New Testament: Its Transmission, Corruption, and Restoration*, 3d enlarged ed. New York: Oxford University Press, 1992, pp. 95–106.

same in both verses. However, knowing that two different Greek words for "coming" were used, it would be interesting to discover what each word meant, and the other instances in which each word was used in the New Testament. The technique of studying where, how many times, and in what context certain key Hebrew and Greek words and phrases are used in scripture was used extensively in the development of this book.

Rule 6. The historical context and setting in which a book or epistle in the Bible is written is extremely important to understand the deeper, hidden meaning behind the text.

With the knowledge that a letter Paul wrote to the Ephesians was written while he was sitting in a Roman jail, light is shed upon his revelation of the armor of God in Ephesians chapter 6. Perhaps Paul was looking at the armor of a Roman guard standing next to his cell as he penned the descriptions of the various pieces of God's armor. Likewise, knowing that the Roman Empire had taken over Palestine, where Jesus Christ lived and ministered, would shed light upon the reason why the Jewish leaders reacted toward Jesus the way they did as recorded in the gospels. The Pharisees, priests, and scribes were no doubt extremely pleased that the Roman Empire was allowing them to continue their sacrifices in the temple. The arrival of Jesus Christ preaching about a different kingdom and the fulfillment of the ceremonial law of Moses was an unwelcome hindrance.

Understanding the context and time in which Revelation was written is also very important. John wrote the book while on Patmos, an island prisoner of the Roman Empire. This sheds light upon perhaps why so much of his letter to the seven churches had to be so heavily veiled in symbolism. Some of the content was in opposition to the rule of the Roman Empire, and if John had referred to them directly, his revelation may have been suppressed, never reaching its intended recipients.

Additional Points of Reference

In addition to these rules, the reader is encouraged to keep the following points in mind as progression is made through this book:

- The prophetic model presented in this book is in no way associated with a "preterist" approach to prophetic interpretation. In addition, the author has no affiliation with the Seventh Day Adventist church.
- While the use of the terms "rapture" and "tribulation period" are commonly understood among those who study prophecy, these two concepts will be referred to as "the catching-up of believers" and "Daniel's 70th week", respectively, throughout the book.

- The book has been purposely structured to unveil information in a particular order. To realize the full benefit of this structure, each chapter should be read in the order presented.
- The *Anno Domini*, or "In the Year of our Lord", system of dating was established in 525 AD by a monk named Dionysius Exiguus. Although the AD and BC system of dating is the dominant system of dating used in the world today, almost all scholars agree that Dionysius was incorrect in his dating of the birth of Jesus Christ, for many reasons. Because of this, most of the BC and AD dates used throughout the book will be qualified with "approximately".
- Scripture quotations, unless otherwise noted, are from the New English Translation of the Bible (NET). The scripture is quoted by permission, copyright © 2003 Biblical Studies Press, L.L.C. All scriptures quoted will be indented from the left. All other non-scripture quotations will be indented from both the left and the right, and footnoted.
- Throughout this book, Hebrew, Greek, and Latin words and phrases will be analyzed. They have been presented in their transliterated English form rather than in the original language, and they are presented in *italicized* font.

Cognitive Dissonance Versus Impartial Evaluation

Cognitive dissonance is the psychological discomfort felt when a discrepancy arises between what one already knows or believes, and new information or interpretation that is presented. Beyond mere discomfort, cognitive dissonance can ultimately result in resistance and rejection of the new information that is in conflict with what one has been taught or believes.

In all likelihood, most who read this book will have already been taught, and may have therefore already developed a belief in, certain aspects of Bible prophecy. Perhaps the reader has studied other books and videos on prophecy which now shape the views that are held. This was definitely the case with this author, and only through dedicated independent study did new insights arise.

When Paul and Silas entered the Macedonian city of Berea, they were confronted by a surprising attitude among the Jews there. In contrast to the Jews of Thessalonica, the Berean Jews:

> Act 17:11 . . .were **more open-minded** than those in Thessalonica, for they eagerly received the message, **examining the scriptures carefully every day to see if these things were so.**

The views that will be presented in this book will likely be new information to the reader, and the natural reaction will be discomfort and resistance. My prayer is that the reader, like the Berean Jews, will first be open to consider the information that is presented herein with impartiality, then be inspired to delve deep into the Word of God to test what has been presented.

Current Events

The production of this book was overlapped by two of the most horrible natural disasters in history: the Sumatran earthquake and resulting tsunami on December 26, 2004, and Hurricane Katrina on August 29, 2005, the latter of the two occurring just days before the official date of publication. In both cases, unfathomable destruction and humanitarian catastrophe was broadcast over the airwaves, available 24 hours a day. The scenes that I witnessed were almost too unbearable to watch, as tears welled up in my eyes more than once. Those who provided eyewitness reports from both sites of destruction described what they saw as being as bad as "Armageddon", "like hell on Earth", and "of Biblical proportions". Unfortunately, the catastrophe and chaos resulting from the tsunami and Hurricane Katrina will pale in comparison to the global catastrophe to come.

Never would I have dreamed that the writing of this book would be accompanied by such unwelcome corroboration of what is described in the Bible. Chapters 7 and 18 will detail the similarities between what happened with the Sumatran tsunami disaster and what will likely happen in the future. Yet, as bad as these recent disasters have been, even more ominous disasters are currently brewing. Mount St. Helens is coming back to life, with its lava dome growing again and reports of hundreds of earthquakes underneath the volcano. Plankton and other sea life along the coastal regions are showing up dead, sea beds are deteriorating, and water temperatures are rising: all signs of rising seismic and volcanic activity. The New Madrid fault zone in the center of the United States has recently been showing increasing seismic activity, a fault which in 1811 and 1812 produced the first, second, and fourth largest contiguous United States earthquakes in history.

In addition, the massive supervolcano under Yellowstone National Park is slowly rising, and has been doing so for many years. Fish are dying in lakes and rivers as the water is heated by the underlying magma getting closer to the surface. Over 300 elk were either dead or dying due to what scientists believe is sulfur permeating the air surrounding the park. Trees around the park are dying due to the rising sulfur in the ground. Visitors are also complaining of the intense smell of sulfur, so bad that they cannot vacation there for more than a couple days. Certain parts of the park, normally accessible by visitors, are being blocked because the ground is too hot to walk on. New mudspots and geysers are springing up on a daily basis, and the number of earthquakes around the caldera have been increasing steadily in recent years. These are all signs that pressure is intensifying under Yellowstone National Park.

So many are oblivious to these developments, unaware that Yellowstone National Park even houses one of the largest supervolcanoes on the earth. The time seems to be growing very short before catastrophe will overtake not only the North American continent, but the entire globe. That is what this book is about, so without further delay, it is time to begin the journey into Earthquake Resurrection: Supernatural Catalyst for the Coming Global Catastrophe.

David Lowe
September 5, 2005

- SECTION I -

THE FUTURE HOPE OF BELIEVERS

Dream Journal – David Lowe

Sunday, April 21, 2002

It's actually Tuesday, April 23, 2002, so I am a couple days late in recording this dream. That I am still able to remember what happened in such detail is a testament to how vivid this dream was. It seems like the images are branded into my memory; I can still see the incredible scenes in my mind when I close my eyes...

- CHAPTER ONE -

I TELL YOU A MYSTERY . . .

1.1 The Moment of the Ages

A significant moment in history is inevitably approaching. It is a moment in the strictest sense of the word, occupying the same amount of time as the shutter of an eyelash. Or perhaps the flapping of the wings of a hummingbird. In Greek, it is *atomos*, the smallest lapse of time that can be imagined. One scientist calls it "The Omega Point".

It is a moment about which the apostles of Christ left tantalizingly few details, yet what details they did leave are sufficient that libraries could be filled with the books, essays, and articles that have been written about it. This moment has been speculated about, pontificated upon, and analyzed from many angles, yet its mysteries still haunt even the most astute scholars.

In this moment, the hope of every believer in Jesus Christ throughout the ages will be realized. The central theme of the Christian faith is enveloped within this moment, yet it is still shrouded in mystery. That it will happen is not the mystery, but how. It is indeed ironic that the central hope of Christianity–the bedrock of the faith– is also its deepest mystery.

The brevity of the moment will be surpassed by the profound impact it will leave on the earth and its inhabitants. On the earth, topographical devastation and utter chaos; it will be forever scarred as a result of the convergence of a supernatural power in a natural world. For the earth's surviving inhabitants, shock, grief, and desperation will prevail. The moment will be comprised of a three-stage event that will affect every covenant member of the faith throughout history. It will alter the course of history and plunge the world into a period of wrath and vengeance foretold by the prophets of the Lord.

In the chapters to follow, the reader will embark on an intense study of the scriptures that describe this future three-stage event. The first stage will be the resurrection of the dead in Christ. The second stage will be the transformation of the bodies of believers. These two stages will take place simultaneously in that moment. The third stage will be the forcible catching up of all living believers.

It is this third stage upon which so much focus has been placed. In popular books and movies, the "rapture" receives much of the attention due to its mysterious description in the Bible. Images come to mind of movies such as "Left Behind" and "A Thief in the Night": a car is left without occupants; clothing draped on the seat; a frantic teenager comes home looking for parents but finds only an iron left running on the ironing board; bed sheets are thrown back only to reveal vacated pajamas; news reports of millions of people disappearing; planes falling out of the sky because the pilot has disappeared. What has been neglected in these popular books and movies, however, are the first two stages of the event: the resurrection and the transformation, and what consequences will be felt as a result of each.

Because the prophetic record is so broad, complex, and interwoven, a narrow and detailed focus on just a few topics is desirable. The primary focus of this model will be on the time leading up to the future three-stage event, the event itself, and the time just after the event. Those expecting a commentary on what will take place during Daniel's 70th week, such as the beast, the false prophet, the mark of the beast, the image of the beast, and the battle of Armageddon, will be best suited to look elsewhere.

First, a foundation will be laid with a discussion of this three-stage event, incorporating Greek and Hebrew word studies. Next, a prophetic model will be introduced explaining how this three-stage event may take place and what will happen on the earth as a result of the event. The prophetic model will be based upon an interesting pattern contained in the scriptures. After the introduction of this prophetic model, a unique study of the where this event fits within the chronology of the Book of Revelation will follow. This study will provide confirmation of the foundation and the model, and will take the traditional interpretation of Revelation chapters 4 through 7 to a new level. These chapters will never be viewed the same way again.

1.2 The Importance of Prophecy

The importance of the study and understanding of prophetic scripture has a solid basis throughout the Bible. It was stressed not only by the apostles and prophets, but by Jesus Christ. If the understanding of the prophetic scriptures relating to the first coming of Jesus Christ to the earth was important, then likewise, discernment of those relating to his second coming are at least equally important. Below are some important reasons why all believers should have a solid understanding in prophetic scripture.

1. Jesus honored the disciple's quest for prophetic knowledge.

Near the end of the ministry of Jesus Christ, some of his disciples came to him privately and asked him about the signs of his coming and signs of the end of the age:

> Mat 24:3 As he was sitting on the Mount of Olives, his disciples came to him privately and said, "Tell us, when will these things happen? And what will be the sign of your coming and of the end of the age?"

Jesus did not rebuke these disciples or call them sign-seekers. Instead of telling them to be more concerned with other issues, Jesus gave them one of the most profound prophetic discourses in all of scripture, spanning Matthew chapters 24 and 25. This sincere quest for knowledge and discernment in the disciples was not suppressed or discouraged. Believers today can therefore be assured that the quest for understanding of his second coming is a worthy pursuit.

2.   Jesus rebuked the Jewish leaders for <u>not</u> discerning the prophetic signs.

In contrast, Jesus himself rebuked Jewish leaders of his day for failing to discern the signs of the first coming of the Messiah. On one occasion, Jesus was confronted by the Pharisees and Sadducees, who asked him to produce a sign from heaven that he was who he claimed to be. Jesus complemented their ability to discern weather patterns, but rebuked them for their inability to evaluate the spiritually significant signs of that present time. Instead of a sign from heaven, Jesus hinted only at the sign of Jonah the prophet, who was a model of the death, burial, and resurrection of Christ.

On another occasion, Jesus wept over the entire city of Jerusalem because they failed to discern the time in which they were living–a time when the Lord himself visited them with a physical presence:

> Mat 19:44 They will demolish you—you and your children within your walls—and they will not leave within you one stone on top of another, **because you did not recognize the time of your visitation from God**."

How could his contemporaries have recognized the time of their visitation from God? By studying the prophetic scriptures in Daniel. The final four verses of Daniel chapter 9 detail the precise amount of time from the announcement to rebuild the temple in Jerusalem until the coming of the Messiah to be 483 years. If they would have calculated the number of years, they would have known that the time in which Jesus was living were the days the Messiah was to appear on the earth. Believers today should also be watching the signs for the second coming.

3.   Believers are exhorted to look for the Lord's next appearing.

Paul exhorted believers to continue to assemble together for meetings, but to do so even more as they saw the day of the coming of Jesus Christ approaching:

> Heb 10:25 not abandoning our own meetings, as some are in the habit of doing, but encouraging each other, and even more so because you see the day drawing near.

How were the people to know that the day of Christ's coming was drawing near? Is there any other way to do this but to understand the prophetic scriptures of the Old and New Testament? In another passage, Paul admonished his readers that the Lord will return for those who are eagerly waiting for his second appearing:

Heb 9:28 so also, after Christ was offered once to bear the sins of many, **to those who eagerly await him he will appear a second time**, not to bear sin but to bring salvation.

4.   Prophets of old searched the scriptures for the coming of the Messiah.

Possibly the most robust passage concerning the study of prophetic scripture is one penned by the apostle Peter in his first epistle. In explaining how the prophets both wrote and studied their own prophecies in searching for the promised salvation of God, Peter revealed the following:

I Pet 1:10 Concerning this salvation, the prophets who predicted the grace that would come to you **searched and investigated carefully**.

I Pet 1:11 They **probed into what person or time** the Spirit of Christ within them **was indicating** when he testified beforehand about the sufferings appointed for Christ and his subsequent glory.

I Pet 1:12 They were shown that **they were serving not themselves but you**, in regard to the things now announced to you through those who proclaimed the gospel to you by the Holy Spirit sent from heaven—things angels long to catch a glimpse of.

This is an awesome revelation regarding the diligence of the prophets in studying the prophecies of the coming salvation. In recording the prophecies of the Old Testament, they were not serving themselves, but all who would read them through the inspiration of the Holy Spirit in the future. Peter also confirmed that the prophecies of scripture are not the product of man, but divinely inspired:

II Pet 1:20 Above all, you do well if you recognize this: No prophecy of scripture ever comes about by the prophet's own imagination,

II Pet 1:21 for **no prophecy was ever borne of human impulse**; rather, **men carried along by the Holy Spirit spoke from God**.

The careful searching and investigation of the prophets for the first coming of Christ, in concert with the guidance of the Holy Spirit, should be a model for believers in studying the second coming of Christ.

5.   The prophetic word is a shining light in a dark place.

Jesus said there will be an end to the present age, and provided many signs for which to look just before that end would come. The exhortation was to be diligent and sober, always watching for the coming of the Lord. In his first epistle, Peter reminded his readers to pay special attention to the prophetic word:

I Pet 1:19 Moreover, we possess **the prophetic word as an altogether reliable thing**. You do well if you pay attention to this as you would to a **light shining in a murky place**, until the day dawns and the morning star rises in your hearts.

He equated the study of the prophetic word with a person who sees a welcomed light in a dark and murky place. Imagine being in a dark room, stumbling around, unable to see the surroundings. The prophetic word is the light, and human understanding is the dark place. The most important proof of the inspiration of the Bible is its revelation of future events before they occur. The Lord stands outside of the time domain, viewing past, present, and future simultaneously. He revealed what would take place to his apostles and prophets, who recorded them for all to read in the future.

6.   Daniel read prophetic scrolls to learn about the 70-year captivity in Babylon.

Just before an angel of the Lord visited Daniel with arguably the greatest prophetic revelation in the Bible, Daniel was studying prophetic scripture. While in Babylonian captivity, Daniel was reading a prophecy in Jeremiah just before his intense prayer for the nation and the great revelation he received in response to his prayer:

Dan 9:1 In the first year of Darius son of Ahasuerus, who was of Median descent and who had been appointed king over the Babylonian Empire—

Dan 9:2 in the first year of his reign I, Daniel, **came to understand from the sacred books** that, according to the word of the LORD **disclosed to the prophet Jeremiah**, the years for the fulfilling of the desolation of Jerusalem were <u>seventy</u> in number.

Dan 9:3 So I turned my attention to the Lord God to implore him by prayer and requests, with fasting, sackcloth, and ashes.

The prophecy in Jeremiah that Daniel was reading was in the 25th chapter:

Jer 25:11 This whole area will become a desolate wasteland. **These nations will be subject to the king of Babylon for seventy years.**'

Jer 25:12 "'But when the <u>seventy years</u> are over, I will punish the king of Babylon and his nation for their sins. I will make the land of Babylon an everlasting ruin. I, the Lord, affirm it.

Imagine Daniel's excitement and anticipation of the deliverance of the Jewish people from the Babylonians, as the 70 years were almost complete. As a result of his study and prayer, the angel Gabriel came and revealed the important prophecy of the 70 weeks. Daniel's study of the prophetic scripture, as well as his intercessory prayer for his nation and people, are a model for believers today.

Clearly, the study of Bible prophecy was not discouraged, but was actually lauded as one of the most important aspects in the development of the faith of believers. This should be a source of great encouragement as it is now time to embark upon an intense study of prophetic scripture.

Myself, my wife, my mother and
father, and my brother and
sister-in-law were gathered
together in our new house for an
occasion of some sort. We met
at our house before leaving, and
all were sort of mingling about
and quietly talking in the
dining room. As I was standing
and talking to someone, I
noticed something out of the
corner of my eye through the
living room window...

- CHAPTER TWO -

THE MYSTERY OF THE RESURRECTION OF THE DEAD

The apostle Paul revealed mysteries throughout his epistles which before that time had not been revealed to the prophets of old. With the advent of the church, God chose to reveal these mysteries to Paul. In the next four chapters, three specific mysteries will be examined, and will serve as an important foundation for the emerging prophetic model. The three specific mysteries to be explored in the next four chapters are:

1. The resurrection of the dead – Chapters 2 and 3
2. The transformation of the perishable bodies of all believers into imperishable bodies – Chapter 4
3. The catching up of all believers into the air to meet the Lord, including both the resurrected dead in Christ and the remaining living believers – Chapter 5.

2.1 Paul's Revelation of Jesus Christ

This major three-stage event was recorded by Paul in his letters to Thessalonica and Corinth. Many times throughout his epistles, the reader will come across the word "mystery" or *musterion* in Greek. Paul, by his own admission, was very well-educated, but that was not the origin of the revelation of the mysteries about which he wrote. On several occasions, he claimed to have received what he preached and what he revealed to his readers directly from Jesus Christ:

Gal 1:11 Now I want you to know, brothers and sisters, that the gospel I preached is **not of human origin**.
Gal 1:12 For I did not receive it or learn it from any human source; instead **I received it by a revelation of Jesus Christ**.

Eph 3:8 **To me**—less than the least of all the saints—**this grace was given**, to proclaim to the Gentiles the unfathomable riches of Christ
Eph 3:9 and **to enlighten everyone about God's secret plan**—a secret that has been hidden for ages in God who has created all things.

Most are familiar with Paul's encounter with Jesus Christ on the road to Damascus, in which he spoke directly to Paul from heaven. But was this what Paul was referring to when he said he received his amazing revelations of the mysteries that had been hidden from the beginning of the world? Much detail is provided regarding what happened to Paul on the road to Damascus, and it seems from Luke's description in Acts chapter 9 and from Paul's descriptions of the experience later in that same book, that the encounter was a relatively brief one. Paul carried on a short conversation with Jesus, and he was told to go into the city of Damascus. There were witnesses to the encounter who saw and heard what happened, but didn't understand any of the words that were spoken.

So, when did Paul receive his revelation directly from Jesus Christ, if not on the road to Damascus? Twice in his first epistle to the Corinthians, Paul told his readers that he had personally met with Jesus:

I Cor 9:1 Am I not free? Am I not an apostle? **Have I not <u>seen</u> Jesus our Lord?** Are you not my work in the Lord?

I Cor 15:8 Last of all, as though to one born at the wrong time, **he [Jesus Christ] <u>appeared to me</u> also**.

According to these verses, Paul claimed to have seen the physical resurrected Jesus Christ. Paul may have been referring to what happened on the road to Damascus, but according to Acts chapter 9, Paul saw a bright light and heard a voice. After the brief experience, he was blind and had to be led into Damascus. If he was blinded by the light, how could this have been the point at which he saw Jesus? When later recounting the Acts chapter 9 experience in Acts chapter 26 to King Agrippa, Paul claimed that the Lord told him he would appear to him again in the future:

Act 26:16 But get up and stand on your feet, for I have appeared to you for this reason, to designate you in advance as a servant and witness to the things you have seen **<u>and</u> to the things in which <u>I will appear to you</u>**.

So, when was it that Jesus appeared to Paul? After Paul's conversion and restoration of sight in Damascus, he revealed in his letter to the Galatians that he went to Arabia:

Gal 1:15 But when the one who set me apart from birth and called me by his grace was pleased
Gal 1:16 to reveal his Son in me so that I could preach him among the Gentiles, I did not go to ask advice from any human being,
Gal 1:17 nor did I go up to Jerusalem to see those who were apostles before me, **but right away I departed to Arabia**, and then returned to Damascus.

It is difficult to match the time of Paul's visit to Arabia with the historical narrative in Acts chapter 9. The most likely spot is between verses 22 and 23, when Luke wrote that after "many days" he went to Jerusalem. How long Paul stayed in

Arabia is not revealed, but to travel such a long distance, it would be logical to conclude that he stayed there for a least a moderate length of time.

But there is more to Paul's visit to Arabia. He further states in his epistle to the Galatians that Mount Sinai, where Moses received the revelation of the Ten Commandments and other laws, as well as the revelation of the heavenly temple and all its articles, is in Arabia:

> Gal 4:25 Now Hagar represents **Mount Sinai in Arabia** and corresponds to the present Jerusalem, for she is in slavery with her children.

Mount Sinai is in Arabia, the geographic area that is currently occupied by Saudi Arabia. Mount Sinai is not located in the Sinai Peninsula, its traditional location. There is currently a wealth of information available on the Internet and in books written by Robert Cornuke[1] and Lennart Moeller[2], among others, which provide convincing evidence that Mount Sinai has been discovered in modern-day Saudi Arabia. Their eyewitness accounts reveal that the top of this mountain is completely charred and burnt black, which matches with the account of God's appearance in fire and smoke on the top of the mountain in Exodus chapter 19.

In addition, the government of Saudi Arabia has made the remote mountain area off-limits. Could it be that Paul, in his journey into Arabia, went to Mount Sinai, the same mountain on which first Moses, and later Elijah, met with the Lord? Could it be that the amazing mysteries Paul explained throughout his epistles were revealed to him by Jesus Christ at that mountain? This possibility will become more intriguing in the chapters to follow.

So why did the Lord reveal these mysteries to Paul at the time he did? Why didn't Jesus specifically refer to the catching up of believers while he was on earth? There are two strong reasons for the timing of the revelation of the mysteries:

1. The church, or the body of Christ, had not yet been birthed. While there may not be a concrete date for the birth of the church, the consensus belief is that it began on the day the baptism of the Holy Spirit was poured out on the 120 upper room believers as they spoke in foreign languages with power and fire as described in Acts chapter 2. How could the mystery of Christ and the church, as described in Ephesians chapter 5, be explained without the church being in existence?
2. The Gentiles had not yet been grafted into the new covenant. Much of the Acts of the Apostles explains how Gentiles were welcomed into the new covenant, receiving the Holy Ghost in Acts chapters 10 and 19. How could the mystery of the grafting in of Gentile believers into the covenant, and Israel's partial spiritual blindness and re-grafting, be revealed before the Gentiles were actually grafted in?

---

[1] Cornuke, Robert (2000). *In Search of the Mountain of God: The Discovery of the Real Mt. Sinai.* Nashville: Broadman and Holman Publishers.
[2] Moeller, Lennart (2002). *The Exodus Case: New Discoveries Confirm the Historical Exodus.* Copenhagen: Scandinavia Publishing House.

These mysteries simply could not have been revealed until the death, burial, resurrection, and ascension of Jesus Christ were accomplished, and until the gifts of the Holy Spirit were given and received.

2.2 What is a Resurrection from the Dead?

What exactly is meant by a resurrection from the dead, or to be raised to life, as described in scripture? A human experiences death when the spirit is separated from the physical body. When the Old Testament patriarchs died, such as Abraham, Isaac, Ishmael, and Jacob, the KJV states that they "gave up the ghost". Similarly, when Ananias and Sapphira died after lying to the Holy Spirit, they "gave up" or "yielded up the ghost". When Christ died on the cross:

Mat 27:50 Then Jesus cried out again with a loud voice and **gave up his spirit**.

Hence, a person dies when the eternal human spirit is separated from the physical body. In Ecclesiastes chapter 12, Solomon provided what may be a clue to the point at which the spirit is separated from the physical body:

Ecc 12:6 **before the silver cord is removed**, or the golden bowl is broken, or the pitcher is shattered at the well, or the water wheel is broken at the cistern—
Ecc 12:7 and **the dust returns to the earth as it was, and the life's breath [spirit] returns to God who gave it**.

Many believe the reference to the silver cord is some type of connector between the spirit and the physical body. Once it is severed, the death of the physical body takes place. When that happens, the spirit returns to the Lord who provided it, and the physical body returns to the dust from which it was formed.

A resurrection of the physical body, therefore, is simply the return of the eternal human spirit to the physical body. The connection between the physical body and the spirit is supernaturally restored. This was how the resurrection of Jairus' daughter was described in Luke chapter 8:

Luk 8:55 **Her spirit returned**, and she got up immediately. Then he told them to give her something to eat.

In the descriptions of resurrections back into mortal bodies throughout the Bible, the spirit was commanded to return to the bodies of the individuals who had died. In each case, the mortal body of the person raised to life had not decomposed to the point at which a resurrection would be impossible. Only three to four days, at most, had passed in each case, so the physical body was still intact and eligible for resurrection to mortality. The difference between a resurrection back into a mortal body and a resurrection to an immortal body will become clear in the remainder of this chapter and the next two chapters.

2.3 Old Testament Resurrections Into Mortal Bodies

There are several examples of the resurrection of the dead back into mortal bodies throughout the Bible. In each case, their spirits were miraculously rejoined with their mortal bodies, and they went on to live a longer life, only to die yet again in the future. A brief synopsis of each resurrection of the dead back into a mortal body throughout the Bible is provided below:

1.   The son of the widow in Zarephath of Sidon (I Kings chapter 17)

The prophet Elijah was staying at the house of a widow who had a son. The son developed a sickness and died. The woman carried the boy to Elijah and confronted him about her son's death. Since a prophet of the Lord was staying with her, she believed Elijah was responsible for the death. Elijah took the boy up to his guest room, laid him on his bed, and stretched his body over the boy's body three times. The Lord answered Elijah's prayer to restore his spirit to him, and the boy was raised to life.

2.   The son of the Shunamite woman (II Kings chapter 4)

Elisha the prophet, protégé of Elijah the prophet, was staying in the home of a couple who had no children. Elisha wanted to do something for the woman to show his appreciation for her hospitality, so he prophesied to her that she would conceive a son, and she did. Later in life, the boy sustained a head injury while working in the field with his father. The woman cared for the boy, but he died in her arms at noon that day. The woman was furious and went to Mount Carmel to confront Elisha. After his servant Gehazi was unable to bring the boy to life by placing Elisha's staff on top of him, Elisha went up into the upper room of the woman's house and saw the boy lying on the same bed in which he formerly slept while he stayed with her. Elisha laid on top of the boy and prayed to the Lord, and the boy sneezed seven times and came back to life.

These first two accounts of resurrection back into mortal bodies are confirmed in the New Testament:

> Heb 11:35 and **women received back their dead raised to life**. But others were tortured, not accepting release, to obtain resurrection to a better life.

3.   A dead man thrown into Elisha's tomb (II Kings chapter 13)

The prophet Elisha died and was buried in a tomb. The Moabite army was invading Israel, and a man that was killed was being prepared for burial. As the men buried him, they spotted a raiding army in the distance. Not having time to bury the man before the army would be upon them, they hurriedly tossed the corpse into the tomb of Elisha the prophet. When the corpse fell on Elisha's bones, the man miraculously came to life and stood up on his feet. The anointing that was on Elisha was so powerful even after he died that it raised the dead.

4. Jonah the prophet in the Mediterranean Sea (Jonah chapters 1-2)

Some may be surprised that Jonah appears in this list. A favorite story taught in Sunday School is the story of Jonah being swallowed by the large fish, but there is another side to this story that is not taught in Sunday School. While it is by no means certain that Jonah died after being thrown into the sea, the prayer of Jonah recorded in Jonah chapter 2 reveals some interesting information. Most understand the story that after Jonah was thrown overboard, a huge fish came and swallowed him while he was still alive. This is possible, but note the prayer of Jonah in the stomach of the fish:

> Jon 2:2 and said, "I called out to the LORD from my distress, and he answered me; from **the belly [beten] of Sheol** I cried out for help, and you heard my prayer.
> Jon 2:3 You cast me into **the deep waters**, into **the middle of the sea**; the ocean current **engulfed me**; all the mighty waves you sent swept over me.

Jonah said he was in the deep waters, covered by the waves of the sea. This could not take place while he was inside the fish. Furthermore, Jonah said he was in the "belly of Sheol". The Hebrew word for belly is *beten*, which means the hollow or inner womb. *Sheol* is synonymous with the grave or, more specifically, the underworld of the dead. Was Jonah claiming to have actually gone to this place, or was he simply being poetic? He continued:

> Jon 2:6 I went down to **the bottoms of the mountains**; the **gates of the netherworld barred me in <u>forever</u>**; but you **brought me up from the Pit**, O Lord, my God.

The prophet stated he was at the bottom of the mountains, which would be in the bottom of the sea, and the netherworld barred him in. Then, he claimed that he was in the pit, or the grave. It is interesting that the Lord brought him up, or raised him, from the pit. In addition, just before being thrown overboard, the men who were going to perform the act reacted as follows:

> Jon 1:14 So they cried out to the Lord, "Oh, please, Lord, don't let us die on account of this man! **Don't hold us guilty of shedding innocent blood.** After all, you, Lord, have done just as you pleased."

The men who threw him overboard knew that Jonah was going to die, so much so that they asked the Lord not to hold the guilt of his innocent blood against them. Rather than the traditional interpretation, it appears that after being thrown overboard, Jonah quickly sank to the bottom of the sea and died. The Lord then sent a great fish to swallow Jonah's body to preserve it. Otherwise, the body would have experienced decay and been scavenged by sea creatures. After three days and nights, Jonah was resurrected while inside the fish, then prayed the prayer recorded in Jonah chapter 2 before being spewed out of the mouth of the fish.

During Christ's ministry, he stated that the people who asked him for a sign would receive only the sign of Jonah the prophet, who was three days and three nights in the belly of the great fish. Just like Jonah, Jesus stated that he would be three days and three nights in the heart of the earth. As prophesied by David, the Lord would not allow his Holy One to suffer corruption, nor did Jonah experience corruption of his flesh, because it was preserved in the belly of the fish. The sign of Jonah, therefore, was that just as Jonah died and was preserved in the belly of the fish for three days and three nights, so Jesus would die and be preserved in the heart of the earth for the same period of time. Neither suffered the decay of their flesh during that time period.

2.4 New Testament Resurrections Into Mortal Bodies

5.   The widow's son at Nain (Luke chapter 7)

Jesus was traveling through the town of Nain followed by his disciples and a large crowd. As they approached the town gate, they encountered a large crowd in a funeral procession to bury the son of a widow who had just died. When Jesus saw her weeping, he had compassion on her, and told the procession to halt. Jesus spoke to the dead man and commanded him to get up. At this command, the dead man sat up and started speaking. This miracle resurrection caused great fear to grip all those who witnessed it.

6.   The daughter of Jairus the synagogue ruler (Luke chapter 8)

The twelve-year-old daughter of Jairus, a synagogue ruler, had fallen sick and died. Jairus petitioned Jesus to come heal her sickness just before she died, but as he was asking him, he was informed that the girl had just died. When Jesus heard this, he told them the girl would be healed and proceeded to go to his house. Those mourning when he arrived were told she hadn't died, but was only sleeping. They derided Jesus for the proclamation, because they knew she was dead. When Jesus commanded the girl to rise up, her spirit returned to her and she got up immediately. Again, this story reveals that Jesus was able to command the dead to rise and have them obey.

7.   Lazarus, friend of Jesus and brother of Mary and Martha (John chapter 11)

Jesus was sent a message that his friend Lazarus of Bethany was sick and dying. When he received it, he did not leave for Bethany to heal him. Since Bethany was only two miles from Jerusalem, many people went there to console the family on the death, but not Jesus. He loved Mary, Martha, and Lazarus, so his absence was probably a shock to the family. Indeed, when Jesus arrived four days after Lazarus died, there were questions as to why he didn't come and do something to save his friend Lazarus from dying. But Jesus had different plans:

Joh 11:4 When Jesus heard this, he said, "This sickness will not lead to death, but **to God's glory, so that the Son of God may be glorified through it.**"

As this famous and moving story goes, Jesus commanded Lazarus to come out of the tomb after being dead four days. A Jewish custom of the day held that the human spirit of a person who had died remained with the body for three days. At the fourth day, when decomposition began, the spirit would leave the body, never to return.[3] It is possible that this custom was in the minds of those in attendance, which Jesus also knew. A resurrection of the dead at that point, therefore, would have to be considered an unequivocal demonstration of the supernatural power of God by those in attendance in the person of Jesus, in order to bring God glory.

8. The disciple Tabitha in Joppa (Acts chapter 9)

A well-loved disciple of Christ named Tabitha had fallen sick and died in the city of Joppa. Simon Peter was staying in the nearby town of Lydda when he was notified of her death. Tabitha's body had been washed and placed in an upper room, and when Peter arrived, widows were weeping and showing him cloths and garments Tabitha had made. Peter, seeing the tears of the women and their love for her, sent them all out of the room. He then knelt down beside the body and prayed, then simply told the woman to get up. She obeyed.

9. The young man Eutychus who fell out of a window (Acts chapter 20)

Picture an upstairs meeting room crowded with people waiting to hear a message by the apostle Paul. He was leaving the next day, and so he extended his message until the midnight hour. One man named Eutychus fell asleep during the message while he was sitting in a window opening of the third story room. He fell out of the window and was picked up dead by the people on the ground. Paul quickly went down to where he was, threw himself on top of the young man, and he lived again. There is some debate as to whether the boy actually died, since Paul did not pray or command the dead to rise. However, it is evident that a miracle occurred because the text records that the boy "recovered" and was taken home alive after the incident.

In summary, the bodies of these nine individuals had not decomposed beyond the point of irreparable decay. These were resurrections back into mortal, corruptible bodies. All of these individuals died again later in their lives, most likely of natural causes. They were resurrected and lived out the rest of their lives. This is in contrast with the resurrection of Jesus Christ from the dead, which was a resurrection into an immortal, incorruptible body. First Corinthians chapter 15 states that Jesus Christ was the "firstfruits" of this type of resurrection of the dead:

I Cor 15:22 For just as in Adam all die, so also all will **be made alive in Christ**.

---

[3] Leviticus Rabbah 18.1: "Bar Kappara taught: Until three days [after death] the soul keeps on returning to the grave, thinking that it will go back [into the body]; but when it sees that the facial features have become disfigured, it departs and abandons it [the body]."

I Cor 15:23 But each in his own order: **Christ, the firstfruits**; then when Christ comes, those who belong to him.

Since there were several resurrections recorded in the Bible before Jesus was resurrected, then the "firstfruits" resurrection referred to in I Corinthians chapter 15 must mean something different: a resurrection into an immortal, incorruptible body. In addition, even after Jesus' resurrection into an immortal body, in which death and the grave were conquered, there were at least two other resurrections back into mortal bodies: Tabitha and Eutychus. This clearly reveals a difference between a raising to life, in which the spirit returns to a mortal body, and a resurrection into a new, incorruptible body.

2.5 Eyewitnesses to Christ's Resurrection to Immortality

Throughout the Old Testament, there are numerous prophecies, parallels, and patterns of a man who would suffer a sacrificial death. Isaiah saw him as the suffering servant. Moses saw him as the snake hanging on a pole. Abraham saw him as the lamb provided by the Lord. David saw him as a man surrounded by his enemies in Psalm chapter 22. Daniel was told by the angel Gabriel that a future anointed one would be cut off, or killed. Throughout the New Testament, there are detailed eyewitness accounts of his birth, life, death, and resurrection. Even Caiaphas, the Jewish high priest during the three and one half years of Jesus' ministry, prophesied that Jesus would die for the sins of all people:

Joh 11:51 (Now he [Caiaphas] did not say this on his own, but because he was high priest that year, he prophesied that **Jesus was going to die** for the Jewish nation,

Joh 11:52 and not for the Jewish nation only, but to gather together into one the children of God who are scattered.)

The four gospels provide detailed accounts of his suffering and crucifixion, all of which fulfilled prophecies in the Old Testament. Therefore, it is upon the most sure and sound evidence that one stands, the Word of God, in declaring the belief that Jesus Christ suffered and died on a cross.

In addition, there is solid biblical eyewitness evidence of his physical, bodily appearance for 40 days after his resurrection, which took place three days and nights after his death. According to Paul in I Corinthians chapter 15, Jesus was seen alive by over 500 men in one setting, and was also seen by the twelve apostles, James, and all of his other apostles, and finally by Paul himself. Armed with the experience of seeing the risen Christ with their own eyes, touching him, eating with him, and speaking with him, the disciples of Christ set the world on fire with bold proclamation of his resurrection in the power of the Holy Spirit. Throughout Acts and their epistles, the pervading message of the apostles was that Christians have hope because of the resurrection of the dead of Jesus Christ, of which they were eyewitnesses:

Acts 3:15 You killed the Originator of life, **whom God raised from the dead. To this fact we are witnesses**.

Act 4:33 With **great power** the apostles were giving **testimony to the resurrection of the Lord Jesus**, and great grace was on them all.

Act 17:2 Paul went to the Jews in the synagogue, as he customarily did, and on three Sabbath days he addressed them from the scriptures,
Act 17:3 **explaining and demonstrating** that the Christ had to suffer and **to rise from the dead**, saying, "This Jesus I am proclaiming to you is the Christ."

I Pet 1:16 For we did not follow cleverly concocted fables when we made known to you the power and coming of our Lord Jesus Christ; no, **we were eyewitnesses of his grandeur**.

This bold proclamation of his resurrection was the underpinning truth of their message, which spread all over the inhabited world.

2.6 Summary and Conclusion

A summary of key points to remember from this chapter include:

- The three key events Paul revealed, which had previously been a secret hid from the foundation of the world, are the resurrection of the dead in Christ in which the spirit is reunited with the physical body, the transformation of the bodies of all living believers into immortal bodies, and the catching up of believers into the air.
- There is a distinct difference between the resurrection of the dead back into the mortal body and the resurrection into immortal bodies. The Bible contains at least nine specific examples of resurrection back into the mortal body.
- The death of Jonah the prophet, and his subsequent resurrection three days and three nights later, was a dramatic preview of the death, burial, and resurrection of Jesus Christ.
- After the resurrection of Jesus Christ into an immortal body, there were at least two more resurrections of the dead back into mortal bodies: Tabitha and Eutychus. This is clear proof of the difference between the two types of resurrections.
- The most important tenet of the Christian faith is the resurrection of Jesus Christ from the dead. Without it, the Christian faith is dead and vain.
- Jesus Christ was the firstfruits of the resurrection into immortal, glorified bodies. The Bible is full of eyewitness accounts of the resurrected Jesus Christ, as well as patterns and parallels in the Old Testament.

The chapter to follow will closely examine the resurrection of the dead into immortal bodies as described in the Bible. These include the resurrection of Jesus Christ, the "many saints" just after the resurrection of Jesus, and, in the future, the two witnesses during Daniel's 70th week.

The conversation I was having ended abruptly, but the others continued to stand and talk. I slowly moved closer to the window, still unsure of what caught my attention outdoors under the overcast morning sky. My hand touched the window pane, and my face moved closer to the glass. Feeling the coolness of the glass against my cheeks, I squinted my eyes to make out what I saw in the distance. *"what in the world..."*

Earthquake Resurrection Prophetic Model Timeline Progression

Weeks 1-69	Week 69 Ends; GAP Between Week 69 and Week 70			Week 70 Begins		
457BC - 27AD	**31AD**		**31AD - PRESENT**	**FUTURE TIME**		

457BC - 27AD	27AD	31AD	31AD	Opening of the First Five Seals - Birth Pains Begin					Sixth Seal	Confirmation / Strengthening of the Covenant	Sealing of the 144,000 Children of Israel	Enormous Group Before the Throne
				1	2	3	4	5				
Decree of Artaxerxes Longimanus, Weeks 1-69 of Daniel's 70 Weeks Prophecy	Transfer of the Priesthood of Melchizedek at Christ's Baptism	Earthquake Resurrection of Christ and the "Many Saints"	Christ's Ascension to the Right Hand of God	Spirit of Religious Domination in Christ's Name	Spirit of War and Bloodshed	Spirit of Financial Oppression	Spirit of Death, Disease, and Famine	Persecution and Death of Believers	Future Earthquake Resurrection of the Dead in Christ, Transformation and Catching Up			
Dan 9:24-25	Luk 3-4	Mat 27	Act 1, Rev 4-5	Rev 6:1-11					1 The 4, 1 Cor 15	Daniel 9:27	Rev 7	
Ch. 5		Ch. 3, 6	Ch. 10, 13	Ch. 12	Ch. 13		Ch. 14		Ch. 4, 5, 7		Ch. 9, 15, 16	

This chart will be presented throughout the book at the beginning of each chapter. Highlighted and in bold font will be the section of the timeline upon which the chapter to follow will be focused.

- CHAPTER THREE -

THE RESURRECTION TO IMMORTALITY

Continuing with the first stage of the future three-stage event, this chapter will analyze the two historic and four future resurrections of the dead to immortality. The firstfruits of the resurrection of the dead was Jesus Christ. But in the New Testament, there is not just this one, but six recorded resurrections of the dead to immortality. Two of these have already taken place in history, while four are prophesied future resurrections:

1. The resurrection of Jesus Christ. (Matthew 27:53; 28:1-10; Mark 16:1-11; Luke 24:1-12; John 20:1-18)
2. The resurrection of the "many saints" in Jerusalem after Jesus' resurrection. (Matthew 27:50-54)
3. The resurrection of the "dead in Christ" just before the catching up of all believers. (I Thessalonians 4:13-17; I Corinthians 15:50-54)
4. The resurrection of the two witnesses. (Revelation 11:3-13)
5. The resurrection of the martyrs from Daniel's 70th week. (Revelation 20:4)
6. The resurrection of "the rest of the dead". (Revelation 20:5; Daniel 12:2-3)

These six resurrections of the dead to immortality will be explored in this chapter.

3.1 The Sign of Jonah the Prophet

Several times throughout his ministry, Jesus told his twelve disciples privately that he was going to rise from the dead after three days. But, he did not directly announce it to the public so explicitly. Instead, he provided the people with clever prophetic signs of his resurrection. Twice during Christ's ministry, it is recorded that the Pharisees and scribes asked him for a sign. One of these requests for a sign is recorded in both Matthew and Luke, and came after an important miracle. According to those gospels, Jesus had just healed a blind and mute man who was demon-possessed:

> Mat 12:22 Then they brought to him a demon-possessed man who was blind and mute. Jesus healed him so that he could speak and see.

A person who is blind and mute can neither see, speak, nor hear. The reaction of those who witnessed this miracle is extremely important. First, the reaction of the common people:

Mat 12:23 All the crowds were amazed and said, "Could **this one** be the Son of David?"

Why would the people, after this particular miracle, ask this question? It was a Jewish custom that only the Messiah will be able to heal a blind mute, because a person that cannot see, hear, or speak wouldn't be able to respond in any way to the Messiah's commands to be healed. Therefore, the Messiah would have to be speaking directly to the demon inside the person. This is why the crowds asked if Jesus was "the Son of David", a Messianic term. In essence, the people knew that this man had to be the Messiah by his ability to perform this particular miracle. So, the Pharisees knew that there was only one other possibility. Note their response to the crowd's question about Jesus being the Son of David, the Messiah:

Mat 12:24 But when the Pharisees heard this they said, "He does not cast out demons **except by the power of Beelzebul**, the ruler of demons!"

This accusation reveals the desperate condition of the religious leaders. They knew full well, even better than the common people, that the power to do this miracle could only come from God through the Messiah. Unless they could make the people somehow believe that Jesus was in league with Satan himself, the Jewish leaders would have been forced to acknowledge that he was the Messiah.

Jesus responded to the claim that he performed the miracle by being in league with Beelzebul with words that are some of the most debated and misunderstood words in the Bible. First, he made clear the absurdity of Satan casting out his own demons, destroying the power of his own kingdom. Second, he explained the consequences of the accusation that they had just leveled upon him:

Mat 12:31 For this reason I tell you, people will be forgiven for every sin and blasphemy, but the **blasphemy against the Spirit will not be forgiven**.

Mat 12:32 Whoever speaks a word against the Son of Man will be forgiven. But whoever speaks against the Holy Spirit **will not be forgiven**, either in this age or in the age to come.

With their backs to the wall, the Pharisees had to save face before the people by denying Jesus was the Messiah in performing this miracle, attributing his power to Satan himself. In doing so, they sealed their fate by assigning to Satan what the Holy Spirit had just done. This is the sin of blasphemy against the Holy Spirit, and it cannot be forgiven. In danger of losing all credibility with the people gathered around this scene, notice the reaction of some of the Pharisees and experts in the law:

Mat 12:38 Then some of the experts in the law along with some Pharisees answered him, "Teacher, **we want to see a sign from you**."

Still defiant, they asked Jesus for a sign. This came just after Christ provided the ultimate sign: casting the demon out of a person who could not see, speak, or hear.

What they desired was a sign that the source of his power was not from Satan. A sign that he was clearly deity, such as calling down fire from heaven like Elijah, or some other supernatural, unmistakable sign from God. Note the response Jesus gave them:

Mat 12:39 But he answered them, "An evil and adulterous generation asks for a sign, but no sign will be given to it **except the sign of the prophet Jonah**.

Mat 12:40 For just as Jonah was in the belly of the huge fish for three days and three nights, **so the Son of Man will be in the heart of the earth for three days and three nights**.

There was going to be no fireball from heaven that day for the Pharisees and experts who refused to believe, indeed, who had just committed the unforgivable sin. The sign they would receive, however, was the sign of Jonah the prophet. Jesus meant that the three days and nights Jonah spent in the belly of the great fish would be a picture of his death, burial, and resurrection from the dead. If they were not going to accept his miracles, or the words of the prophets fulfilled through him, as proof he was the Messiah, then the only sign their generation was going to receive was the sign of his death, burial, and resurrection in the same pattern as Jonah.

3.2 The Sign of the Rebuilding of the Temple

This, however, was not the only time the Jewish leaders asked Jesus for a sign. John's gospel records Jesus cleansing the temple near the beginning of his ministry. Just as he responded with the sign of Jonah, Jesus made a veiled reference to his death and resurrection:

Joh 2:19 Jesus replied, **"Destroy this temple and in three days I will raise it up again."**

Once again, they did not understand Jesus was referring to his own body. They thought he was referring to the literal temple in Jerusalem. Incredibly, instead of using the sign of his resurrection from the dead as a sign he was the Messiah, the leaders of the Jews subsequently used these statements to accuse Jesus and ultimately send him to his death:

Mat 26:59 The chief priests and the whole Sanhedrin were trying to find false testimony against Jesus so that they could put him to death.

Mat 26:60 But **they did not find anything**, though many false witnesses came forward. Finally two came forward

Mat 26:61 and declared, "This man said, 'I am able to destroy the temple of God and rebuild it in three days.'"

This false charge in front of Caiaphas the high priest led to Caiaphas' request for Jesus to identify himself as the Christ, the Son of God. When Jesus answered him, instead of believing, Caiaphas condemned him as a blasphemer. This ultimately led to his death on the cross, where their spiritual ignorance about the sign of his resurrection continued even as he hung dying in front of them:

Mat 27:39 Those who passed by defamed him, shaking their heads
Mat 27:40 and saying, "You who can **destroy the temple and rebuild it in three days**, save yourself! If you are God's Son, come down from the cross!"

The Jews turned the sign of rebuilding the temple in three days to try to get him to come down off the cross, instead of its intended meaning of the death of his body and its resurrection after three days. Instead of understanding the redemptive value of his death and the power of the resurrection, they wanted to see Jesus come off the cross. Surely, God would save his own Son by bringing him off the cross, wouldn't he? This would once and for all show he was God's Son, thwart the death sentence, and prove he was the prophesied Messiah to deliver Israel from Roman domination. This was the role of the Messiah in their minds. Even after his death and burial, the Jewish leaders remembered the sign Jesus gave them:

Mat 27:62 The next day (which is after the day of preparation) the chief priests and the Pharisees assembled before Pilate
Mat 27:63 and said, "Sir, **we remember** that while that deceiver was still alive he said, '**After three days I will rise again.**'
Mat 27:64 So give orders to secure the tomb until the third day. **Otherwise his disciples may come and steal his body and say to the people, 'He has been raised from the dead,' and the last deception will be worse than the first.**"

3.3 The Resurrection Moment

Jesus was dead for good in their minds, and their problem solved. But remembering his prediction of rebuilding the temple in three days, they thought the disciples would use it as a cover story to steal his body and point to an empty tomb to prove Jesus indeed had risen from the dead. However, no matter how secure they made the tomb, it would not be able to stop his resurrection:

Mat 28:5 But the angel said to the women, "Do not be afraid; I know that you are looking for **Jesus, who was crucified.**
Mat 28:6 He is not here, **for he has been raised**, just as he said. Come and see the place where he was lying.
Mat 28:7 Then go quickly and tell his disciples, '**He has been raised from the dead**. He is going ahead of you into Galilee. You will see him there.' Listen, I have told you."

Neither this passage nor any of the other four gospel accounts record the actual moment of his resurrection. What they record are the women coming to the tomb early on the first day of the week, and seeing an angel descend from heaven and roll the stone away. The angel informed them that he had already been raised.

The closest to the actual moment of his resurrection recorded in scripture is actually before it happened, as recorded in Matthew chapter 27. Although Jesus was the first to rise to immortality, he wasn't the only person to rise from the dead at that time.

3.4 The Resurrection of the "Many Saints"

Matthew chapter 27 contains the one and only account of an unnamed group of "many saints" who also rose from the dead that day:

Mat 27:50 Then Jesus cried out again with a loud voice and gave up his spirit.

Mat 27:51 Just then the temple curtain was torn in two, from top to bottom. The earth shook and the rocks were split apart.

Mat 27:52 And tombs were opened, and **the bodies of many [pollois] saints who had died were raised**.

Mat 27:53 **(They came out of the tombs after his resurrection and went into the holy city and appeared to many people.)**

Mat 27:54 Now when the centurion and those with him who were guarding Jesus saw the earthquake and what took place, they were extremely terrified and said, "Truly this one was God's Son!"

The mysterious resurrection of this group, and their appearance to many people in Jerusalem, is the subject of much speculation and conjecture. Of the four gospel accounts, this story is only found in the Matthew account of the crucifixion and resurrection of Jesus. The traditional belief about these saints is that they consisted of all the righteous saints from Adam until the thief on the cross whom Jesus stated would be with him in paradise that day.

However, additional scriptural evidence reveals that the resurrection of the saints in Matthew chapter 27 after Jesus' resurrection did not include all of the righteous dead from Adam to the thief on the cross. First, the verse states that many, not all, of the tombs of the saints were opened. The Greek word for "many" is *polus*, and is used hundreds of times in the New Testament to describe a noun, such as "many people", "many waters", "many days", and "many years". Here, it is used with "saints" to describe those saints which came out of their tombs. The use of *polus* effectively restricts it to a part of the Old Testament saints, not all.

In addition, there is strong evidence that the righteous dead from Adam until the thief on the cross are still dead and in the grave, and will be part of the resurrected "dead in Christ". This evidence is found in two separate passages of the New Testament, both written after the events of Matthew chapter 27. First, Peter's address on the day of Pentecost:

Act 2:29 "Brothers, I can speak confidently to you about our forefather **David**, that **he both died and was buried, and his tomb is with us to this day**.

Peter "confidently" stated that King David was both dead and buried, not yet resurrected from the dead. He then stated that it was common knowledge that his tomb was still there, not one of the tombs that was broken open as described in the events of Matthew chapter 27. Furthermore, Peter provided even more proof that David had not yet been raised and taken to heaven as one of the "many saints":

Act 2:34 For **David did not ascend into heaven**, but he himself says, 'The Lord said to my lord, "Sit at my right hand

Act 2:35 until I make your enemies a footstool for your feet."'

Here, Peter confirms what he had stated earlier: that David was still dead and buried, not yet resurrected and taken to heaven in bodily form.

The second passage providing confirmation that only many, not all, of the Old Testament saints were raised in the Matthew chapter 27 event is found in Hebrews, where Paul revealed the following information in his listing of the heroes of faith:

> Heb 11:4 By faith **Abel** offered God a greater sacrifice than Cain, and through his faith he was commended as righteous, because God commended him for his offerings. And through his faith he still speaks, **though he is dead**.

This verse reveals that Abel was still dead after the Matthew chapter 27 event, and clearly he would be considered one of the righteous dead saints, because he was "commended as righteous" by his faith through his offerings. From these passages, it is clear that at least two righteous men who died before the resurrection of Christ were still dead after the raising of the "many saints": David and Abel. If these two men were still dead, then it follows that others were still dead.

Some may question whether these "many saints" were simply raised to life back into their mortal bodies, rather than into immortal bodies like the one possessed by Jesus. Could they not have been raised, lived out the rest of their lives, then died again just as some the previous individuals who were raised back into their mortal bodies? For one very important reason, this cannot be the case: the decomposition factor.

These "many saints" surely consisted of individuals who had been dead for several, perhaps hundreds of years. At the very least, most were dead for more than four days. Therefore, their bodies would have been decomposed beyond the point of a resurrection back into their mortal bodies. Recall the nine resurrections from the dead back into mortal bodies discussed in the previous chapter. Each of these nine accounts featured individuals whose bodies had only been dead four days at most. Therefore, when their spirits returned to their bodies, they came back into a body that was not decayed or decomposed. In contrast, the resurrection experienced by the "many saints" would require a resurrection into a new, glorified body. The key is that they were raised to life after Christ's resurrection:

> Mat 27:53 (They came out of the tombs **after his resurrection** and went into the holy city and appeared to many people.)

Because they were raised after Christ had risen, the doctrine that Christ was the firstfruits of the resurrection of the dead to immortality is obeyed. First Christ was raised to immortality, then these "many saints" after him. There may be an important future purpose of these "many saints" during Daniel's 70th week, which is considered in detail in chapter 16.

3.5 The Resurrection of the Two Witnesses

The third resurrection of the dead to immortality recorded in the New Testament is the two witnesses of Revelation chapter 11, a resurrection that has yet to take place but is described in detail. The two witnesses are described as two individuals who will appear on the earth during Daniel's 70th week to give a testimony and prophesy for exactly 1,260 days. A great deal of detail about their specific mission is provided in Revelation chapter 11, however, their specific identity is kept hidden. When their time of testimony is completed, they will be killed by the beast from the abyss:

Rev 11:9 For three and a half days those from every people, tribe, nation, and language will look at their corpses, because they will not permit them to be placed in a tomb.

Rev 11:10 And those who live on the earth will rejoice over them and celebrate, even sending gifts to each other, because these two prophets had tormented those who live on the earth.

Rev 11:11 But after three and a half days **a breath of life from God entered them, and they stood on their feet**, and tremendous fear seized those who were watching them.

Rev 11:12 Then they heard a loud voice from heaven saying to them: "Come up here!" So the two prophets went up to heaven in a cloud while their enemies stared at them.

It would not be fruitful to dwell on the identity of the two witnesses, about which many an essay has been written. However, there are some interesting passages in the Old Testament in which clues are provided regarding their current activities and whereabouts. Revelation 11:4 makes reference to a passage in Zechariah chapter 4, which provides details on these two men:

Zec 4:2 He asked me, "What do you see?" I replied, "I see a menorah of pure gold with a receptacle at the top and seven lamps, with fourteen pipes going to the lamps.

Zec 4:3 There are also **two olive trees beside it**, one on the right of the receptacle and the other on the left."

Zec 4:11 Next I asked the messenger, "**What are these two olive trees on the right and left of the menorah?**"

Zec 4:12 Before he could reply I asked again, "What are these **two extensions of the olive trees**, which are emptying out the golden oil through the two golden pipes?"

Zec 4:13 He replied, "Don't you know what these are?" And I said, "No, sir."

Zec 4:14 So he said, "These are **the two anointed ones who stand by the Lord of the whole earth**."

A study of the chapters surrounding the passage from Zechariah chapter 4 reveals that the two olive trees are Joshua the high priest, and Zerubbabel the governor, under whom much of the temple destroyed by the Babylonians was rebuilt. Whether these two men are equivalent to the two witnesses of Revelation is not addressed. However, Zechariah chapter 4 reveals that they have golden oil flowing through them, emptying out into two golden pipes. Interestingly, these two witnesses are called the two olive trees and lampstands that stand before the Lord of the earth in Revelation chapter 11:

Rev 11:4 (These **are the two olive trees and the two lampstands** that stand before the Lord of the earth.)

These two men, therefore, are currently in heaven with continuous golden anointing oil flowing through them. The Hebrew term *vene-hayyitshar*, translated in Zechariah 4:14 above as "anointed ones", literally means "sons of fresh oil". When they are sent to the earth during Daniel's 70th week, therefore, they will have been receiving continuous fresh oil of anointing through their bodies until that time.

When these men are killed, the inhabited world responds with celebration and gift-giving. Perhaps they are blamed for the severe trumpet judgments that come on the earth during their 1,260 day period of testimony. Their dramatic resurrection will be immediately followed by a powerful earthquake that will level one tenth of the city of Jerusalem and kill 7,000 people. Not only will they be resurrected from the dead, but they will be taken up to heaven in a cloud, similar to the public ascension of Jesus Christ as recorded in Acts chapter 1, and similar to the description of the future resurrection of the dead in Christ in I Thessalonians chapter 4.

3.6 The Future Resurrection of the Dead in Christ

First Corinthians chapter 15 and I Thessalonians chapter 4 contain famous and important passages describing the future resurrection of the dead of those who belong to Christ, and those who are dead in Christ:

I Cor 15:22 For just as in Adam all die, so also in Christ all will **be made alive**.
I Cor 15:23 But each in his own order: Christ, the firstfruits; then **when Christ comes, those who belong to him**.

I The 4:16 For the Lord himself will come down from heaven with a shout of command, with the voice of the archangel, and with the trumpet of God, and **the dead in Christ will rise** first.

Who will make up the "dead in Christ"? The traditional belief about the resurrection of the dead in Christ generally states the following:

1. The dead in Christ includes only believers who died after his death on the cross. They are dead in Christ because they died after the new covenant of Christ was established.
2. All those righteous souls who died under the old covenant before Christ came, meaning all those from Adam until the thief on the cross, are not part of the dead in Christ.
3. All the righteous dead were raised when the "many saints" were raised just after Jesus' resurrection, as recorded in Matthew chapter 27 and discussed above.

As previously shown, however, at least two righteous men, Abel and David, were still dead after the events of Matthew chapter 27. Many saints, not all, were raised and walked the streets of Jerusalem. A passage from Hebrews chapter 11 will shed light on the dilemma of who will be part of the future resurrection of the dead in Christ:

> Heb 11:13 These all died in faith without receiving the things promised, but they **saw them in the distance and welcomed them** and acknowledged that they were strangers and foreigners on the earth.
>
> Heb 11:39 And these all were **commended for their faith, yet they did not receive what was promised.**
> Heb 11:40 For God had provided something better for us, **so that they would be made perfect together with us**.

These passages offer the suggestion that the righteous Old Testament heroes will be included with the "dead in Christ". Verse 39 states that the heroes of faith did not receive what was promised during their lifetime. However, God provided something better, so they could be made perfect "together with us". Therefore, these heroes of faith are made perfect with those considered to be the "body of Christ", or all those who died after Jesus Christ was crucified. If they are to be made perfect "together" with a future group of people, then these saints must be resurrected together with the "dead in Christ" referred to in I Thessalonians chapter 4.

The future resurrection of the dead in Christ, therefore, will include not only all those who died in covenant relationship with Christ after his death, but also all the Old Testament saints from Adam until the thief on the cross who were made perfect with "us", all post-crucifixion believers. The resurrection of this group will also be studied in-depth in chapter 6.

3.7 The Resurrection of Daniel's 70th Week Martyrs

Those who will be beheaded and martyred during Daniel's 70th week will be resurrected at the end of that seven-year period. In Revelation 20:4, it is revealed that those who were beheaded for the testimony of Christ they held, and who had not received the mark of the beast in their hand or forehead, will be raised just prior to the 1,000-year period in which Satan is bound in the abyss and Christ reigns with the saints:

> Rev 20:4 Then I saw thrones and seated on them were those who had been given authority to judge. I also saw **the souls of those who had been beheaded** because of the testimony about Jesus and because of the word of God. These had not worshipped the beast or his image and had refused to receive his mark on their forehead or hand. **They came to life** and reigned with Christ for a thousand years.

These persons are not part of the caught-up believers or resurrected dead in Christ. However, they will be resurrected from the dead into immortal, incorruptible bodies and reign with Jesus Christ for 1,000 years on the earth.

3.8 The Resurrection of "The Rest of the Dead"

The final future group to be resurrected from the dead to immortal bodies will be a group called "the rest of the dead":

Rev 20:5 (The **rest of the dead** did not come to life until the thousand years were finished.)

After the 1,000-year incarceration of Satan in the abyss, all the dead who, up to that point, had not been resurrected, will come to life. Comparing this group with the other groups who will have been raised prior to this point, they must consist of:

1.   The righteous mortals who will die during the 1,000-year period, and
2.   All the u̲nrighteous throughout history until the end of the 1,000-year period

There will be some individuals who survive Daniel's 70th week and move into the period of 1,000 years in which Christ and the saints reign on the earth during Satan's incarceration in the abyss. These will be mortals who will die during the 1,000-year period in either a righteous or unrighteous state. All of the previous five resurrections to immortality will have consisted only of righteous individuals. However, some of the "rest of the dead", according to Revelation chapter 20, will be thrown into the lake of fire:

Rev 20:12 And I saw **the dead, the great and the small**, standing before the throne. Then books were opened, and another book was opened—the book of life. So the dead were judged by what was written in the books, according to their deeds.

Rev 20:15 **If anyone's name was not found written in the book of life, that person was thrown into the lake of fire.**

This is the only resurrection of the dead which will include unrighteous individuals. They will rise and stand before the great white throne and be judged according to their deeds. Those thrown into the second death will eternally abide in the lake of fire.

The following table will help to summarize the two historic, and four future resurrections of the dead to immortality:

Person/Group	Righteous or Unrighteous?	Time Frame
Jesus Christ	Righteous	Firstfruits of the Resurrection
The "Many Saints" of Matthew 27	Righteous	From Adam until the Thief on the Cross (Partial)
The "Dead in Christ"	Righteous	From Adam until the Moment of Catching-up/Resurrection Event (Remainder)
The Two Witnesses	Righteous	During Daniel's 70th Week
Daniel's 70th Week Martyrs	Righteous	During Daniel's 70th Week
"The Rest of the Dead"	BOTH Righteous & Unrighteous	Righteous: From the End of Daniel's 70th Week until the End Satan's 1,000-Year Incarceration Unrighteous: From Cain until the End of the 1,000 Year Incarceration of Satan

3.9 Resurrection: Faith Versus Science

The resurrection of Jesus Christ from the dead into immortality is arguably the single most significant and momentous event in human history. It is the central theme of the "gospel", or good news for humanity:

I Cor 15:12 Now if Christ is being preached as raised from the dead, how can some of you say there is no resurrection of the dead?

I Cor 15:13 But if there is no resurrection of the dead, then not even Christ has been raised.

I Cor 15:14 And **if Christ has not been raised**, then our preaching is **futile** and your **faith is empty**.

Paul reasoned that the entire system of Christian faith is dependent on the reality that Jesus Christ rose from the dead by the power of God and conquered the power of death. Without it, the Christian faith–the hope of resurrection and eternal life–is empty. While redemption by his shed blood on the cross is absolutely necessary to atone for sin, without the resurrection from the dead, Jesus Christ would be viewed as just another human being who lived and died. A revolutionary, a prophet, and a miracle-healer, but not a risen Savior.

As a result of its importance, opponents of Christianity vigorously attack the idea of the resurrection of Jesus Christ. The underlying reason why modern science denies the possibility of a resurrection of the dead is because it requires the supernatural. Consider this statement about modern science's attitude toward natural death of the human body by Frank Tipler, Professor of Mathematical Physics at Tulane University:

One is accustomed to hear that the message of science is: we are mechanistic puppets of blind, impersonal, and deterministic natural laws; nothing remotely like a personal God exists; and when we're dead, we're dead, and that's the end of it. The latter has indeed been the message of science for a very long time now.[1]

While Mr. Tipler admittedly did not agree with this view, he stated that the overriding belief of his contemporaries is that the deterministic laws of the natural world, consisting of visible phenomena and known information, is all there is to life. Those who give credence to the startling announcements from scientists of new discoveries about life, which now appear in the headlines on an almost daily basis, must realize their denial of the supernatural is underlying the conclusions that they draw. Like modern science, Christians should have a belief that underlies their worldview. A belief based on scripture that encompasses not only the visible world, but also the world not visible to the human eye:

II Cor 4:18 because we are not looking at what can be seen but at **what cannot be seen**. For what can be seen is temporary, but **what cannot be seen is eternal**.

Heb 11:3 By faith we understand that the worlds were set in order at God's command, so that **the visible has its origin in the invisible**.

This truth is manifest in the mysteries of quantum physics. Quantum particles are so tiny and chaotic that they seemingly do not even exist, yet they also appear to be the building blocks of larger particles which can be seen. It almost appears that all detectable matter has its counterpart in antimatter, but the net result still washes to "nothing". During creation, did God achieve "something from nothing" by introducing a negative and positive balance of matter, such that the physical property of conservation of mass was maintained, while still allowing for the "creation" of visible matter?

For example, to create something out of nothing, the nothingness must be split into equal parts of negativeness and positiveness, such that the positive matter plus the negative matter still obeys mass conservation. The mortal world can then be shaped and formed from essentially "nothing" which is only the positive (visible) matter, while the negative (invisible) matter must also exist, but remains undetectable without the spiritual power to access it. Indeed, the visible has its origin in the invisible, just has Paul explained in Hebrews.

However, because scientists cannot test what they cannot observe, they deny the supernatural, invisible elements of the universe and try to explain them with natural phenomena, which falls far short. As a result, they conclude that they simply cannot yet explain these mysteries without additional technological advancement. Yet the Word of God reinforces for the believer that the invisible qualities of the Lord are the explanation of these and all other mysteries:

Rom 1:20 For since the creation of the world **his invisible attributes**—his eternal power and divine nature—have been clearly seen, because they are understood through what has been made. So people are without excuse.

---

[1] Tipler, Frank J. (1994). *The Physics of Immortality*, p. 2. New York: Doubleday.

Col 1:17 He himself is before all things and **all things are held together in him**.

The attitude of science about the supernatural is a direct contradiction to the Christian faith. As noted above, Paul argued that the Christian faith is useless without the reality of the resurrection of the dead, a supernatural event. Wise men throughout history have consistently rejected the idea, and will continue to do so as long as they rely on their own understanding, which is based on what they see, rather than faith.

The faith versus science battle is one that has been fought for centuries. Paul tried to convince the wise men of Athens about the invisible God:

Act 17:24 The God who made the world and everything in it, who is Lord of heaven and earth, does not live in temples made by human hands,

Act 17:28 For **in him we live and move about and exist**, as even some of your own poets have said, 'For we too are his offspring.'

Act 17:31 because he has set a day on which he is going to judge the world in righteousness, by a man whom he designated, **having provided proof to everyone by raising him from the dead**."

His attempt to explain the origin of life and the reality of an unseen God was concluded with a reference to the resurrection of Christ. Note their reaction in the next verse when Paul introduced the resurrection of the dead:

Act 17:32 Now when they heard about the resurrection from the dead, **some began to scoff**, but others said, "We will hear you again about this."

Little has changed today. The wise men of science still scoff at the resurrection of the dead. While the resurrection of Jesus Christ is probably one of the most documented and detailed events of ancient history, unbelievers still attempt to provide incredibly inadequate explanations for what happened other than a supernatural resurrection. These explanations include hallucination by his disciples, theft of the body by his disciples, the notion that he was never killed, and several others. This is the same attitude that has existed for nearly 2,000 years: attempts to explain the supernatural with a natural explanation. The discoveries of science are useful only for a partial understanding of the natural phenomena in the world:

I Cor 13:12 For **now we see in a mirror indirectly**, but then we will see face to face. **Now I know in part**, but then I will know fully, just as I have been fully known.

In the end, it is only the Christian faith that will prevail. Through faith alone can man understand the mystery of the resurrection of the dead. That faith is rooted in what science cannot observe, which is why faith and naturalistic science cannot harmonize:

Heb 11:1 Now faith is being sure of what we hope for, **being convinced of what we do not see**.

I Cor 2:5 so that **your faith would not be based on human wisdom but on the power of God.**

That power of God on which the Christian faith is based is his power to raise the dead, the power to create the universe and everything visible and invisible within it, and the power to sustain and hold together his creation. The secular scientific community will unfortunately continue to reject the possibility of a supernatural realm, and denigrate those who believe in it, because it lies outside the realm of what they can observe.

3.10 Summary and Conclusion

A summary of key points to remember from this chapter include:

- Jesus provided two distinct signs of his deity to the common people of his day: the rebuilding of the temple of his body and the sign of Jonah inside the belly of the great fish for three days and three nights. Both signs were referring to his approaching death, burial, and resurrection.
- As described in Matthew chapter 27, and *only* Matthew chapter 27, "many saints" were also resurrected from the dead into immortal bodies after Christ's resurrection. These saints were some, but not all, of the righteous dead from Adam until the thief on the cross.
- The bodies of the "many saints" were likely decomposed beyond the point of a resurrection back into a mortal body. Such a condition would require that they be raised into glorified, immortal bodies.
- A third resurrection from the dead into immortal bodies is described in Revelation chapter 11, when the two witnesses are dramatically resurrected in front of the whole world after lying dead in the streets of Jerusalem for three and a half days.
- The future resurrection of the dead in Christ will include, except for the "many saints" described in Matthew chapter 27, all the righteous from Adam until the future three-stage event described in I Corinthians chapter 15 and I Thessalonians chapter 4.
- The battle between faith and science has its foundation in the suppression of the resurrection of the dead. If science can convince people that there is no supernatural God, then there is no Creator and no supernatural resurrection of the dead. The battle with science is won by the spoken Word of God from the mouth of the believer in proclamation of their faith.

Having a solid understanding of each of these resurrections will be beneficial to the step-by-step development of this prophetic model. An investigative mind may have noticed an interesting parallel in connection with the resurrection of Jesus Christ, the "many saints" after Jesus' resurrection, and the resurrection of the two witnesses. This parallel will be explored in depth in chapters 6 and 7. The next chapter, however, will continue the foundation of the model with an exploration of the transformation of the perishable body into an imperishable one, the second stage of the future three-stage event.

The double-paned, latticed living room window did not provide adequate vision, and there was a glare that further obscured my view. Still going unnoticed by the others, I quickly walked toward the dining room, stealing a glance through each window as I passed. In the dining room would be an unobstructed view of my backyard and the surrounding landscape through a full-length sliding glass door. Arriving at the door, I grabbed the outer frame with both hands and pressed my nose to the surface. Though still in disbelief, there could now be no mistaking what I saw...

Earthquake Resurrection Prophetic Model Timeline Progression

	Weeks 1-69				Week 69 Ends; GAP Between Week 69 and Week 70	Week 70 Begins		
	457BC - 27AD	27AD	31AD	31AD	31AD - PRESENT		FUTURE TIME	
					Opening of the First Five Seals – Birth Pains Begin	Sixth Seal		
Event	Decree of Artaxerxes Longimanus, Weeks 1-69 of Daniel's 70 Weeks Prophecy	Transfer of the Priesthood of Melchizedek at Christ's Baptism	Christ's and "Many Saints" Earthquake Resurrection	Christ's Ascension to the Right Hand of God	1 – Spirit of Religious Domination in Christ's Name; 2 – Spirit of War and Bloodshed; 3 – Spirit of Financial Oppression; 4 – Spirit of Death, Disease, and Famine; 5 – Persecution and Death of Believers	Future Earthquake Resurrection of the Dead in Christ, Transformation and Catching Up	Confirmation / Strengthening of the Covenant; Sealing of the 144,000 Children of Israel	Enormous Group Before the Throne
Scripture	Dan 9:24-25	Luk 3-4	Mat 27	Act 1; Rev 4-5	Rev 5:1-11	I The 4; I Cor 15	Daniel 9:27	Rev 7
Chapter	Ch. 8		Ch. 3, 6	Ch 10, 11	Ch 12 / Ch 13 / Ch 14	Ch. 4, 5, 7	Ch 9, 15, 16	

- CHAPTER FOUR -

THE TRANSFORMATION TO IMMORTALITY

The two previous chapters focused on the different types of resurrection of the dead, both those in which the dead are raised back into a mortal body and those in which the dead are raised into immortal bodies. Continuing with the important foundation for the prophetic model that will be presented, this chapter will focus on the transformation of the bodies of believers from perishable to imperishable.

4.1 The Likeness of His Resurrection

Paul's first epistle to the Corinthians includes the most important passage describing the mysterious transformation of the mortal body to immortality. Although it is not as detailed as the passage in I Thessalonians chapter 4, it contains some very important clues about what happens to the mortal bodies of the dead in Christ, as well as the bodies of the living, at the moment in which the transformation takes place:

> I Cor 15:51 Listen, I will tell you a mystery: We will not all sleep, but **we will all be changed—**
> I Cor 15:52 **in a moment, in the blinking of an eye**, at the last trumpet. For the trumpet will sound, and **the dead will be raised imperishable, and we will be changed**.
> I Cor 15:53 For this perishable body must put on the imperishable, and this mortal body must put on immortality.

Take note that, in this passage, Paul did not refer to the believer being caught up in the clouds, or meeting the Lord Jesus in the air as he does in the I Thessalonians chapter 4 passage. But he provided several clues as to what will happen to the mortal body at the time of this event, and how quickly it will happen. In a different epistle, Paul revealed that the believer will be resurrected into the likeness of Christ's resurrection:

> Rom 6:5 For if we have become united with him in the likeness of his death, **we will certainly also be united in the likeness of his resurrection**.

To be united in the likeness of his resurrection means that the bodies of believers will be identical in structure and feature to the resurrected body of Jesus Christ. Paul provided more clues about this event in his letter to the Philippians in perhaps the most unknown and unheralded verse of New Testament prophecy:

> Php 3:20 But our citizenship is in heaven—and we also await a savior from there, the Lord Jesus Christ,
> Php 3:21 who will **transform these humble bodies** of ours <u>**into the likeness of his glorious body**</u> by means of that power by which he is able to subject all things to himself.

According to this passage, the body of the believer will be a glorified body exactly like Jesus possessed after his resurrection. The four gospels, particularly Luke and John, provide detailed descriptions of his abilities in his resurrected, glorified body in the 40 days before his ascension to heaven. From these descriptions, an understanding of what it will be like to have these bodies is evident, and will be explored in depth. But before this, the reason for the transformation must be examined.

4.2 The Seed Must Die

Paul declared in I Corinthians chapter 15 that flesh and blood cannot inherit the kingdom of God. This is because all human flesh and blood is corrupt and perishable. It became corrupt when Adam sinned and introduced the curse of death to all humanity through his blood:

> I Cor 15:21 For since **death came through a man**, the resurrection of the dead also came through a man.
> I Cor 15:22 For just **as in Adam all die**, so also in Christ all will be made alive.

Think of a mortal, fleshly body as computer hardware, such as the monitor, printer, central processing unit, disk drives, scanner, and keyboard. All these parts will eventually either wear down and die or become obsolete, and will need to be replaced. Think of the human spirit, however, as the God-breathed software that is invisible and cannot be destroyed. Software cannot be destroyed once it is created unless the user deletes the data from the storage device, but the disks or drives on which it is stored can be destroyed. The software can be moved anywhere quickly by electronic transmission, but the hardware must be moved physically. It is the same way with the human spirit. Once the spirit is created by God, it can never be destroyed, even though the physical outer shell eventually breaks down and dies:

> Ecc 12:7 and the dust returns to the earth as it was, and the life's breath returns to God who gave it.

> Ecc 12:7 before the dust also return to the earth as it was, and **the spirit [rûach] return to God who gave it.** (LXX)

The NET renders the Hebrew *rûach* as "life's breath" above, but "spirit" may be a better translation in this case, as rendered by the Septuagint (LXX) version of the Old Testament. The prophet Isaiah provided a perfect explanation of what the human spirit is:

Isa 57:16 For I will not be hostile forever or perpetually angry, for then **man's spirit** would grow faint before me, **the <u>life-giving breath I created</u>**.

The human spirit is eternal because it is initially given by an eternal God, and it returns to God who gave it when the corruptible outer shell dies. As explained above, this corruptibility was birthed by man's sin, not because God designed the body to be corruptible.

In attempting to convey the mystery of the resurrection of the dead in I Corinthians chapter 15, Paul used the analogy of a seed dying followed by the birthing of the new body:

I Cor 15:36 Fool! What you sow will not come to life unless it dies.

I Cor 15:37 And what you sow is not the body that is to be, **but a bare seed**— perhaps of wheat or something else.

I Cor 15:38 But God gives it a body just as he planned, and **to each of the seeds a body of its own**.

I Cor 15:42 **It is the same with the resurrection of the dead**. What is sown is **perishable**, what is raised is **imperishable**.

When a seed is planted in the ground, that seed must die before what is to grow forth from it can do so. Once that seed dies, the transformation into a tree, a stalk of corn, or any other kind of vegetation, can begin. This is what Paul meant in verses 36 and 37. He then equated this with the human body. Paul was expanding on the teaching of Jesus about the death of the seed:

Joh 12:24 I tell you the solemn truth, unless a kernel of wheat falls into the ground and dies, it remains by itself alone. But if it dies, it produces much grain.

The seed of the body has inside it the software–a soul and spirit–that is able to be birthed into an imperishable body. When the perishable body dies, the transformation can begin.

4.3 Resurrecting a Body That Has Decayed

Many wonder just how God could resurrect a dead body that has rotted to bones and dust. Some bodies have been cremated, their ashes thrown to the wind or poured into rivers or lakes. So just how will God be able to put all the pieces back together again if they are scattered all over the earth? For some, the seemingly elusive answer to these questions hinders their acceptance of a faith in Jesus Christ. Many believe that the dust and ashes will have to be re-gathered from wherever they may be and be reformed into their original state in order for a resurrection to take place. But which particles will be re-gathered and resurrected? The ones present at birth? Just prior to death? Somewhere in between? While God can perform what seems impossible for man, these questions can be answered by going back to the creation of the first man.

The smallest unit of matter retaining the characteristics of a particular chemical element is an atom, which consists of electrons, protons, and neutrons. The physical body is made up of 28 elements, all of which can be found in the dust of the ground, including oxygen, carbon, hydrogen, nitrogen, calcium, phosphorus, potassium, sulfur, sodium, magnesium, and several others in trace amounts.

At the subatomic level, scientists have discovered that individual particles do not have a specific identity that distinguishes them from any other particle of the same type. It does not make sense to refer to "that" electron as being here at one moment and there at another moment. It only makes sense to say than "an" electron was at both places. For example, one could not find an oxygen atom, look at its subatomic particles, and conclude that it looks any different than any other oxygen atom. So, a water molecule consisting of two hydrogen atoms and one oxygen atom cannot be distinguished from any other water molecule. They are interchangeable and have no separate identity. This is true of all other atoms in the universe as well. A hydrogen atom in a water molecule could be interchanged with a hydrogen atom anywhere else in the universe. Put another way, every hydrogen atom is an exact duplicate of itself.

Given this reality, the resurrection of a human body need not be as perplexing as it may at first seem. God need only use interchangeable atomic particles of which the universe consists to reform a physical body. The initial human being, of course, was created in the likeness of God using the chemical elements in the soil of the ground:

Gen 2:7 The Lord God formed the man **from the soil of the ground** and breathed into his nostrils the breath of life, and the man became a living being.

Because all human beings consist of these same atomic particles, all that will be required to form the resurrection body is a collection of the these atoms, which can still be found in the soil. It will not be necessary for God to reconstruct the exact chemical elements of which each particular human being consisted while living, which may have been thrown into a river and carried into the ocean, or eaten by a worm, which in turn was eaten by a bird, which was eaten by a cat, which was eaten by a dog, etc. Again, this is because atomic particles are identical to and can be interchanged with atomic particles of the same type.

What makes a person unique is not necessarily their physical body, which eventually decays to dust, but rather that person's intangible personalities and traits. These are contained within the soul, the genetic information which makes every person unique, and the spirit, the eternal body which can neither be destroyed nor viewed within the three-dimensional universe. When the resurrection takes place, the reformed physical body will be joined with the eternal soul and spirit, which Paul in I Corinthians chapter 15 called a "spiritual body":

I Cor 15:44 . . .if there is a natural body, there is also a spiritual body.

This spiritual body includes the genetic material that is God-breathed, of which an omniscient God would possess intimate knowledge for each and every human being. Did not Jesus state that the Lord knows the number of hairs on each head? If so, then he certainly has knowledge of the genetic material of which each person consists. God need only reform a physical body within the framework of the eternal spiritual body resulting in the re-creation of a body in his perfect image, just as Adam was initially created in a perfect state.

It is much easier to understand, therefore, how God will be able to resurrect a physical body if one remembers:

1. That the physical part of the human body is simply a collection of chemical elements which are found in the earth,
2. That no particular atomic or subatomic particle has an individual identity that would distinguish it from another atomic or subatomic particle of the same type, for example, no hydrogen atom is different from any other hydrogen atom.
3. That it will not be necessary to re-gather the exact physical particles of which a specific human consisted while alive in order to reconstruct a physical body for a reunion with the spiritual body,
4. That the human "spiritual body" is eternal, containing both an eternal spirit, and a soul, the genetic information which contains the unique traits and personalities of each individual, and
5. That the Lord holds together all things, and because he controls all things, he will be able to transform the human body into the likeness of his glorified resurrection body.

4.4 "We Will Not All Sleep"

After Paul established the foundation of the comparison of the human body to a seed that must die in order to bring forth a new glorified body, he next revealed information that had up to that point been hidden:

I Cor 15:51 Listen, **I will tell you a mystery**: We will **not all sleep**, but we will **all be changed [allagesometha]**—

Who is the "we" to whom Paul is referring? By studying the context of I Corinthians chapter 15, as well as Paul's other epistles, it can be discerned that it is the body of believers, the body of Christ, who have accepted the sacrifice of Jesus Christ on the cross, repented of their sin, and been made partakers of the new covenant. Jesus simply called it being "born again"–death to the fleshly man but life to the spiritual man. Those born again believers, whether dead or alive, will experience the transformation at that moment.

Notice that Paul said not all believers will sleep. Who has not heard the joke at one time or another that there are only two certainties in life: death and taxes? Some believe that everyone will die based on the following verse from Hebrews:

Heb 9:27 And just as people are appointed to die once, and then to face judgment,

Is there a contradiction, then? No, because the context of passage in which this verse appears is simply comparing the necessity for Christ to die once for the sins of all, and that humans are appointed to die once. It does not, however, state that all humans will die.

The root Greek word for "changed" used by Paul in this passage is *allaso*. The meaning of the verb is to exchange one thing for another, or to transform it. *Allaso* is used only six times in the New Testament, and twice in this passage.

4.5 "In the Blinking of an Eye"

I Cor 15:52 in a moment [en atomoi], in the blinking of an eye [en ripei ophthalmou] . . .

The change to the imperishable body will occur in a "moment". In describing the change, Paul used a Greek word that is found nowhere else in the New Testament: *atomos*. The word is a combination of the negative *a* and the verb *temno*, which means to cut. The word *atomos*, then, applies to something that is indivisible–that cannot be cut. Paul is attempting to convey that the amount of time it will take to change to immortal bodies is so small that it cannot be cut or made any smaller.

He further elaborated by giving an everyday example of the blinking of an eye. The Greek verb used is *ripto*, which means to throw or bat. Combined with the reference to the eye, Paul meant that the amount of time needed to perform the change will be the same amount of time it takes to bat an eyelash. Greek writers used this verb in other instances to describe the flapping of a wing, the twinkling of a star, or one of the hundreds of quivers made by a harp string when it is played.

4.6 "At The Last Trump"

I Cor 15:52 . . .at the last trumpet [salpiggi]. For the trumpet will sound, and the dead will be raised imperishable, and **we will be changed [allagesometha]**.

The change will take place at the *eschatei salpiggi*, or the "last trump". Paul did not elaborate on the meaning of the last trump, so students of prophecy are left to try to discern what he meant. One way to do this is to understand Paul's background and the background of his readers. Another way is to compare this scripture with other scriptures. Both of these approaches will yield stunning results to be explored later.

It is not likely that Paul had in mind the seventh trumpet judgment of Revelation chapter 11:

Rev 11:15 Then **the seventh angel blew his trumpet**, and there were loud voices in heaven saying: "The kingdom of the world has become the kingdom of our Lord and of his Christ, and he will reign for ever and ever."

Paul's first letter to the Corinthians was written many years before John's revelation of the trumpet judgments in Revelation chapters 8, 9, and 11. Therefore, his Corinthian readers would not have understood what the "last trump" meant if he was referring to something that had not yet been revealed to John in his Revelation vision. In addition, there is no other specific reference in the entirety of scripture to a last or final trumpet to which this reference by Paul can be compared.

The trumpet Paul may have been referring to was the last trumpet blasts during the Feast of Trumpets, the Jewish feast day called Rosh Hashannah, or the Head of the Year. On this feast day, there are one hundred blasts of the trumpet as the Jewish new year is celebrated. This feast was one of the seven feasts established by the Lord:

Lev 23:23 The Lord spoke to Moses:

Lev 23:24 "Tell the Israelites, 'In the seventh month, on the first day of the month, you must have a complete rest, a memorial **announced by loud horn blasts**, a holy assembly.

Num 29:1 "'On the first day of the seventh month, you are to hold a sacred assembly. You must not do your ordinary work, for it is **a day of blowing trumpets for you.**

Jewish tradition established one final trumpet blast of this feast, called *tekiah gedolah* in Hebrew. Paul, whose background in Judaism was impeccable, had full knowledge of this feast and the other six major feasts. It is the final trumpet blast of Rosh Hashannah, which is a secular holiday still celebrated in Israel today, to which Paul may have been referring. It is interesting to note that when Moses met with the Lord on Mount Sinai just before the giving of the law, there was the sound of the blowing of a horn:

Exo 19:19 When **the sound of the horn** grew louder and louder, Moses was speaking and God was answering him with a voice.

As mentioned earlier in this chapter, Exodus chapter 19 will be explored further as the introduction of this prophetic model progresses. Paul's reference to this last trump, however, has interesting possibilities given the knowledge that Paul went to Arabia, the location of Mount Sinai and the location in which this historic horn sounding took place.

4.7 "This Perishable Body Must Put on the Imperishable"

I Cor 15:53 For this perishable body must put on the imperishable [aphtharsia], and this mortal body must put on immortality [athanasian].

Paul further elaborated on the transformation by stating that the perishable body must put on an imperishable body. The Greek word for "imperishable" is *aphtharsia*, which means the perpetual absence of corruption and decay, or eternal purity. The

Greek word for "immortal" in this passage is *athanasia*, meaning the impossibility of experiencing mortal death. There are two major clues about how the transformation into an immortal body will be accomplished in Philippians chapter 3:

Php 3:21 who will **transform [metaschematisei] these humble bodies of ours** into the likeness [summorphon] of his glorious body . . .

First, the transformation of the body of the believer will be performed by Jesus Christ, and will be into the likeness of his glorified resurrection body. That transformation will be from a body of humiliation into the body of his glory. The Greek *metaschematizo*, or transformation, is used only five times in the New Testament. Paul used the word in the Philippians passage above, but three times in II Corinthians chapter 11, one of which describes what the angelic being Satan, is able to do:

II Cor 11:14 And no wonder, for even **Satan disguises [metaschematizetai] himself as an angel of light**.

The KJV renders it "transform" instead of "disguise". *Metaschematizo* is used in this passage to describe a masquerading or cloaking ability. Paul stated that Satan is able to transform or disguise himself as an angel of light, which reveals an interesting ability of angels. Other passages in the New Testament provide evidence that angels have the ability to shape-shift or morph into human form:

Heb 13:2 Do not neglect hospitality, because through it **some have entertained angels without knowing it**.

According to this verse, angels have the ability to appear as human beings without their guests knowledge that they are angels. Apparently, angels have the ability to transform their bodies into what appear to be human bodies. Jude also revealed an interesting account of what happened to some of the angels in heaven when they chose to leave their abode in heaven, morph into human form, and commit sins:

Jud 1:6 You also know that the angels who did not keep within their proper domain but **abandoned their own place of residence [oiketerion]**, he has kept in eternal chains in utter darkness, locked up for the judgment of the great Day.

The Greek *oiketerion*, translated as "place of residence" above, is found in only one other place in the New Testament. Interestingly, it is another passage which describes the body which the believer will put off in order to put on the transformed body:

II Cor 5:2 For in **this earthly house [oiketerion] we groan**, because we desire to put on **our heavenly dwelling**,

When the meaning of *oiketerion* as used in the verse from II Corinthians chapter 5 is applied to the verse in Jude, the meaning is further illuminated. Those angels were disrobed from their angelic bodies when they left their initial domain in the heavenly realm, and are now kept in eternal chains for judgment. What can be learned from these passages that can be applied to the glorified bodies believers will receive? A glorified body will be able to transform from spirit form into human form and back again at will. While this may seem hard to believe, it is the same actions Jesus took in his glorified body after his resurrection, which will be explored in depth below.

The second major clue provided in Philippians 3:21 is how the transformation from the humble bodies into which humans are born into glorious bodies will take place. Paul revealed how Jesus Christ will be able to perform the transformation:

Php 3:21 . . . by means of that power [energeian] by which he is able **to subject [hupotasso] all things to himself**.

What is this power? *Energeian*, according to Thayer's Greek Definitions, is used only in the New Testament Greek to describe supernatural power, whether of Jesus Christ or Satan. One such occurrence is found in Paul's letter to the Ephesians:

Eph 1:19 and what is the incomparable greatness of his power toward us who believe, as displayed in the **exercise [energeia] of his immense strength [kratos ischus]**.

Eph 1:20 This power he **exercised [energeo] in Christ <u>when he raised him from the dead</u>** and seated him at his right hand in the heavenly realms

God exercised the power about which Paul was speaking, the power with which Christ is able to subject all things to himself, when he raised Christ from the dead. This same power will be on display when the transformation of the bodies of believers takes place.

In Philippians 3:21, Paul stated that Christ is able to subject "all things" to himself. It is interesting to note some of the other passages in the New Testament which reveal Jesus Christ's relationship to all things:

Col 1:16 for all things in heaven and on earth were created by him—**all things, whether visible or invisible** . . . **<u>all things</u> were created through him and for him**.

Col 1:17 He himself is **before <u>all things</u>** and **<u>all things</u> are held together in him**.

Heb 2:8 You put **<u>all things</u> under his control** . . .

Heb 1:2 . . . whom he appointed **heir of <u>all things</u>** . . .

Heb 1:3 . . . **he sustains <u>all things</u> by his powerful word** . . .

Jesus Christ created all things both visible and invisible, is heir of all things, has control over all things, holds together all things, and sustains all things. That basically covers the gamut of the entire universe. It is through his complete supernatural power over all things both visible and invisible that he will be able to perform the transformation. From the tiniest proton, neutron, electron, lepton, or quark, to the largest and most evil invisible principality in Satan's kingdom, Jesus Christ has total dominion, power, and authority over all things.

4.8 "Into the Likeness of His Glorious Body"

> Php 3:21 who will transform these humble bodies of ours **into the likeness of [summorphon]** his glorious body . . .

The phrase "into the likeness of" is very interesting. The transformation will be from the humble body into the "likeness" of Christ's body. The Greek adjective *summorphon* for "likeness" connotes that believers will inherit all of the essential attributes that make his body glorious. Within the first five books of the New Testament, there is a detailed record of the activities of Jesus while in his glorified, post-resurrection body. These activities provide startling clues about abilities believers will have in the imperishable, glorious bodies into which they will be transformed. Not only did he display the basic qualities of human beings, including the ability to see, hear, speak, taste, touch, and smell, but he also displayed the following supernatural abilities:

1. The ability to cloak or disguise his identity

> John 20:14 When she had said this, she turned around and saw Jesus standing there, but she did not know that it was Jesus.
> John 20:15 Jesus said to her, "Woman, why are you weeping? Who are you looking for?" Because she thought he was the gardener, she said to him, "Sir, if you have carried him away, tell me where you have put him, and I will take him."
> John 20:16 Jesus said to her, "Mary." She turned and said to him in Aramaic, "Rabboni" (which means Teacher).

Mary clearly turned around and saw Jesus Christ standing in front of her, according to verse 14. Yet she was not able to recognize who he was, a man who had changed her life by casting seven evil spirits out of her body. There are many explanations as to why she was unable recognize him, but the most apparent explanation is that Jesus had somehow shielded her eyes from recognizing him. This is what happened in the second example of Jesus' ability to hide his identity:

> Luk 24:13 Now that very day two of them were on their way to a village called Emmaus, about seven miles from Jerusalem.
> Luk 24:14 They were talking to each other about all the things that had happened.
> Luk 24:15 While they were talking and debating these things, Jesus himself approached and began to accompany them
> Luk 24:16 (but **their eyes were kept [ekratounto] from recognizing him**).

The Greek verb for "kept" above is *krateo*, which is an interesting verb in the context of this verse. *Krateo* means "to take hold of" or "to have power over". In this case, it means Jesus had a supernatural power over their eyes to the point that they were temporarily unable to recognize him. Later in the narrative, after Jesus blessed and broke the bread at their table, their eyes were opened, and they recognized him:

Luk 24:31 At this point **their eyes were opened [dienoichthesan] and they recognized him**. . .

The Greek *dienoichthesan* for "opened" is found nowhere else in the New Testament. It is a very interesting verb that means to open thoroughly what had been closed, or to stimulate or rouse understanding of something. In the context of this encounter, it means that Jesus released the control over their eyes and roused an understanding in them, so that they were able to recognize who he was.

2.   The ability to move through walls–to materialize and dematerialize

Joh 20:19 On the evening of that day, the first day of the week, the disciples had gathered together and **locked the doors of the place** because they were afraid of the Jewish leaders. Jesus came and stood among them and said to them, "Peace be with you."

The disciples were shut up and locked into the place where they were staying, hiding from the Jewish leaders. The body of Jesus was gone and they feared they would be blamed for its theft. The doors were locked, and there was no way to get into the place unless the doors were completely bashed down. But Jesus simply came and stood in the middle of them. Barring an unmentioned secret passage, he would have had to somehow dematerialize from his fleshly body, pass through the walls, then re-materialize into human form when inside the room. This happened not once, but twice, the second occurrence eight days later:

Joh 20:26 Eight days later the disciples were again together in the house, and Thomas was with them. **Although the doors were locked**, Jesus came and stood among them and said, "Peace be with you!"

This ability seems to suggest that natural world obstacles such as walls, doors, solid rock, metal, and others will not be obstacles for the immortal, glorified bodies of believers. It also seems to suggest that believers will be able to move into and out of both the higher and lower dimensions at will.

3.   The ability to vanish from sight while sitting with disciples

Luk 24:30 When he had taken his place at the table with them, he took the bread, blessed and broke it, and gave it to them.
Luk 24:31 At this point their eyes were opened and they recognized him. Then he **vanished [aphantos] out of their sight**.

The Greek *aphantos*, for "vanished" is made up of two base words. The *a* in front of *phantos* is simply a negative participle, meaning "not". The *phantos* ending is very interesting, because it is derived from the base word *phainos* or *phos*, which means "light", or "to shine forth light". Therefore, *aphantos* means to be taken out of sight or be made invisible, a word from which the English word "phantom" is derived. Another way of wording the phrase "he vanished" would be to say "he became invisible" or "he became a phantom in front of them".

Jesus Christ displayed the ability to dematerialize from a physical body to a spiritual body, then to materialize back into a physical body, in a moment's time. Whether it was vanishing from sight while sitting amongst the disciples, or moving through physical walls, this trait was the key. These appearances highlight Christ's ability to transcend the limitations of the flesh while abiding within the constructs of the three-dimensional physical world.

Jesus told his disciples that he was not a spirit, but that he had "flesh and bones". The immortal body will not, therefore, be floating around in the atmosphere without any substance or structure. It will clearly have normal features of the human body, but will not be limited only to those features. This is difficult to fathom while confined within the dimensions of length, width, height, and time, but remember these promises:

> I Joh 3:2 Dear friends, we are God's children now, and what we will be has not yet been revealed. We know that whenever it is revealed **we will be like him**, because <u>we will see him just as he is</u>.

4.9 Summary and Conclusion

Some important points to remember from this chapter include:

- The mortal human body must die in order to put on the immortal body promised for the believer because it was born into sin through Adam. Paul analogized this with the concept of the seed dying in the earth before it produces fruit.
- The physical body, though decayed or cremated, can be reconstructed because all humans consist of the same chemical elements that are found in the ground. The spiritual body is eternal and contains the unique genetic information with personalities and traits that will be joined with a glorious resurrection body.
- Not all believers will be dead when the transformation event takes place. It will happen as quickly as the eye blinks, and at the sound of the last trump, a possible reference to the Feast of Trumpets.
- Philippians 3:21 contains two important clues about the transformation into immortality: (1) that believers will be transformed into a body just like Jesus had after his resurrection, and (2) that Jesus will be able to accomplish the transformation due to his absolute supernatural power over all things.
- God utilized massive power and immense strength when he raised Christ from the dead, and will use the same power and strength to transform the bodies of believers.
- Jesus, in his glorified resurrection body, displayed not only natural abilities, but supernatural abilities to cloak his identity, to move into and out of different

dimensions, and to vanish from sight. Transformed believers will be in his likeness and will therefore possess the same qualities.

As this chapter detailed, Christ has the ultimate power over all things in the universe to accomplish the transformation of the bodies of believers into glorified bodies. The event that follows the resurrection and transformation will be explored in the next chapter: the sudden catching up of all living, transformed believers.

Our house was built in January 2000, and was one of the first homes to be constructed on our street. The landscape, therefore, was still clear of other houses, trees and buildings, reserved for future additions. Looking out the back of our house, there was nothing but open fields until the lone north-south street in the area interrupted them. A small wildlife reserve to the left, a barren plain directly in front, and two ponds toward the right. But what I saw was beyond the immediate landscape of our house, toward the east. As my brain began to process what my eyes were seeing, an intense fear gripped me...

Earthquake Resurrection Prophetic Model Timeline Progression

| | Weeks 1-69 | Week 69 Ends; GAP Between Week 69 and Week 70 | Week 70 Begins |

Time Period	Event	Scripture	Chapter
45BC - 27AD	Decree of Artaxerxes Longimanus, Weeks 1-69 of Daniel's 70 Weeks Prophecy	Dan 9:24-25	Ch. 3
27AD	Transfer of the Priesthood of Melchizedek at Christ's Baptism	Luk 3-4	Ch. 3, 6
31AD	Christ's and the "Many Saints'" Earthquake Resurrection	Mat 27	Ch. 3, 6
31AD	Christ's Ascension to the Right Hand of God	Act 1; Rev 4-5	Ch. 10, 11
31AD - PRESENT — Seal 1 (Opening of the First Five Seals – Birth Pains Begin)	Spirit of Religious Domination in Christ's Name	Rev 6:1-11	Ch. 12
Seal 2	Spirit of War and Bloodshed	Rev 6:1-11	Ch. 13
Seal 3	Spirit of Financial Oppression	Rev 6:1-11	Ch. 13
Seal 4	Spirit of Death, Disease, and Famine	Rev 6:1-11	Ch. 13
Seal 5	Persecution and Death of Believers	Rev 6:1-11	Ch. 14
Sixth Seal	Future Earthquake Resurrection of the Dead in Christ, Transformation and Catching Up	I The 4; I Cor 15	Ch. 4, 5, 7
FUTURE TIME	Confirmation / Strengthening of the Covenant	Daniel 9:27	Ch. 9, 15, 16
FUTURE TIME	Sealing of the 144,000 Children of Israel		Ch. 9, 15, 16
FUTURE TIME	Enormous Group Before the Throne	Rev 7	

- CHAPTER FIVE -

THE MYSTERYIOUS SUDDEN CATCHING UP OF BELIEVERS

In the previous three chapters, two revelations of the apostle Paul that will occur simultaneously were examined: the resurrection of the dead in Christ, and the transformation of the perishable body into imperishable. The third will be examined in this chapter, which is the climax of the event: the catching up of all resurrected and transformed believers into the air. While this event is specifically taught only in I Thessalonians chapter 4, there are certain prophetic patterns and parallels elsewhere in the Bible which may be alluding to the event, which will also be explored. In addition to the patterns and parallels, there are several specific examples of prophets and apostles being snatched up or carried away by the Lord which serve as a precedent for the catching up of living believers in the future.

5.1 The Latin *Rapiemur* and the Greek *Harpazo*

The popular English word for this event is "rapture", a word derived, as are so many English words, from the Latin language. In fact, when St. Jerome, who lived from approximately 347 to 419 AD, penned the Latin Vulgate translation of scripture, he used the verb *rapiemur* in I Thessalonians 4:17 as follows:

I The 4:17 Deinde nos qui vivimus qui relinquimur simul **rapiemur [suddenly caught up]** cum illis in nubibus obviam Domino in aera et sic semper cum Domino erimus. (Latin)

I The 4:17 Then we who are alive, who are left, will be **suddenly caught up [rapiemur]** together with them in the clouds to meet the Lord in the air. And so we will always be with the Lord.

Rapiemur is derived from the root verb *rapio*, which means to carry off or to seize someone or something. The English words "rapt" and "rapture" stem from this Latin verb. Therefore, the English term "rapture" was appropriately borrowed from the Latin Vulgate as a description of what will happen at that moment based on I Thessalonians 4:17.

The Greek term for "suddenly caught up" is *harpazo*, which means to seize or snatch up something suddenly with great force without the consent of the owner. The specific usage of the verb in I Thessalonians 4:17 is *harpagesometha*, the future passive indicative tense. Compare the transliterated Greek to the English translation below:

I The 4:17 epeita hemeis oi zontes hoi perileipomenoi hama sun autois **harpagesometha [suddenly caught up]** en nephelais eis apantesin tou kuriou eis aera kai houtos pantote sun kurio esometha (Greek)

I The 4:17 Then we who are alive, who are left, will be **suddenly caught up [harpagesometha]** together with them in the clouds to meet the Lord in the air. And so we will always be with the Lord.

The verb *harpazo* is used a total of 17 times in the New Testament in a variety of ways, with several referring to the sudden nonconsensual seizure of human beings. The purpose of the above presentation of both the Greek and Latin translation of this verse is to stress that language should not be a barrier to understanding any concept that is established in scripture. Whether a particular English word is or is not found in the Bible is of no importance. What is of paramount importance, however, is whether the *concept* is found. The original language in which the text was written reveals that the concept of the sudden catching up is rock solid.

5.2 The Forcible Catching Up of Old Testament Prophets

In addition to the future catching up of believers, there are examples in both the Old and New Testament which provide solid precedent for this event. In some of these examples, the person was in a visionary state, or out of the body. In other accounts, there is no indication of any other state than a normal state of mind. Each passage bolsters the case that the prophesied massive catching up of believers in the future both can and will happen exactly as described in I Thessalonians chapter 4, just after the resurrection of the dead in Christ. Below some of the passages, the Latin Vulgate and the transliterated Greek versions of the passage are provided to facilitate word studies.

1. The disappearance and translation of Enoch

    Gen 5:22 After he became the father of Methuselah, Enoch walked with God for three hundred years, and he had other sons and daughters.
    Gen 5:23 The entire lifetime of Enoch was three hundred and sixty-five years.
    Gen 5:24 Enoch walked with God, and **then he disappeared [ayin] because God took him away [lâqach].**

    Gen 5:24 kai euhresthsen enwc tw qew kai ouc hurisketo oti **meteqhken [took him away]** auton o qeoV (LXX)

In describing this event, the Hebrew simply states that Enoch was no more, or was no longer present or visible. The NET renders the verb *ayin* with the pronominal "he" as "he disappeared". The phrase "God took him away" uses the common Hebrew verb *lâqach* or "took". There is an interesting parallel passage describing this event in Hebrews chapter 11:

> Heb 11:5 By faith Enoch was **taken up [metetethe]** so that he did not see death, and **he was not to be found because God took him up [metetheken]**. For before **his removal [metatheseos]** he had been commended as having pleased God.

The Greek *metatheseos* means to transpose two things, one for another, or to exchange one thing for another. In using this verb, both the author of Hebrews, and the Greek Septuagint translation of Genesis 5:24, are trying to convey the idea that Enoch was physically and suddenly removed from sight. One interesting description of Enoch's departure outside the Bible is found in the writings of Josephus the Jewish historian:

> Enoch succeeded him, who was born when his father was one hundred and sixty-two years old. Now he, when he had lived three hundred and sixty-five years, **departed and went to God**; whence it is that they have not written down his death.[1]

A second source describes the departure of Enoch as a whirlwind with chariots of fire and horses[2]. While it is not known whether this is accurate, it is almost exactly the same description that is given of the departure of Elijah to heaven.

2. Obadiah's words to Eljiah just prior to the incident with the prophets of Baal on Mount Carmel

> I Kin 18:12 But when I leave you, **the Lord's Spirit will carry you away so I can't find you.** If I go tell Ahab I've seen you, he won't be able to find you and he will kill me. That would not be fair, because your servant has been a loyal follower of the Lord from my youth.

Notice that Obadiah seemed to be keenly aware of the Spirit's ability to snatch up Elijah physically and take him somewhere else, as well as Elijah's favor with the Lord to afford such an opportunity. Perhaps this was a foretelling of what would later happen to Elijah.

3. Elijah's translation in a chariot of fire and a whirlwind

---

[1] Flavius Josephus, "Antiquities of the Jews", Book I, Chapter 3.4.
[2] "The Book of Jasher", Chapter 3, Verse 36, J.H. Parry & Company, Salt Lake City, 1887.

II Kin 2:11 As they were walking along and talking, suddenly a fiery chariot pulled by fiery horses appeared. They went between Elijah and Elisha, and **Elijah went up to heaven in a windstorm.**
II Kin 2:12 While Elisha was watching, he was crying out, "My father, my father! The chariot and horsemen of Israel!" Then he could no longer see him. He grabbed his clothes and tore them in two.

Elijah joined Enoch as one of only two men in the Bible who did not die a natural death. In I Kings chapter 18, Obadiah exclaimed his fear that the Lord would carry away Elijah so that he could not find him, and in II Kings chapter 2, that came to pass. These two men had such an anointing and alliance with the Lord that they were taken alive into heaven. Another Old Testament prophet experienced a supernatural catching up: Ezekiel.

4.   The snatching away of Ezekiel to see visions in Jerusalem

Eze 8:1 In the sixth year, in the sixth month, on the fifth of the month, as I was sitting in my house with the elders of Judah sitting in front of me, **the hand of the Sovereign Lord touched me.**
Eze 8:2 I saw a form that appeared to be a man. From his waist downward he was like fire, and from his waist upward he looked like a bright glowing substance.
Eze 8:3 The form of a hand stretched out and **grabbed me by the hair of my head**. Then a wind **lifted me up into the air** and brought me in visions from God **to Jerusalem**, to the door of the inner gate which faces north. This was the location of the statue which provokes to jealousy.

Notice that Ezekiel was apparently calmly sitting in his house with several elders with him. Suddenly, without his consent, he was snatched up forcibly and taken in the air to Jerusalem. This must have been a physical snatching rather than a visionary state because he was grabbed by his hair and lifted into the air.

5.3 The Forcible Catching Up of New Testament Individuals

5.   The catching up and transportation of Philip the evangelist

Act 8:38 So he ordered the chariot to stop, and both Philip and the eunuch went down into the water, and Philip baptized him.
Act 8:39 Now when they came up out of the water, **the Spirit of the Lord snatched [herpasen] Philip away**, and **the eunuch did not see him any more**, but went on his way rejoicing.
Act 8:40 Philip, however, **found himself at Azotus**, and as he passed through the area, he proclaimed the good news to all the towns until he came to Caesarea.

Act 8:39 hote de anebesan ek tou hudatos pneuma kuriou **herpasen [snatched]** ton philippon kai ouk eiden auton ouketi ho eunouchos eporeueto gar ten hodon autou chairon (Greek)

Act 8:39 cum autem ascendissent de aqua Spiritus Domini **rapuit [snatched]** Philippum et amplius non vidit eum eunuchus ibat enim per viam suam gaudens (Latin)

According to Acts chapter 8, an angel told Philip to leave Samaria and go into the southern desert area of the country. Philip obeyed, and there met a representative of the Ethiopians in a chariot, who was returning from a visit to Jerusalem. The Spirit commanded Philip to go over to the chariot, and as he did, he overheard the Ethiopian man reading from the prophet Isaiah. Philip took that opportunity to explain the entire gospel story to him as they traveled. When they came upon some water, they stopped and Philip baptized the man.

As they were coming up out of the water, something supernatural happened. The Spirit of the Lord suddenly snatched Philip away, and the Ethiopian man was left standing there by himself. Philip was suddenly and forcibly, without his consent, snatched away from where he was. The Greek *harpazo* was used to describe the event. The Ethiopian man did not see Philip any longer–he simply vanished from before his eyes. The Spirit of the Lord took the physical body of Philip, dematerialized it, and transported it to the nearby town of Azotus.

6.   The catching up of the man-child, Jesus Christ

Rev 12:5 So the woman gave birth to a son, a male child, who is going to rule over all the nations with an iron rod. Her child **was suddenly caught up [herpasthe]** to God and to his throne,

Rev 12:5 kai eteken huion arsen hos mellei poimainein panta ta ethne en rhabdo sidera kai **herpasthe [suddenly caught up]** to teknon autes pros ton theon kai pros ton thronon autou (Greek)

Rev 12:5 et peperit filium masculum qui recturus erit omnes gentes in virga ferrea et **raptus [suddenly caught up]** est filius eius ad Deum et ad thronum eius (Latin)

This passage is a reference to the ascension of Jesus Christ to heaven, where he was bodily lifted up in front of many witnesses into the clouds. The passage from Revelation is symbolic, but by comparing scripture with scripture, it is clear that the woman is the nation of Israel, or the Hebrew people, and the male child is Jesus Christ. This awesome event was recorded in two separate passages:

Luk 24:50 Then Jesus led them out as far as Bethany, and lifting up his hands, he blessed them.

> Luk 24:51 Now during the blessing he departed and **was taken up into heaven**.
>
> Act 1:9 After he had said this, while they were watching, <u>he was lifted up</u> and a cloud hid him from their sight.
> Act 1:10 As they were still staring into the sky while he was going, suddenly two men in white clothing stood near them
> Act 1:11 and said, "Men of Galilee, why do you stand here looking up into the sky? This same Jesus who has been **taken up from you into heaven** will come back in the same way **you saw him go into heaven**."

In his resurrected, immortal body, Jesus was caught up into heaven before the disciples on the Mount of Olives. The promise of the two men in white clothing was that not only was Jesus "taken up from you into heaven", but that he would one day return to the earth in the exact same manner they visibly witnessed him ascend into the sky above.

With his ascension complete, all three mysterious events that the apostle Paul declared await believers were fulfilled by Jesus: the resurrection of the dead, the transformation of the body from perishable to imperishable, and the catching up of believers into the clouds.

7. Paul's catching up into the third heaven paradise

> II Cor 12:1 It is necessary to go on boasting. Though it is not profitable, I will go on to visions and revelations from the Lord.
> II Cor 12:2 I know a man in Christ who fourteen years ago (whether in the body or out of the body I do not know, God knows) **was caught up [harpagenta] to the third heaven**.
> II Cor 12:3 And I know that this man (whether in the body or apart from the body I do not know, God knows)
> II Cor 12:4 **was caught up [harpazo] into paradise** and heard things too sacred to be put into words, things that a person is not permitted to speak.
>
> II Cor 12:4 oti **herpage [caught up]** eis ton paradeison kai ekousen arrehta rhemata ha ouk exon anthropo lalesai (Greek)
>
> II Cor 12:4 quoniam **raptus [caught up]** est in paradisum et audivit arcana verba quae non licet homini loqui (Latin)

In this account, Paul stressed that he did not know whether he was taken up to the third heaven in his physical body, or whether his spirit was temporarily separated from his physical body and taken up to paradise. This may be similar to what Ezekiel experienced when he was grabbed by his hair and taken in visions to Jerusalem. Whatever the case, the Greek verb *harpazo* was again used to describe the act. It was sudden, it was forcible, and it was without his consent.

5.4 The Catching Up of All Believers to Meet Jesus Christ in the Air

The catching up of believers, as described in I Thessalonians chapter 4, will include both the resurrected dead in Christ and all remaining living believers, both of which will be transformed into immortal bodies. This may be the most recognized prophetic passage among those who study Bible prophecy, but there are several key phrases that will be beneficial to explore:

I The 4:13 Now we do not want you to be uninformed, brothers and sisters, about those who are asleep, so that you will not grieve like the rest **who have no hope**.

I The 4:14 For if we believe that **Jesus died and rose again**, so also we believe **that God will bring with him** those who have fallen asleep as Christians.

First, Paul stated why he needed to write regarding those among the Thessalonians who had died. It seems there was some confusion among them as to the fate of those who had passed on. Paul stated that there is a hope for those who have died in Christ not shared by those who do not believe that Jesus died and rose again. While he certainly wasn't stating they shouldn't mourn the loss of life, he reminded them that the mourning should be tempered with a hope that unbelievers do not possess.

Second, the hope for the dead is stated in the next verse. God will bring with him those who had a personal relationship with Christ at his return. That hope is predicated upon the fact that Jesus himself both died and rose again. Paul echoed this doctrine in his first letter to the Corinthians:

I Cor 15:17 And **if Christ has not been raised**, your faith is useless; you are still in your sins.

I Cor 15:18 Furthermore, those who have fallen asleep in Christ have also perished.

I Cor 15:19 For **if only in this life we have hope in Christ**, we should be pitied more than anyone.

I Cor 15:20 But now Christ has been raised from the dead, the firstfruits of those who have fallen asleep.

One might question how God could bring those who had fallen asleep with him, if he is going to raise them from the dead later. How can he both bring them with him before he raises them from the dead, then afterward raise them from the dead? The answer lies in remembering that human beings are made up not only of a body, but also a soul and spirit:

I The 5:23 Now may the God of peace himself make you completely holy and may **your spirit and soul and body** be kept entirely blameless at the coming of our Lord Jesus Christ.

As explained earlier, though the body must go into the ground and die, the spirit does not. It is the eternal part of the current existence of the human being, and when a Christian dies, the soul and spirit is taken to be with the Lord:

II Cor 5:8 Thus we are full of courage and would prefer **to be away from the body and at home with the Lord.**

Php 1:23 I feel torn between the two, because I have a desire **to depart and be with Christ, which is better by far,**
Php 1:24 but it is more vital for your sake that I **remain in the body.**

Paul stated that if he were to die, he would be with Christ. However, his physical body would obviously remain on the earth and decompose to the bone stage and eventually to dust. Therefore, when he stated that God will bring those who have died with him when Christ comes, he must have been referring to the eternal part of the human being. It follows, then, that the Lord will return with the soul and spirit of the dead in Christ, resurrect their dead physical bodies, and transform them. Then, their soul and spirit will be joined with their resurrected and transformed bodies, which will all transpire in the briefest of moments. Next, Paul revealed what has become the most inspiring and yet controversial prophetic passage in the Word of God.

5.5 "By the Word of the Lord"

I The 4:15 For we tell you this **by the word of the Lord,** . . .

What Paul was preparing to reveal was by the *logos tou kurio*, or "word of the Lord". When this phrase is used throughout the New Testament, it always refers to the gospel message proclaimed by the apostles as they preached in different cities, except in this occurrence. This is the only occurrence in which a new doctrine from a divine prophetic utterance follows *logos tou kurio*.

What did Paul mean by stating he had received a word from the Lord? It could have been given to Paul directly from the Lord, or it could have been from another person or persons in the form of one of the vocal spiritual gifts: foreign languages, interpretation of foreign languages, or prophecy. This is not the only direct revelation from the Lord that Paul claimed to have received. One of the most important doctrines in Christianity, the eating of bread and wine in remembrance of Christ's death until he returns, also had its source directly from the Lord:

I Cor 11:23 For **I received from the Lord** what I also passed on to you, that the Lord Jesus on the night in which he was betrayed took bread,

Paul's claim of direct revelation was examined in a previous chapter, including the possibility that he went to Mount Sinai in Arabia and received revelation at the same place that Moses and Elijah met with the Lord directly. He separated his own apostleship from the other twelve apostles by stating he received it by a revelation of Jesus Christ:

Gal 1:11 Now I want you to know, brothers and sisters, that the gospel I preached is not of human origin.

Gal 1:12 For I did not receive it or learn it from any human source; instead I **received it by a revelation of Jesus Christ**.

5.6 "We Who Are Alive, Who Are Left"

Paul began his revelation of the word of the Lord by stating the general premise of what he had received:

I The 4:15 . . . that **we who are alive, who are left [perileipomenoi] until the coming [parousian] of the Lord**, will surely not **go ahead [phthasomen]** of those who have fallen asleep.

The revelation was meant to provide comforting words concerning the Thessalonian believers who had died: that living and remaining believers would not go to be with the Lord when he comes before those who had already died. The Greek word describing those who are alive at the time is *perileipomenoi*, which is a combination of two other Greek words. *Peri* is simply a preposition that means "about" or "because", and *leipo* means "to leave" or "to be lacking". In this case, those who are alive are further described as remaining or surviving until the coming of the Lord.

The Greek *parousia* is used to describe the "coming" of the Lord. Rather than the English word "coming", however, this word would be better translated as "presence". *Parousia* is used many times in the New Testament to describe Christ's future coming:

Mat 24:27 For just like the lightning comes from the east and flashes to the west, so **the coming [parousia] of the Son of Man** will be.

II The 2:1 Now regarding **the arrival [parousias] of our Lord Jesus Christ** and our being gathered to be with him, we ask you, brothers and sisters,

However, this Greek word is not to be restricted only to the physical second coming of the Lord, as if that were its only meaning. There are several uses of the noun *parousia* for the coming of other people:

I Cor 16:17 I was glad about **the arrival [parousiai] of Stephanus, Fortunatus, and Achaicus** because they have supplied the fellowship with you that I lacked.

II Cor 7:6 But God, who encourages the downhearted, encouraged us by the **arrival [parousiai] of Titus**.

This is important because *parousia* should not be reserved only for the final earthly arrival of Christ at the end of Daniel's 70th week. In fact, the apostle Peter used it to describe Christ's presence while he was still on the earth:

II Pet 1:16 For we have not by following artificial fables made known to you the power and **presence [parousian]** of our Lord Jesus Christ: but we were eyewitnesses of his greatness.

Peter was an eyewitness of the power and the *parousia*, or power and presence of Jesus while he was on earth. This could only be referring to his presence during his earthly ministry, not a future coming or presence.

The final clause of I Thessalonians 4:15 states that those alive and remaining until the coming of the Lord will not go ahead of those who have died. The Greek verb *phthasomen* means to precede, to attain to, or to anticipate. In this case, it means that those alive and remaining at the coming of Christ will not be with Jesus prior to the resurrection of the dead. Both groups will meet him in the air at the same time.

5.7 The Shout of Command and The Trumpet of God

After the general statement about the word of the Lord he had received, in the next two verses, Paul specifically stated what will happen when the Lord returns for the body of believers on the earth:

I The 4:16 For the Lord himself will come down from heaven **with a shout of command**, with the voice of the archangel, and **with the trumpet of God**, and the dead in Christ will rise first.

I The 4:17 Then we who are alive, who are left, will be suddenly caught up together with them in the clouds to meet the Lord in the air. And so we will always be with the Lord.

The Lord will give a shout of command when he comes down from heaven. If this were considered a cause, then the first effect or reaction on the earth to this shout of command is that the dead in Christ will rise from the dead. This is very interesting given Jesus' own words in describing the raising of the dead:

Joh 5:25 I tell you the solemn truth, a time is coming—and is now here—**when the dead will hear <u>the voice of the Son of God</u>**, and **those who hear will live.**

Could it be that the voice of the Son of God that will cause the dead to live is the same as this shout of command that the Lord will utter as he descends from heaven? A dramatic example of a shout of command that caused a dead man to rise was Lazarus. Notice there was both a shout and a command, just as will occur when he descends from heaven to raise the dead to immortality:

Joh 11:43 When he had said this, he **shouted in a loud voice, "Lazarus, <u>come out</u>!"**

Joh 11:44 The one who had died came out, his feet and hands tied up with strips of cloth, and a cloth wrapped around his face. Jesus said to them, "Unwrap him and let him go."

The trumpet is a key connector between the passages from I Thessalonians chapter 4 and I Corinthians chapter 15. In both passages, the dead are raised after the sound of the trumpet:

I Cor 15:52 . . . at the last **trumpet [salpiggi]**. For **the trumpet will sound [salpisei]**, and **the dead will be raised imperishable** . . .

I The 4:16 For the Lord himself will come down from heaven . . . with **the trumpet [salpiggi] of God [theos]**, and **the dead in Christ will rise first.**

These trumpet sounds are generally regarded to be related. Why? Because the next event described in each verse is the resurrection of the dead. In the I Corinthians passage, the dead will be raised imperishable, and in the I Thessalonians passage, the dead in Christ will be raised after the trumpet sound was described. The trumpet of God and its implications will be further analyzed in the chapter to follow.

5.8 "Will Be Suddenly Caught Up Together With Them"

While several different examples of the sudden and forcible catching up of individuals throughout scripture were examined earlier in this chapter, there are other uses of the Greek verb *harpazo* which will help illuminate what will happen when living believers are caught up according to the description in I Thessalonians chapter 4. The specific individuals examined earlier who experienced *harpazo* as described in the New Testament were Jesus Christ, Philip the evangelist, and Paul. Consider the following uses of the verb in Jesus' own ministry:

Mat 13:19 When anyone hears the word about the kingdom and does not understand it, the evil one comes and **snatches [harpazei] what was sown in his heart**; this is the seed sown along the path.

Joh 10:28 I give them eternal life, and they will never perish; no one will **snatch [harpasei] them from my hand.**

The first verse characterizes the preaching of the word to someone who hears it being quickly snatched out of their heart by the devil before they can understand what they have heard. The second verse characterizes believers as abiding in Christ's hand from which they can never be snatched. Another interesting use of the verb is found in the book of Jude:

Jud 1:23 save others by **snatching them [harpazontes]** out of the fire; have mercy on others, coupled with a fear of God, hating even the clothes stained by the flesh.

This may be the best verse to illustrate the kind of quick seizure that believers will experience at the catching-up event. Jude exhorted his readers to have a heart for saving certain unbelievers as if they were snatching them out of a fire. In the same way, Jesus Christ will quickly snatch up all the transformed believers from whatever

67

remains in the wake of the resurrection of the dead and the changing of the bodies of the righteous resurrected and living believers.

The catching-up event will include all believers, both those resurrected dead in Christ and those believers who will be living at that moment:

I The 4:17 Then we who are alive, who are left, will be **suddenly <u>caught up together</u>** with them in the clouds to meet the Lord in the air.

The believers who are living at the time of the resurrection of the dead will be caught up *together* with the resurrected dead in Christ. Therefore, all believers will be alive and in transformed, immortal bodies when the sudden catching-up event occurs. This is in contrast to most movies and books which describe the catching-up event as happening only to living believers. According to this verse, both those alive in Christ and those dead in Christ prior to that moment, will be caught up together to meet the Lord in the air.

5.9 Changed or Caught Up in a Moment?

Because of the similarities between the "transformation" in I Corinthians chapter 15 and the "catching up" in I Thessalonians chapter 4, the assumption is usually drawn that the sudden catching up, or *harpazo*, will happen "in a moment, in the blinking of an eye", just as the resurrection and transformation event. But this is not necessarily the case. The passage from I Corinthians chapter 15 does not state that the sudden catching up will happen at that moment, but only the change from mortal to immortality:

I Cor 15:51 . . .We will not all sleep, but we will all **be changed—**
I Cor 15:52 **in a moment**, in the blinking of an eye . . .

I The 4:16 . . .and the dead in Christ will rise first.
I The 4:17 **Then we who are alive, who are left, will be suddenly caught up** together with them in the clouds . . .

The I Corinthians chapter 15 passage does not mention the catching-up event, and the I Thessalonians chapter 4 passage does not mention the changing, or transformation event. However, by carefully comparing the two verses, it can be stated that the catching-up event does not happen at the same moment of the changing event. The popular books and movies depicting this event commonly portray people disappearing on the earth, leaving behind whatever they are doing, such as cars being left without a driver, ambling down a highway and killing other people.

This need not be, however. It is possible that there will be a short period of time for the living believers who had just been changed to first come to a point at which they could be caught up without causing harm to others. Perhaps those driving automobiles are changed in the blinking of an eye, but are allowed to bring their cars to a safe stop before being caught up? Remember that, in their transformed state in the likeness of Christ's resurrection body, they will still possess all the basic human qualities they had prior to the transformation. Perhaps some intervening event causes them to first bring their cars to a stop? These possibilities afford that the imminent death and carnage that would be caused by people disappearing from airplanes and automobiles could be mere fantasy. What a bittersweet event it would be if, in the process of being caught up to be with the Lord, the car you were driving was allowed to plow into a van and kill several people. The scripture is clear that the transformation will occur in the briefest of moments, but not the catching up.

5.10 An Old Testament Model of the Catching Up?

Exodus chapter 19 contains a pattern that may have provided Paul the divine inspiration for the mystery of the resurrection of the dead and the catching up of believers. Exodus chapter 19 describes the children of Israel, who had just miraculously passed through the Red Sea by the hand of God, encamped at Mount Sinai. The Lord was preparing to meet with Moses to give him the law.

But before Moses could meet with him, the Lord gave him several instructions to tell the people. Moses went down from the mountain and repeated what the Lord told him. At this point, several interesting similarities between this passage and the I Thessalonians chapter 4 passage are evident.

1.   Sanctification and washing

Exo 19:14 Then Moses went down from the mountain to the people, and **sanctified the people**, and they **washed their clothes**.

I The 4:14 For **if we believe that Jesus died and rose again**, so also we believe that God will bring with him those who have fallen asleep as Christians.

Just as the people of Israel were to be sanctified and wash their clothes before their meeting with the Lord near the mountain, so the believers in Jesus Christ's death and resurrection will participate in the events of this day, whether living or dead. Paul explained both the sanctification and washing of which a believer partakes in his letter to the Ephesians:

Eph 5:25 Husbands, love your wives just as Christ loved **the church** and gave himself for her

Eph 5:26 to **sanctify her by cleansing her with the washing of the water** by the word,

2.   The third day and the resurrection of the dead

Exo 19:15 And he said to the people, "Be **ready by the third day**. Do not go near your wives."

Exo 19:16 And **on the third day in the morning** there was thunder and lightning and a dense cloud on the mountain . . .

I The 4:16 . . . and **the dead in Christ will rise** first.

The Lord told Moses to have the people ready on the third day, because on that day, he was going to descend onto the top of Mount Sinai. It is very interesting that Jesus Christ, the firstfruits of the resurrection of the dead into an immortal body, repeatedly foretold of his resurrection from the dead on the third day:

Luk 9:22 saying, "The Son of Man must suffer many things and be rejected by the elders, chief priests, and experts in the law, and be killed, and **on the third day be raised.**"

Christ's resurrection to immortality, as the pattern for the future resurrection of the dead in Christ, occurred on the third day. This is paralleled by the Lord's announcement that he was going to descend on Mount Sinai on the third day.

3.   The trumpet sound of God's voice

Exo 19:16 And on the third day in the morning there was thunder and lightning and a dense cloud on the mountain, and **the sound of a very loud horn**; all the people who were in the camp trembled.
Exo 19:19 When **the sound of the horn** grew louder and louder, Moses was speaking and God was answering him with a voice.

I The 4:16 For the Lord himself will come down from heaven with a shout of command, with the voice of the archangel, and with **the trumpet of God** . . .

On Mount Sinai, the Lord's presence was accompanied by an extremely loud sounding horn. In fact, the passage seems to indicate that the Lord's voice was the sound of the horn. Similarly, at the Lord's appearance at the resurrection and catching-up event, the trumpet of God will be heard in the earth.

4.   The Lord's descent

Exo 19:18 Now Mount Sinai was completely covered with smoke because **the Lord had descended on it** in fire; and its smoke went up like the smoke of a great furnace, and the whole mountain shook greatly.

I The 4:16 For **the Lord himself will come down from heaven** with a shout of command . . .

Just as the Lord descended from the heavens onto the top of Mount Sinai, the Lord will descend from heaven at the resurrection and catching-up event.

5.   The catching up of believers to meet the Lord

> Exo 19:20 And the Lord came down on Mount Sinai, on the top of the mountain; and **the Lord summoned [qara] Moses to the top of the mountain, and Moses went up**.

> I The 4:17 Then **we who are alive, who are left, will be suddenly caught up [harpagesometha]** together with them in the clouds to meet the Lord in the air.

Moses was "summoned", or called up to the top of the mountain, then went up to meet the Lord. In the same manner, believers will be caught up, or summoned, into the air to meet the Lord. The roots of the Hebrew word *qara* for "summoned" are extremely interesting. According to the highly respected Hebrew dictionary by Brown, Driver, and Briggs, this is a primitive root verb whose basic meaning is that of accosting a new acquaintance. It is a common verb appearing hundreds of times in the Old Testament, but its root meaning matches nearly perfect with the Greek *harpazo*, or sudden forcible snatching.

While the Exodus chapter 19 account may not be an exact parallel of what is described by Paul in I Thessalonians chapter 4, it is a very good pattern, or model, of the event Paul described. The harmony between the two passages is hermeneutically striking and convincing. Recall the previous discussion of the source of Paul's revelation, though, and the pattern becomes even more intriguing. It was shown that Paul not only received his revelation directly from Jesus Christ, but that he went to Arabia. Furthermore, it was shown from Galatians chapter 4 that Mount Sinai is in Arabia.

With all the similarities between these two passages, the fascinating possibility that Paul actually went to Mount Sinai in Arabia and there received the revelation from Jesus Christ gains even more merit. Imagine Paul, at the same mountain in Arabia where the Lord descended after the deliverance from Egypt, receiving the revelation of the Lord's future descent to catch up believers. Could it be that this is where Jesus actually appeared to Paul, and where he received revelation of this mystery?

Another Old Testament passage that Paul may have been drawn to is recorded in Isaiah chapter 26. The prophet Isaiah was anticipating the vindication of the Lord against the wicked and his justice for their deeds. The Lord was preparing to act in vengeance, but the wicked were not able to discern it. Isaiah closed the chapter with a word of encouragement:

> Isa 26:19 Your **dead will come back to life; your corpses will rise up**. Wake up and shout joyfully, you who live in the ground! For you will grow like plants drenched with the morning dew, and **the earth will bring forth its dead spirits**.
> Isa 26:20 **Go, my people! Enter your inner rooms!** Close your doors behind you! **Hide for a little while, until his angry judgment is over!**

Just as in I Thessalonians chapter 4, the resurrection of the dead preceded the command of the Lord for his people to enter their inner rooms. Furthermore, in agreement with a catching up of believers prior to Daniel's 70th week, Isaiah described the hiding as occurring until the Lord's angry judgment is over. Remember this important passage from Isaiah, as it will be further explored throughout the book.

5.11 Summary and Conclusion

Some key points to remember from this chapter include:

- Whether or not a particular English word is found in a particular translation of the Bible is not important. Rather, whether a particular concept is taught is paramount.
- There are several examples of believers being suddenly and supernaturally caught up and taken away in both the Old and New Testament. In the Old Testament, Enoch, Elijah, and Ezekiel. In the New Testament, Philip, Jesus, and Paul.
- Paul described the source of his revelation of the future resurrection of the dead in Christ and catching up as being "by the word of the Lord". It was a direct revelation from the Lord.
- *Parousia* is a Greek noun that means "presence" and should not be reserved only for the final presence of the Lord when he comes back to earth. In fact, Peter used the verb to describe the earthly presence of Christ.
- The descent of the Lord on Mount Sinai has several powerful similarities to the "word of the Lord" provided by Paul in I Thessalonians chapter 4. The Exodus chapter 19 account is an impressive model of the future resurrection and catching-up event.

The important foundation of the resurrection of the dead, the changing of the bodies of believers to imperishable bodies, and the sudden catching up of all transformed believers into the air to meet the Lord, should now be firmly established. It is time to move on to the discovery that was the driving force behind this book: earthquake resurrections. The common thread uniting the three resurrections to immortality explored in chapter 3, as well as its implications for the future of the earth and its inhabitants, will be thoroughly examined in the next chapter.

- SECTION II -

EARTHQUAKE RESURRECTION
PROPHETIC MODEL

I kept staring in unbelief, unable to tear my eyes away from the scene outside, yet I knew I had to warn the others. There was no sound yet, and the others still had not seen it. But there was not much time left until it would be upon us. Suddenly, the realization that I was going to die hit me, and that fear caused me to turn my back to the glass door and slowly slide down to the floor with my back against the glass.

Earthquake Resurrection Prophetic Model Timeline Progression

Weeks 1-69				Week 69 Ends; GAP Between Week 69 and Week 70		Week 70 Begins
457BC - 27AD	27AD	31AD	31AD – PRESENT		FUTURE TIME	

Opening of the First Five Seals - Birth Pains Begin

				Seal 1	Seal 2	Seal 3	Seal 4	Seal 5	Sixth Seal			
Decree of Artaxerxes Longimanus Weeks 1-69 of Daniel's 70 Weeks Prophecy	Transfer of the Priesthood of Malchizedek at Christ's Baptism	**Earthquake Resurrection of Christ and the "Many Saints"**	Christ's Ascension to the Right Hand of God	Spirit of Religious Domination in Christ's Name	Spirit of War and Bloodshed	Spirit of Financial Oppression	Spirit of Death, Disease, and Famine	Persecution and Death of Believers	Future Earthquake Resurrection of the Dead in Christ, Transformation and Catching Up	Confirmation / Strengthening of the Covenant	Sealing of the 144,000 Children of Israel	Enormous Group Before the Throne
Dan 9:24-25	Luk 3-4	Mat 27	Act 1, Rev 4-5	Rev 6:1-11					1 The 4, 1 Cor 15	Daniel 9:27		Rev 7
Ch. 8	Ch. 3, 6		Ch. 10, 11	Ch. 12		Ch. 13		Ch. 14	Ch. 4, 5, 7			Ch. 9, 15, 16

- CHAPTER SIX -

EARTHQUAKE RESURRECTION

To this point in the book, a mysterious three-stage event that will occur when the Lord returns for those who have entered into the new covenant relationship with him has been examined in detail. First, the resurrection of the dead in Christ. Second, the transformation of the bodies of all believers into immortal and glorified ones like Christ's. Third, the sudden catching up of all believers into the air to meet the Lord. These four chapters will provide a strong foundation for the rest of the book. In this chapter, the resurrection of the dead will be examined closer, and from a different viewpoint. From this examination, an intriguing pattern will become evident.

First, the meaning of the trumpet of God will be explored, followed by a comparison of the three descriptions of resurrections of the dead into immortal bodies that are recorded in the Bible. The chapter will close with a brief examination of the Shroud of Turin. Shocking connections between its image and the biblical account of the death and resurrection of Jesus Christ will be explored. The evidence presented in this chapter and the next will form the basis of the prophetic model that will be defended in this book.

6.1 "The Trumpet of God"

In the previous chapter, the trumpet of God was briefly examined in terms of its initiation of the sequence of the three-stage event that has been studied thus far. Just what could Paul have meant by the "trumpet of God" in I Thessalonians 4:17? Does the idea of God Almighty placing a gold or silver trumpet to his mouth come to mind? Given his omnipotence, the idea of the Creator of the universe placing a literal trumpet to his mouth in heaven seems a bit unnecessary. Could it be that the trumpet of God is actually his voice rather than a trumpet that he places to his mouth and blows?

Fortunately, there is a wealth of scripture that will shed some light on these questions. The first is Exodus chapter 19, in which the scene is set for the giving of the Ten Commandments. The following is the Septuagint version of the passage:

> Exo 19:16 And it came to pass on the third day, as the morning drew nigh, there were voices and lightnings and a dark cloud on Mount Sinai. **The voice of the trumpet [salpiggo] sounded loud**, and all the people in the camp trembled.

Exo 19:17 And Moses led the people forth out of the camp to meet God, and they stood by under the camp.

Exo 19:18 Now Mount Sinai was altogether in smoke, because God had descended upon it in fire; and the smoke went up like the smoke of a furnace, and the people were exceedingly amazed.

Exo 19:19 And **the sounds of the trumpet [salpiggo] were growing much louder**. Moses spoke, and **God answered him with a voice.**

It is clear from this famous account that the voice heard from the mountain was the sound of a trumpet. As God spoke to Moses, his voice reverberated and shook Mount Sinai, and the people were extremely terrified. When Paul recounted this spectacle in the letter to the Hebrews, the voice of the trumpet is again mentioned:

Heb 12:18 For you have not come to something that can be touched, to a burning fire and darkness and gloom and a whirlwind

Heb 12:19 and **the blast of a trumpet [salpiggos] and a voice uttering words** such that those who heard begged to hear no more

The trumpet and the voice are again combined in describing God's communication to the Israelites. Another example of supernatural communication and trumpets is found in Revelation, when John encountered the Lord on the isle of Patmos:

Rev 1:10 I was in the Spirit on the Lord's Day when I heard behind me **a loud voice like a trumpet [salpiggo],**

Rev 4:1 After these things I looked, and there was a door standing open in heaven! And **the first voice I had heard speaking to me like a trumpet [salpiggo]** said: "Come up here so that I can show you what must happen after these things."

Revelation chapter 1 states that John heard the resurrected Jesus Christ speaking to him, who would have been seated at the right hand of God after his ascension. In both cases, John described the voice he heard as a loud trumpet blast.

6.2 The Voice and the Shaking

In each of the verses explored above, the Greek nouns *salpiggi* or *salpiggo* are used to describe a trumpet or the sound of the trumpet. These Greek words are also found in the two prophetic passages in I Corinthians and I Thessalonians in describing the sound just before the dead are resurrected:

I Cor 15:52 in a moment, in the blinking of an eye, at the last **trumpet [salpiggi]**. For **the trumpet will sound [salpisei], and the dead will be raised imperishable,** and we will be changed.

I The 4:16 For the Lord himself will come down from heaven with a shout of command, with the voice of the archangel, and with **the trumpet [salpiggi] of God [theos]**, and **the dead in Christ will rise first**.

According to Strong's Concordance, these words are associated with the reverberation and vibration sound made by a trumpet when it is blown. These Greek words have root word origins that are too interesting and important to bypass. Again according to Strong's Concordance, one root word is *salos*, which means the quavering or billowing of the waves on the sea, and is used but once in the New Testament:

Luke 21:25 "And there will be signs in the sun and moon and stars, and on the earth nations will be in distress, anxious over the roaring of the sea and **the surging waves [salou]**.

A second root word for the Greek *salpiggo* is *saino*, which means to be shaken, troubled or disturbed. *Saino*, too, is used but once in the New Testament:

I The 3:3 so that no one **would be shaken [sainesthai]** by these afflictions. For you yourselves know that we are destined for this.

But it gets even more interesting. The Greek *saino* for "would being shaken" is derived from the Greek verb *saleuo*, which according to Strong's Concordance means to waver, shake, or agitate. This verb is used several times in the New Testament, but it also has a primary root verb. That primary verb is *seio*, which means to rock or vibrate to and fro, to cause to tremble or tremor, or to cause to shake or quake. One important verse that was discussed in the previous chapter uses this verb:

Mat 27:51 Just then the temple curtain was torn in two, from top to bottom. **The earth shook [eseisthe]** and the rocks were split apart.

The primary Greek verb *seio* is the word from which the English "seismograph", a device that measures earthquakes, is derived. It is also the root of the Greek noun *seismos*, the common word for earthquake or shaking in the New Testament, and is used in an important verse that was also discussed in the previous chapter:

Rev 11:13 Just then **a major earthquake [seismos] took place** and a tenth of the city collapsed; seven thousand people were killed in **the earthquake [seismos]**, and the rest were terrified and gave glory to the God of heaven.

Using these root words, a pattern of clues begins to form regarding what the trumpet of God may actually be, and what will happen when it is sounded:

• The voice of the trumpet was heard when God spoke to Moses on Mount Sinai and when John heard the voice of the Lord on the isle of Patmos.
• The voice of the trumpet on Mount Sinai was so loud that it caused the earth to shake and vibrate.

- The trumpet of God will be sounded when the Lord descends and the dead in Christ are resurrected.
- The Greek word for the voice of the trumpet is *salpiggo*, which is derived from a verb that is related to the reverberation or vibration sound of a trumpet.
- The Greek *salpiggo* has its roots in *salos, saino, saleuo,* and *seio,* which are all used in the New Testament to describe motion, shaking, quaking, reverberation, or vibration. The Greek word *seismos,* or earthquake, is derived from the primary verb *seio.*

This pattern of clues reveals that the voice of the Lord *is* the sound of a trumpet. The meaning of the Greek word "trumpet" has its roots in motion and vibration, and a trumpet will sound at the resurrection of the dead in Christ, which will be a worldwide resurrection. His voice will sound like the reverberating sound of a trumpet, causing the dead in Christ to awake from death and rise with an imperishable body, and powerful shaking in the surrounding earth. The shout of command may be similar to the command given Lazarus: to "Come forth!" Jesus confirmed that his voice is what would cause the dead to rise:

Joh 5:28 "Do not be amazed at this, because **a time is coming when all who are in the tombs <u>will hear his voice</u>**

Joh 5:29 and **will come out**—the ones who have done what is good to the resurrection resulting in life, and the ones who have done what is evil to the resurrection resulting in condemnation.

This passage is referring to the resurrection of the dead, which has been reviewed in previous chapters. In I Thessalonians 4:16 and I Corinthians 15:52, Paul revealed the mystery of the resurrection of the dead, but Jesus foretold the event by stating that the dead will hear the voice of the Son of God. That voice will not only contain a command to come out of the grave, but will also produce a massive shaking on the earth.

A passage that blends this study together is Hebrews 12:18-21, where Paul provided a short recounting of what took place in Exodus chapter 19 on Mount Sinai. After this description, Paul indicated a future shaking on the earth and in the heavens is coming, comparing it to the shaking of the earth on Mount Sinai:

Heb 12:26 **<u>Then</u> his voice shook [esaleusen] the earth**, but now he has promised, "I will **once more shake [seiso] not only the earth** but heaven too."

This verse follows Paul's account of what happened on Mount Sinai at the giving of the Ten Commandments, discussed above. The verb *esaleusen* is from *saleuo,* meaning to shake or agitate, and the verb *seiso* is from *seio,* meaning to cause to vibrate or quake, both of which were discussed above. This verse is therefore stating that God's voice shaking the earth when he descended on Mount Sinai is an example of the a future *seiso,* or shaking, that is to come on the earth.

Now recall the scene when the Lord descended on Mount Sinai to give the Ten Commandments in Exodus chapter 19. Several parallels between this scene and Paul's revelation of the mystery of the resurrection and catching-up event, including the voice of the trumpet sounding, were provided. An even more conspicuous picture develops:

1. Paul spent time in Arabia, and indicated that Mount Sinai is in Arabia.
2. Paul revealed the mystery of the resurrection of the dead and the catching up of believers.
3. The Exodus chapter 19 account of the scene when the Lord descended on Mount Sinai has several interesting parallels to Paul's revelation of the mystery of the resurrection and catching-up.
4. Paul provided an account of the Exodus chapter 19 scene in Hebrews chapter 12.
5. Paul stated that the voice of the Lord shaking the earth in Exodus chapter 19 was an example of a future shaking of the earth.
6. The first stage of this future shaking of the earth will occur at the resurrection of the dead. The reverberation from the voice of the Lord will result in devastating global earthquake activity.

The prophets searched the scriptures diligently when they were trying to understand the coming anointed one:
> I Pet 1:10 Concerning this salvation, the prophets who predicted the grace that would come to you **searched** and **investigated** carefully.
> I Pet 1:11 **They probed into** what person or time the Spirit of Christ within them was indicating when he testified beforehand about the sufferings appointed for Christ and his subsequent glory.

The key words are "searched", "investigated", and "probed", all indicative of the kind of study that has been undertaken to understand what the trumpet of God may be. Continuing in this spirit of investigation and probing will be beneficial as the crux of this prophetic model is presented.

6.3 The Resurrection of Jesus Christ and the "Many Saints"

As discussed in chapter 3, there is no actual account of the precise moment of the resurrection of Jesus Christ in the Bible. Those chapter headings for the beginning of Matthew chapter 28, Mark chapter 16, Luke chapter 24, and John chapter 20 should be titled "The Discovery of the Empty Tomb" instead of the traditional title such as "The Resurrection". What is described in each of those passages is the discovery of the empty tomb by Mary, the other women, Peter, and John.

However, Matthew's gospel includes some very important clues about what happened at the moment of the resurrection of Christ. Interestingly, however, these clues about the moment of his resurrection are included within the detailed description of the moment of his *death*:
> Mat 27:50 Then Jesus cried out again with a loud voice and gave up his spirit.
> Mat 27:51 Just then the temple curtain was torn in two, from top to bottom. **The earth shook and the rocks were split apart.**

Mat 27:52 And tombs were opened, and the bodies of many saints who had died were raised.
Mat 27:53 (They came out of the tombs after his resurrection and went into the holy city and appeared to many people.)
Mat 27:54 Now when the centurion and those with him who were guarding Jesus saw the earthquake and what took place, they were extremely terrified and said, "Truly this one was God's Son!"

Notice the words underlined above. To understand the differences in the gospel accounts of the moment Jesus died, it is necessary to look at the other two gospels which record this event in a parallel manner:

Mark:
Mar 15:37 But Jesus cried out with a loud voice and breathed his last.
Mar 15:38 And the temple curtain was torn in two, from top to bottom.
Mar 15:39 Now when the centurion, who stood in front of him, saw how he died, he said, "Truly this man was God's Son!"

Luke:
Luk 23:45 because the sun's light failed. The temple curtain was torn in two.
Luk 23:46 Then Jesus, calling out with a loud voice, said, "Father, into your hands I commit my spirit!" And after he said this he breathed his last.
Luk 23:47 Now when the centurion saw what had happened, he praised God and said, "Certainly this man was innocent!"

John's gospel records that after Jesus died, the Jewish leaders asked Pilate to have the victims' legs broken and the bodies taken off the crosses. This was because they didn't want the bodies to remain on the crosses on the Sabbath Day which was quickly approaching:
Joh 19:30 When he had received the sour wine, Jesus said, "It is completed!" Then he bowed his head and gave up his spirit.
Joh 19:31 Then, because it was the day of preparation, so that the bodies should not stay on the crosses on the Sabbath (for that Sabbath was an especially important one), the Jewish leaders asked Pilate to have the victims' legs broken and the bodies taken down.
Joh 19:32 So the soldiers came and broke the legs of the two men who had been crucified with Jesus, first the one and then the other.
Joh 19:33 But when they came to Jesus and saw that he was already dead, they did not break his legs.
Joh 19:34 But one of the soldiers pierced his side with a spear, and blood and water flowed out immediately.

Take note that John's gospel does not record any earthquake occurring at Jesus' death or shortly after it. Neither do the accounts of Mark and Luke. If any of the gospels should have recorded an earthquake at his death, it should have been John, as he was present at the scene:

> Joh 19:26 So when Jesus saw his mother and the disciple whom he loved standing there, he said to his mother, "Woman, look, here is your son!"
> Joh 19:35 And the person who saw it has testified (and his testimony is true, and he knows that he is telling the truth), so that you also may believe.

John's gospel, however, records no earth shaking whatsoever at the death of Jesus. He cried out "It is finished", bowed his head, and died. John's account then records that the soldiers came along and broke the legs of the two men who were crucified with Jesus to speed up their deaths. Then they came to Jesus and found he was dead. Were they running away in fear because of the earth shaking and the rocks splitting? No. Instead, one of the Roman guards found time to thrust a spear into the side of the Lord, causing blood and water to flow out. Later, Joseph of Arimathea and Nicodemus came and took Christ's body off the cross after petitioning Pilate for permission to do so. Still no mention of an earthquake in John's gospel.

6.4 An Earthquake at His Resurrection

For these reasons, Matthew 27:54 must be a summary of the reaction of the centurion and the guards of the entire death and resurrection sequence as encapsulated within Matthew 27:51-53. Unless the tombs of the "many saints" came open without a shaking of the earth, there had to be an earthquake at the moment of the resurrection of Jesus Christ, not his death. Otherwise, the tombs of the "many saints" would have been open while their dead bodies remained in place during the entire time Christ was also dead in the tomb, three days and three nights. Matthew's gospel states that the saints came out of their graves only after Christ had been raised from the dead. A better explanation is that they came out of their tombs due to a shaking of the earth at Christ's resurrection.

Were these "many saints" raised from the dead back into their mortal bodies? This is not possible, again, because of the decomposition factor. The mortal bodies of these saints were decomposed past the point that they could have been raised back into them. Therefore, they must have been resurrected into an immortal body.

If this interpretation is correct, three things happened just after the moment of the *resurrection* of Christ:

1. There was an earthquake – a shaking of the earth.
2. Tombs in and surrounding the city were opened.
3. Many bodies of the saints who had died were raised from the dead to immortality, and they were seen walking about the streets of Jerusalem.

In order for the earthquake and opening of the tombs to have occurred at the moment of Jesus' *death*, the "many saints" would have been resurrected to immortality *before* him. If they were resurrected before Christ when the earth shaking of Matthew chapter 27 is recorded, then Christ was not the firstfruits of the resurrection of the dead. Scripture states, however, that Christ *was* the firstfruits of the resurrection of the dead, not these saints:

I Cor 15:20 But now Christ has been raised from the dead, **the firstfruits of those who have fallen asleep.**

I Cor 15:21 For since death came through a man, **the resurrection of the dead also came through a man.**

I Cor 15:22 For just as in Adam all die, so also in Christ all will be made alive.

I Cor 15:23 But each in his own order: **Christ, the firstfruits**; then when Christ comes, those who belong to him.

There is no other logical interpretation than to state the resurrection of these saints occurred after the resurrection of Jesus Christ. Therefore, the shaking of the earth, which also caused their tombs to open, must have taken place at the moment of Christ's resurrection.

6.5 The Resurrection of the Two Witnesses

The third and final account of a resurrection from the dead to immortality coinciding with a powerful earthquake is the death and resurrection of the two witnesses. The account in Revelation chapter 11 is surprisingly detailed in its description of what occurs at their death and resurrection:

Rev 11:8 Their corpses will lie in the street of the great city that is symbolically called Sodom and Egypt, where their Lord was also crucified.

Rev 11:9 For three and a half days those from every people, tribe, nation, and language will look at their corpses, because they will not permit them to be placed in a tomb.

Rev 11:11 But after three and a half days **a breath of life from God entered them**, and they stood on their feet, and tremendous fear seized those who were watching them.

Rev 11:12 Then they heard a loud voice from heaven saying to them: "Come up here!" So the two prophets went up to heaven in a cloud while their enemies stared at them.

Rev 11:13 **Just then a <u>major [megas] earthquake [seismos]</u> took place and <u>a tenth of the city collapsed</u>; <u>seven thousand people were killed</u> in the earthquake**, and the rest were terrified and gave glory to the God of heaven.

According to this passage, immediately after the two men rose, a major earthquake took place in the city of Jerusalem with the following effects:

1. One tenth of Jerusalem collapsed
2. Seven thousand people died
3. The people were terrified and gave God glory

Combining these three resurrection events, a common characteristic is the presence of earthquakes immediately after the resurrection. The power released upon the earth when individuals are resurrected appears to be responsible for the earthquakes that are recorded in each case. Indeed, Paul revealed in Philippians chapter 3 that God's resurrection power is dynamic:

Php 3:10 My aim is to know him, to **experience the power of his resurrection** [ten dunamin tes anastaseos autou], to share in his sufferings, and to be like him in his death,

Php 3:11 and so, somehow, to attain to the resurrection from the dead.

Paul also revealed in Ephesians chapter 1 that God displayed immense power and strength in raising Christ from the dead:

Eph 1:19 and what is the incomparable greatness of his power toward us who believe, as displayed in the **exercise [energeia] of his immense strength [kratos ischus]**.

Eph 1:20 This power he **exercised [energeo] in Christ when he raised him from the dead** and seated him at his right hand in the heavenly realms

There may be evidence of that immense strength and power present at the resurrection of Jesus Christ in his burial linen, a cloth that many believe has been preserved since that amazing event.

6.6 The Shroud of Turin - Image of the Resurrection Power?

What many scientists believe is further evidence of the supernatural power of the resurrection of Jesus Christ is the famous Shroud of Turin, the burial linen cloth of Jesus Christ in which Joseph of Arimathea and Nicodemus wrapped him:

Joh 19:40 Then they took Jesus' body and wrapped it, with the aromatic spices, in **strips of linen cloth** according to Jewish burial customs.

Joh 20:6 Then Simon Peter, who had been following him, arrived and went right into the tomb. He saw **the strips of linen cloth** lying there,

Joh 20:7 and the face cloth, which had been around Jesus' head, not lying with the strips of linen cloth but rolled up in a place by itself.

It is not the aim of this section to fully describe the Shroud, nor to exhaustively cover all the reasons why it may or may not be the burial cloth of Jesus Christ. There are literal mountains of material written by experts and available on the Internet that will suffice–a perusal of the site located at www.shroud.com could keep one busy for months. The goal of the sections that follow will be to explore some interesting facts about this shroud, as well as to cite some fascinating quotes by experts which tend to corroborate many scriptures covered by this model up to this point. Whether the shroud is or is not the actual burial linen of Christ should have no bearing on the Christian faith. Its history and characteristics are being explored for the purpose of understanding their significance upon the future resurrection of the dead in Christ and the transformation of the bodies of believers.

What follows are a compilation of some of the most important facts that lead to the conclusion that the Shroud of Turin is indeed the burial shroud of Jesus Christ, and the visible image on the cloth is a photograph of the resurrection event. The facts have been broken down into four sections: the visible wounds, the blood stains, the cloth, and the image.

6.7 The Visible Wounds

Any observer of the Shroud of Turin can look at this piece of cloth and make some simple observations. There is an image of a male resting in death with several evidences of wounds and beatings. What follows is an examination of the characteristics of the shroud in comparison with what is recorded in scripture.

1. The shroud has a photographic image of a man who was killed by crucifixion, a brutal and tortuous death commonly carried out by the Roman Empire.

    Luk 23:33 So when they came to the place that is called "The Skull," **they crucified him** there, along with the criminals, one on his right and one on his left.

2. There are nail holes in the wrists and the feet of the shroud image, with blood stains on the cloth on top of and around the nail holes.

    Joh 20:25 The other disciples told him, "We have seen the Lord!" But he replied, "Unless I see the **wounds from the nails in his hands,** and put my finger into **the wounds from the nails,** and put my hand into his side, I will never believe it!"

3. The man in the shroud image appears to have severe swelling over one eye.

    Joh 18:22 When Jesus had said this, one of the high priest's officers who stood nearby **struck him on the face** and said, "Is that the way you answer the high priest?"

    Joh 19:3 They came up to him again and again and said, "Hail, king of the Jews!" And **they struck him repeatedly in the face**.

4. Blood stains on the forehead and around the back of the head indicate that something spiked and sharp was forced onto his head.

    Joh 19:2 The soldiers braided a **crown of thorns and put it on his head,** and they clothed him in a purple robe.

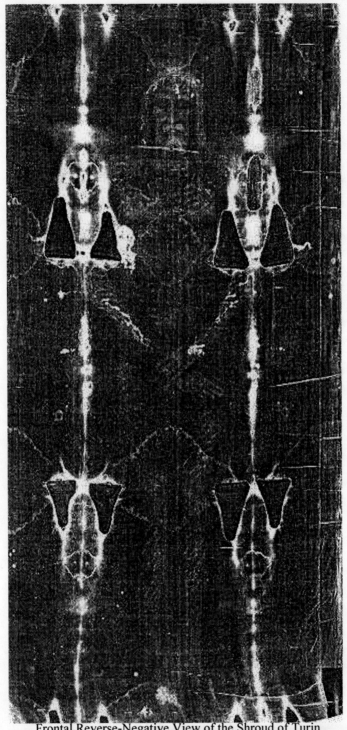

Frontal Reverse-Negative View of the Shroud of Turin
(photo courtesy www.shroud.com)

Dorsal Reverse-Negative View of the Shroud of Turin
(photo courtesy www.shroud.com)

5. The image on the shroud shows many marks of a severe scourging with a whip on the shoulders, back, buttocks, and legs.

    Mar 15:15 Because he wanted to satisfy the crowd, Pilate released Barabbas for them. Then, after **he had Jesus flogged**, he handed him over to be crucified.

6. The scourge marks on the shoulders of the man in the image are blurred, where others on different parts of the body are not, indicating something heavy rubbed against them.

    Joh 19:17 and **carrying his own cross** he went out to the place called "The Place of the Skull" (called in Aramaic Golgotha).

7. There is a considerable amount of blood in the area of the side, depicting a violent wound to the chest area.

    Joh 19:34 But one of the soldiers **pierced his side with a spear**, and blood and water flowed out immediately.

8. The man whose image the shroud depicts did not have his legs broken, which nearly all those crucified by Roman crucifixion experienced in order to speed up the death process.

    Joh 19:32 So the soldiers came and **broke the legs of the two men** who had been crucified with Jesus, first the one and then the other.
    Joh 19:33 But when they came to Jesus and saw that he was already dead, **they did not break his legs**.

6.8 The Blood Stains

Study of the Shroud of Turin has revealed some very interesting facts about the blood stains that are evident on the cloth. Many have tried to discredit the stains as paint or a mixture of chemicals put on by an artist. However, tests have revealed that it is not only real human blood, but the blood of a male. Below are some facts about these blood stains that refute the notion that they are the work of an artist.

1. The blood stains on the cloth are evident in all the places in which Christ was tortured, including the hands, the feet, the back, the forehead, the face, and the side chest wound, with the largest amount of blood stain by the chest.

2. The blood stains captured on the cloth differ from the color variations that form the main image, and are totally separate from the image. The image is part of the cloth, and the blood stains are part of the cloth, but the blood and the image are not parts of each other.

3.   The blood stains have been verified by laboratory testing to contain high levels of the pigment bilirubin. This chemical is produced in the hemoglobin of red blood cells.[1]

4.   Those who have seen the shroud usually comment on how red the blood stains still are. A torture, scourging, and crucifixion would produce a tremendous break-up of red blood cells, and in turn, a very high level of the pigment bilirubin. When mixed with the broken-up red blood cells from the extreme torture, the blood that flowed out would appear to be a very rich red color.[2]

5.   An artist would have had to add the chemical bilirubin to the blood that he put on the shroud, something that is extremely unlikely to begin with, but even more unlikely given the chemical was only discovered in the 20th century.

6.   When a sample of the blood on the shroud was dissolved away, the cloth fibril below was untouched and clean of any body image. If an artist were to create this image, he would have to put the blood on the cloth first, then somehow form the image afterward on top of the blood. This is extremely improbable and very difficult.[3]

7.   The blood has been tested by Italian forensic medicine Professor Pierluigi Baima-Bollone to be human blood, and to be of the blood type AB.[4]

8.   At the Texas University Health Science Center, Dr. Victor Tryon performed further DNA tests on the same threads, and found both X and Y chromosomes, proving the blood is of the male gender.[5]

9.   Two threads of cloth fiber from the foot area were examined at the Genoa Institute of Legal Medicine. According to the Institute's professor, Marcello Canale, the blood stains have *the presence of DNA*, human genetic material.[6]

---

[1] Wilson, Ian (1998). *The Blood and the Shroud*, p. 88-89. London: Weidenfeld and Nicolson.

[2] Adler, Alan D. "The Origin and Nature of Blood on the Turin Shroud", in "Turin Shroud – Image of Christ?" Proceedings of the Symposium of Hong Kong, 3-9 March 1986, Cosmos Printing Press Ltd., Hong Kong, March 1987, p. 57-59.

[3] Wilson, Ian (1998). *The Blood and the Shroud*, p. 89. London: Weidenfeld and Nicolson.

[4] Baima-Bollone, Pierluigi, Mario Jorio & Anna Lucia Massaro, "Identification of the Group of the Traces of Human Blood on the Shroud", Shroud Spectrum International 6, March 1983, pp. 3-6.

[5] Wilson, Ian (1998). *The Blood and the Shroud*, p. 91. London: Weidenfeld and Nicolson.

[6] Ibid, p. 90.

6.9 The Cloth

The Shroud of Turin is linen fabric, the same type of fabric with which Jesus Christ was wrapped after his death. Many interesting microscopic particles have been found on the cloth that all but confirm the shroud was in Jerusalem, Israel at some point in its journey through Europe and the Middle East through the years. The cloth has been through many hands, but there are certain facts that cannot be ignored which point toward it being the same linen cloth with which Christ was wrapped.

1. According to Professor Gilbert Raes of the Ghent Institute of Textile Technology, the shroud cloth could have been manufactured in first-century Palestine. The fabric is definitely linen, and the weave is a rare three-to-one herringbone twill from that time.[7]

2. Dirt was found near the image of the feet on the bottom of the cloth, obviously highly unusual for the work of an artist. Why would an artist put dirt on the *back side* of his canvas, let alone the front side? This dirt contains travertine aragonite limestone found in Jerusalem, Israel today. Testing on the dirt of the shroud and dirt in Jerusalem showed a perfect match.[8]

3. The cloth, carbon-dated by scientists to be in the range of 1260-1390 AD, was *quoted in 1204 AD* to exist in the memoirs of Robert de Clari. There are several problems with radio carbon dating to begin with, but with the shroud, there are additional features which skew the date, such as the bioplastic coating which developed as sort of a natural protective shell on the outside of the shroud. Robert de Clari stated in 1204 AD, a date before the scientific carbon-date, "the shroud, in which Our Lord had been wrapped, which every Friday raised itself upright, so that one could see the figure of our Lord on it."[9]

4. A document called *Otia Imperialia* written by a lawyer named Gervase of Tilbury in 1211 AD, again before the dates provided by the carbon dating, states, "The story is passed down from archives of ancient authority that the Lord prostrated himself with his entire body on whitest linen, and so by divine power there was impressed on the linen a most beautiful imprint of not only the face, but the entire body of the Lord."[10]

---

[7] Wilson, Ian (1986). *The Mysterious Shroud*, p. 34. New York: Doubleday.

[8] Wilson, Ian (1998). *The Blood and the Shroud*, p. 104-106. London: Weidenfeld and Nicolson; quoting Edgar H. McNeal (1936). *The Conquest of Constantinople, translated from the Old French;* Columbia University Records of Civilisation 23. New York.

[9] Ibid, p. 124.

[10] Ibid, p. 139-144.

5. The shroud fibers have a fungal and bacterial bioplastic coating on the outside layers of the cloth due to centuries of handling and exposure to the elements. This coating would also cause the radio carbon dating to register a later date than it in reality possessed.[11]

6. A low-dose radiation event on cellulose fibers, similar to the shroud fibers, would act to stabilize the cloth, which explains how the shroud could be in such great shape, yet date back to the first century.[12]

6.10 The Image

1. The image on the shroud rests on the outer fibers of the linen weave, in a layer thinner than a human hair. The image doesn't penetrate through the rest of the cloth like paint would.[13]

2. The image reverses dark and light shades, and the optimal viewing distance is six to ten feet away, so that if an artist did apply some liquid to its surface to produce the image, he or she would have to stand that far away to see what was being painted.[14]

3. The image itself has three-dimensional qualities, made while the cloth was laying in contact with the body of the man. This technique would be nearly impossible to simulate by an artist.[15]

4. The image not only registers the outer surface of the body, but also the *inside* of the body. According to Michael Blunt, Professor of Anatomy at the University of Sydney, the metacarpal bones in the hands and phalange bones in the fingers are visible.[16]

5. The body was lifted away from the blood that had soaked into the linen cloth, however, no fibrils of the cloth were pulled or scraped in any direction when the body disappeared. This supports the theory that the body dematerialized, then

---

[11] Ibid, p. 224-225.

[12] Little, Kitty. "The Holy Shroud of Turin and the Mystery of the Resurrection", Christian Order, April 1994, p. 226.

[13] Wilson, Ian (1986). *The Mysterious Shroud*, p. 98-100. New York: Doubleday.

[14] Tribbe, Frank C. (1983). *Portrait of Jesus: The Illustrated Story of the Shroud of Turin*, p. 175. New York: Stein and Day.

[15] Wilson, Ian (1986). *The Mysterious Shroud*, p. 100. New York: Doubleday.

[16] Wilson, Ian (1998). *The Blood and the Shroud*, p. 29. London: Weidenfeld and Nicolson.

left the photographic negative image as it collapsed together where the body had been.[17]

6. The image of the man on the shroud was not made by paint or pigment, because there is no natural direction consistent with brush strokes, nor is there any cementation between the fibers.[18]

7. The image could not have been a painting because it resulted from rapid dehydration of the cellulose in the cloth similar to what happens in a fire, but without heat. When chemical decomposition of material is accompanied by heat such as in a fire, substances called pyrols are left behind. Pyrols are in abundance in the parts of the shroud scorched by the various cathedral fires it has suffered through the centuries, but there are no pyrols connected to the image itself.[19]

8. There are more than one hundred dumbbell-shaped marks all over the back side image, from the back to the ankles. The distribution of the marks enable a reasonable interpretation that they were administered by a whipping with a lash having two or three dumbbell-shaped pellets attached to the end.[20]

9. The presence of enough carbon 14 to skew the radio carbon dating could have occurred when the radiation that created the image interacted with the fibers of the shroud. Tests in 1988 involving radiation onto cellulose fibers resulted in the formation of extra carbon 14, which would cause the apparent age of the cloth to appear more recent, or younger, than it truly is.[21]

10. A study of the cloth in Volume 425 of the January 2005 issue of Thermochimica Acta, a chemistry peer-reviewed scientific journal, completely dismissed the aforementioned 1988 radio carbon 14 results. According to the journal, the cloth is much older than those test results indicated, which was 1260 to 1390 AD. Instead, chemist Raymond Rogers measured the loss of vanillin in the cloth, a chemical found in linens made with flax like the shroud, and determined that the

[17] Stevenson, Kenneth, and Gary Habermas (1990). *The Shroud and the Controversy*. Nashville: Nelson.
[18] Wilson, Ian (1998). *The Blood and the Shroud*, p. 77. London: Weidenfeld and Nicolson.
[19] Parker, Shafer. "The Shroud of Turin: Latest Research Bolsters Authenticity", National Catholic Register, 2002.
[20] Wilson, Ian (1998). *The Blood and the Shroud*, p. 32. London: Weidenfeld and Nicolson.
[21] Ibid, p. 233.

cloth was from 1,300 to 3,000 years old. The resurrection of Jesus Christ, nearly 2,000 years ago, fits nicely within the middle of that date range.[22]

11. The very latest evidence on the image involves the fainter second image on the cloth. The shroud was sewn onto a backing in 1534, but was recently removed in order to be examined. There is a second image on the reverse underside of the shroud, only on the top fibrils, a characteristic also possessed by the image on the front side of the shroud. This is yet more extremely important evidence against the theory that the image is a painting.[23]

It is difficult to imagine to whom, other than Jesus Christ, this could belong. How many men in history were crucified? Furthermore, how many of those men crucified were pierced in the side near the heart with large amounts of blood visible in the area of the side? And how many of those men both crucified and pierced in the chest would have blood around their forehead where a crown of thorns would be placed? And how many men in history with all those traits would have a *supernatural*, three-dimensional image photographed onto a burial linen, not only on the front, but the reverse underside? When all the other factors above are added into the equation, along with many others not even considered in this book, the evidence certainly weighs heavily in the favor of this shroud being the actual burial shroud of Jesus Christ.

6.11 The Moment of His Resurrection – What Caused the Image?

This shroud, therefore, is in all likelihood an image of Jesus Christ at the moment of his powerful resurrection from the dead to an immortal body. But what do the experts believe caused the image to form on the cloth in the amazing way that it did? Consider what these experts have noted [emphasis added]:

1. Ian Wilson, art historian and noted author on the Shroud of Turin:
   In the darkness of the Jerusalem tomb the dead body of Jesus lay, unwashed, covered in blood, on a stone slab. Suddenly there is a burst of mysterious power from it. In that instant the blood dematerializes, dissolved perhaps by the flash, while its image and that of the body becomes indelibly fused onto the cloth, preserving for posterity a literal **'snapshot' of the Resurrection**.[24]

---

[22] Rogers, Raymond N. (2005). "Studies on the Radiocarbon Sample from the Shroud of Turin", Thermochimica Acta, Volume 425, Issues 1-2, pp. 189-194.

[23] Govier, Gordon (December 2004). "The Shroud's Second Image", *Christianity Today*, Vol. 48, No. 12, pg. 56; based on research published in the April 2004 by the British Institute of Physics Journal of Optics, and authored by Giulio Fanti and Roberto Maggiolo.

[24] Wilson, Ian (1979). *The Turin Shroud*, p. 211. Middlesex: Penguin Books.

2. Thaddeus Trenn, Director of the Science and Religion Course Programme at the University of Toronto:

    I'm just simply saying I see the X-ray phenomena as a secondary event taking place **after the primary event** that I'm talking about . . .I'm starting with [the notion] there was **a triggering event that will release at the secondary follow-on event such things as the X-rays** . . .my suggestion is that if you were to allow for the possibility that the strong force could be overcome–in other words, an **influx of energy** in the amount we already know that it has to be (1% of the mass)–if that could somehow happen, then certain things would follow. And one of them is that the binding of the protons and neutrons would no longer hold. You would have a separation of the basic nucleons of matter. All your nuclei would come unstuck. And therefore, all these secondary phenomena such as the release of X-rays would take place.[25]

3. Dr. Alan Whanger, professor emeritus of Duke University Medical Center and Director of the Council for the Study of the Shroud of Turin:

    That's why some scientists have suggested that the image resulted from **a controlled nuclear event that occurred at the moment of the Lord's Resurrection**. His body would have given off massive amounts of radiation as it **dematerialized** and passed through the Shroud, leaving a kind of **negative photograph with an X-ray component** relating to the bones resting near the material.[26]

4. Frank J. Tipler, Professor of Mathematical Physics at Tulane University and author:

    In effect, Jesus' dead body, lying in the tomb, would have been enveloped in a sphaleron field. This field would have de-materialized Jesus' body into neutrinos and antineutrinos in a fraction of a second, after which the energy transferred to this world would have been transferred back to the other worlds from whence it came. Reversing this process (by having neutrinos and antineutrinos–almost certainly not the original neutrinos and antineutrinos de-materialized from Jesus' body–materialize into another body) would generate Jesus' resurrection body. **If a body were to de-materialize via this mechanism inside a linen**

---

[25] Trenn, Thaddeus, interviewed by Linda Moulton Howe. "X-File on the Shroud", British Society for the Turin Shroud, Issue, 49, June 1999.

[26] Parker, Shafer. "The Shroud of Turin: Latest Research Bolsters Authenticity", National Catholic Register, 2002.

shroud, it would generate an image just like the image of Jesus seen on the Shroud of Turin.[27]

Earlier, it was stated that the biblical accounts of the resurrection of Jesus Christ do not provide specific details of what happened at the moment of his resurrection. But, if the Shroud of Turin is indeed the linen shroud of Jesus Christ, which the evidence clearly shows, then there is an actual three-dimensional photograph of the moment of Jesus Christ's resurrection to immortality. Scientists state it was a "nuclear event", that it was "instantaneous", and that the body "dematerialized", leaving behind the evidence of the resurrection. If this is indeed what happened at the moment of Jesus Christ's resurrection, the implications for believers in Jesus Christ are literally and figuratively earth-shaking.

6.12 Earthquakes at the Resurrection of the Dead in Christ

Could the nuclear event, which many scientists who have studied the shroud conclude caused its image, have caused a disturbance in the atomic and molecular structure of the surrounding earth at the moment of his resurrection? What these scientists call a nuclear event was actually the power of God raising up the dead, which caused the shaking of the surrounding earth.

It is evident what kind of effect the power of Christ's resurrection had on the shroud, leaving behind an X-ray, three-dimensional photograph at the moment he was being resurrected. Is it possible that this same resurrection power to raise Jesus, the "many saints", and the two witnesses caused the earthquakes that were associated with each of their resurrections? Consider what Dr. Alan Mills, quoted by noted author and Shroud historian Ian Wilson, stated on this question:

> Another hypothesis, put forward by Dr. Allan Mills of Leicester University, suggests that the image might have been created by some type of **electrical discharge** between body and cloth, **associated perhaps with the earthquake activity described by the Evangelist Matthew as having occurred while Jesus' corpse lay in the tomb.**[28] [emphasis added]

Dr. Mills believes that there may be a connection between the electrical discharge that took place at the moment of his resurrection and the earthquake activity described in Matthew's gospel. Another doctor and former nuclear physicist, Kitty Little, further elaborates on this idea:

> The appearance of the image and the properties of the linen of the Shroud can thus be explained if the cause was **the nuclear disintegration** of the atoms in the body. With such a

---

[27] Tipler, Frank. "The Omega Point and Christianity", http://home.worldonline.nl/~sttdc/tipler.htm, accessed September 21, 2004.
[28] Wilson, Ian (1986). *The Mysterious Shroud*, p. 126. New York: Doubleday.

disintegration–a **minor nuclear explosion**–light and energy would also be produced. In the body the main elements involved would be carbon, hydrogen, oxygen and nitrogen, together with smaller quantities of calcium, phosphorus and sulphur. These all have lower molecular weights, and a lower proportion of internal energy, so that the energy liberated would be far less than that from the disintegration of the heavy atoms in nuclear weapons. **It would still be sufficient to move the stone at the entrance to the tomb, and to make the guards think that there had been an earthquake.**

An instantaneous disintegration of the nuclei of the atoms in the body would account for the formation of the image, detail by detail, and the good state of preservation of the linen of the Shroud. It would seem to be the only mechanism whereby the straw-yellow colour could be produced–and the lemon-yellow colour of the serum deposits. It would have to be instantaneous to account for the well-defined image, in terms of the clarity of detail and the range of the radiation causing the image before any collapse of the linen cloth. **The minor earthquake described in the Gospels is also explained.**[29] [emphasis added]

These scientists believe that the earthquake described in the account of the resurrection of Jesus Christ may have been due to the nuclear discharge during the resurrection event. Again, this nuclear event was the power of God, the reverberating, quaking activity that raised the dead and shook the surrounding earth. If the resurrection power to raise Jesus Christ, the "many saints", and the two witnesses caused the earthquakes that were associated with each of their resurrections, then what about the future resurrection of the dead in Christ?

Consider the explosive magnitude of an exponentially larger resurrection of the dead in Christ in the future. Many millions of those who have died in covenant with Jesus Christ throughout history will be instantaneously and simultaneously resurrected from the dead and transformed to immortality with the same dynamic power described in the resurrections of Jesus Christ, the "many saints", and the two witnesses.

With all this supernatural activity happening in a moment's time, might it be possible that severe geologic activity will result, causing a magnetic disturbance and changes to the structure of the earth's surface? If this magnitude of energy is unleashed worldwide at the resurrection event, when the Lord's shout of command and the trumpet sound of God's voice awakens the dead in Christ, then a global shaking would certainly result. Consequently, one would expect massive worldwide earthquakes, volcanic activity due to displaced magma, tsunamic activity due to the

---

[29] Little, Dr. Kitty. "The Application of Scientific Methods to the Turin Shroud", http://www.shroud.com/bsts4607.htm, accessed September 21, 2004.

massive earthquakes, perhaps even a shifting of the earth's magnetic poles or worse, the crust itself, the movement of mountains and islands, and more.

Amazingly, there is a description of these exact consequences at the opening of the sixth seal in Revelation chapter 6:

> Rev 6:12 Then I looked when the Lamb opened the sixth seal, **and a huge earthquake took place**; the sun became as black as sackcloth made of hair, and the full moon became blood red;
> Rev 6:13 and **the stars in the sky fell to the earth** like a fig tree dropping its unripe figs when shaken by a fierce wind.
> Rev 6:14 **The sky was split apart** like a scroll being rolled up, and **every mountain and island was moved from its place**.

Take special notice of the text "a huge earthquake took place" and "every mountain and island was moved from its place". This is perfectly consistent with significant seismic activity, as well as a magnetic or partial crustal pole shift. If crustal, there would not have to be a full 180 degree shift from pole to pole, which would arguably destroy all life on the planet. If a crustal shift resulted with movement consisting of only a few feet or a few miles, then the aforementioned text in Revelation 6:12-14 would be satisfied. Life on the earth would certainly be compromised, but not to the point of extinction.

If the pattern of earthquakes occurring at the resurrection of the dead to immortality continues, then the description of what will happen when the Lamb opens the sixth seal perfectly fits the presumed description of what will take place at the moment of the resurrection of the dead in Christ and transformation to immortality. It will occur within the blink of an eye, it will be accompanied by the voice of God shaking the earth, and it will leave in its wake a catastrophic change to the surface of the earth.

6.13 Summary and Conclusion

Some key points to remember from this chapter include:

- The voice of the trumpet was heard at Mount Sinai when the Lord spoke to Moses.
- The trumpet of God, the last sound before the resurrection of the dead in Christ, will be the voice of God shaking the earth.
- The Greek word for trumpet is *salpiggo*. It has its roots is *salos*, *saino*, *saleuo*, and *seio*, which are all used in the New Testament to describe motion, shaking, quaking, or vibration.
- The writer of Hebrews declared that God's voice once shook the earth at Mount Sinai, and it will shake the earth again in the future.
- At the moment of the resurrection of Christ and the "many saints", there was a *seismos*, or shaking of the earth.

- The tombs of the "many saints" came open after Christ's resurrection. Unless the tombs opened of their own volition and not because of the shaking of the earth, then the earthquake described in Matthew chapter 27 occurred at the resurrection of Christ, not his death.
- There will also be a major earthquake that occurs at the moment the two witnesses are resurrected to immortality in Jerusalem, causing one tenth of the city to fall and 7,000 deaths.
- The best evidence clearly indicates that the Shroud of Turin is indeed the burial cloth of Jesus Christ, bearing the proof of the moment of his resurrection from the dead to immortality.
- According to scientists, the nuclear disturbance in the atmosphere caused by the resurrection event may explain the shaking of the earth described in the Bible. This nuclear disturbance was the power of God's voice when the dead were raised to immortality, causing a shaking of the surrounding earth.
- A worldwide resurrection of the dead in Christ, if accompanied by the same resurrection power described with the biblical accounts of resurrection to immortality, would cause sudden massive and catastrophic changes to the surface of the earth.
- Revelation chapter 6 provides a description of several catastrophic events on the earth occurring just after the opening of the sixth seal. This will occur at the moment of the resurrection of the dead and the changing of the mortal bodies of believers into immortal bodies.

The chapter to follow will more closely examine the events described within the opening of the sixth seal. Two catastrophic events of history, to which Jesus referred in comparing the time of his lightning-quick return to the earth, present a sobering pattern of global devastation that will result. The December 26, 2004 tsunami in Southeast Asia, while admittedly smaller in scale, may be a striking preview to this global devastation, and will be examined in detail. Also included will be the revelation of two very important clues that indicate Daniel's 70th week *must* begin after, and *cannot* begin before, the opening of the sixth seal.

Picture the billowing of waves on the ocean as they roll toward the shore. A wave is the reverberating effect from the pressure that has been impressed upon it, such as from the moon's gravitational force, or a pebble thrown into the middle of a lake. This is what I saw, but infinitely more violent: a billowing and exploding wave coming toward us from the east. However, this wasn't a wave of water, but a wave of ground...

Earthquake Resurrection Prophetic Model Timeline Progression

Weeks 1-69		Week 69 Ends; GAP Between Week 69 and Week 70						Week 70 Begins		
457BC - 27AD	27AD	31AD	31AD - PRESENT					FUTURE TIME		
			Opening of the First Five Seals – Birth Pains Begin							
			1	2	3	4	5			
Decree of Artaxerxes Longimanus, Weeks 1-69 of Daniel's 70 Weeks Prophecy	Transfer of the Priesthood of Melchizedek at Christ's Baptism	Christ's and the "Many Saints" Earthquake Resurrection	Christ's Ascension to the Right Hand of God	Spirit of Religious Domination in Christ's Name	Spirit of War and Bloodshed	Spirit of Financial Oppression	Spirit of Death, Disease, and Famine	Persecution and Death of Believers	Sixth Seal	Future Earthquake Resurrection of the Dead in Christ, Transformation and Catching Up	Confirmation / Strengthening of the Covenant	Sealing of the 144,000 Children of Israel	Enormous Group Before the Throne
Dan 9:24-25	Luk 1-4	Mat 27	Act 1; Rev 4-5	Rev 6 1-11					1 The 4; 1 Cor 15	Daniel 9:27	Rev 7
Ch. 8	Ch. 3, 6		Ch. 10, 11	Ch. 12	Ch. 13		Ch. 14		Ch. 4, 5, 7	Ch. 9, 15, 16

- CHAPTER SEVEN -

THE SIXTH SEAL OF THE SCROLL: GLOBAL CATASTROPHE

This would be a good time to review what has been explored up to this point. In chapters two through five, a future event was analyzed in depth, which will take place in three main stages:

1. Those who have died in a covenant relationship with Jesus Christ, including those who died prior to Christ's death and resurrection, will be resurrected from the dead.
2. The bodies of all living believers, both those who are resurrected and those living at the time of the event, will be transformed from mortal to immortal just like the post-resurrection body of Christ.
3. All believers, in transformed, immortal bodies, will then be suddenly and forcibly caught up into the air to meet Christ.

First Corinthians chapter 15 makes it very clear that the first two stages will happen in the briefest of moments, the time it takes to blink the eye. The amount of time for the catching up in the third stage is not revealed, but it is possible that this catching up will occur a short period of time after the first two stages.

Chapter six featured a closer examination of the three resurrections from the dead to immortality recorded in scripture: Jesus, the "many saints", and the two witnesses during Daniel's 70th week. A common trait within these three resurrections was the presence of earthquakes, a shaking of the surrounding earth. Because the future resurrection of the dead will feature multiple millions of believers throughout the ages, from Adam until the last person to die in Christ prior to the event, the effect on the earth is unknown. However, if the pattern of earthquakes occurring in conjunction with the resurrection of the dead to immortality continues, then a similar earthquake event is virtually certain to happen again at the resurrection and transformation moment.

Additionally, if the severity of the effect on the earth is dependent upon the number of resurrections involved, then the effect on the earth should be considerably greater. When this event happens, though, it will not affect only a small part of Israel, or part of the city of Jerusalem, as with the resurrections of Jesus, the "many saints", and the two witnesses. If believers are buried across the face of the planet, then so scattered will the resurrection energy be. It will affect the entire populated surface of the earth.

7.1 Convergence of the Natural and Supernatural World

All of these events will be completely supernatural, not seen in the natural world. The convergence of supernatural events within the natural world, in such a brief amount of time, will cause incredible things to happen to the natural world. Remember that Jesus was able to move into and out of the normal three spatial-dimension world of length, width, and height, as well as the fourth dimension continuum of space-time, in which humans are currently constrained. The interference between the natural world and the unseen supernatural world is what will be explored in this chapter.

With this in mind, consider again the description of the opening of the sixth seal in Revelation chapter 6, and what happens when it is opened:

Rev 6:12 Then I looked when the Lamb opened the sixth seal, **and a huge earthquake took place**; the sun became as black as sackcloth made of hair, and the full moon became blood red;

Rev 6:13 and **the stars in the sky fell to the earth** like a fig tree dropping its unripe figs when shaken by a fierce wind.

Rev 6:14 **The sky was split apart** like a scroll being rolled up, and **every mountain and island was moved from its place**.

Looking closely at this seal, other than the opening of the seal by the Lamb, there is no cause given for the many effects listed. What follows the opening is a description of some incredible things happening on the earth and in the sky. The first four seals, which will be explored in detail in chapters 12 through 15, all feature some kind of natural effect upon the earth, such as war, disease, and famine. But in each case, the cause is revealed: a white, red, black, and pale green horse with a rider, symbolizing an evil spirit unleashed on the earth. The *unmentioned cause* setting in motion the catastrophic sixth seal events, according to this prophetic model, will be the future three-stage resurrection, transformation, and catching-up event. The convergence of this supernatural event within the natural world will result in the effects seen in Revelation 6:12-14.

7.2 Sudden Destruction: The Days of Noah and Lot

Many may be resistant to the idea that the catching-up event and the beginning of Daniel's 70th week will be ushered in by a worldwide catastrophe that would likely cause the deaths of many people. Yet, that is exactly what both Jesus and Paul stated would be the case. According to Paul, the day of the Lord will be introduced with "sudden destruction":

I The 5:2 For you know quite well that **the day of the Lord** will come in the same way **as a thief in the night.**

I The 5:3 Now when they are saying, "There is peace and security," **then sudden [aiphnidios] destruction comes on them,** like labor pains on a pregnant woman, and they will **surely not escape [ekphugosin].**

In the natural, a thief in the night comes when the people are sleeping, unaware of the sudden destruction coming on them. In the spiritual, those who are not prepared for the coming of the Lord will be caught in an unprepared state, unable to escape what comes upon them. The Greek words used by Paul in explaining the quick destructive power that introduces the day of the Lord are the same used by Jesus when he was explaining the day of the Lord to his disciples:

Luk 21:34 "But be on your guard so that your hearts are not weighed down with dissipation and drunkenness and the worries of this life, and that day close down upon you **suddenly like a trap [aiphnidios].**

Luk 21:35 For it will **overtake [pagis]** all who live on the face of the whole earth.

Luk 21:36 But stay alert at all times, praying that you may have strength to **escape [ekphugein]** all these things that must happen, and to stand before the Son of Man."

Unlike those upon whom the day of the Lord comes like a thief, Jesus stated there will be those who will escape the catastrophic events which introduce the day of the Lord. The same Greek word is used to describe the escape, *ekpheugo*, which was used by Paul in describing the fate of those who will be caught by surprise by the sudden destruction. In addition, both of the passages use *aiphnidios* to describe the swift and severe manner in which the destruction will come. The Greek *pagis* is a noun which means a trap set for animals resulting in their destruction and capture. This noun was used to describe the fate of all those who are not ready at his coming.

Most popular books and movies, based on traditional prophetic models, feature a world in basically the same physical condition after the resurrection and catching-up event as before it. But, if there is any further doubt about whether the time of the coming of the Lord will be a time of catastrophe on the earth, as presented in this chapter, one need only examine Luke chapter 17.

Jesus himself warned that the time of his *apokalupsis*, or revealing, would feature destructive events patterned after those in the days of Noah and Lot. As recorded in Luke chapter 17, Jesus began the warning to his disciples with an explanation of what his appearance in the sky would be like:

Luk 17:23 Then people will say to you, 'Look, there he is!' or 'Look, here he is!' Do not go out or chase after them.

Luk 17:24 For **just like the lightning flashes and lights up the sky from one side to the other,** so will the Son of Man be in his day.

In contrast to those who will be looking for the Lord to first appear on the earth, Jesus stated that he will appear in the sky just as quickly as the lightning flashes through the sky. This description is in agreement with Paul's description of the resurrection and transformation event taking place in a moment, in the blinking of an eye, in which Jesus will return in the sky to catch up all believers who are resurrected and transformed. Jesus continued the discussion by providing two dramatic, historic examples of what will take place on the earth at the time of this lightning-flash appearance:

> Luk 17:26 Just as it was in the days of Noah, **so too it will be in the days of the Son of Man.**
> Luk 17:27 People were eating, they were drinking, they were marrying, they were being given in marriage—right up to the day Noah entered the ark. **Then the flood came and destroyed them all.**

First, he compared the time of his coming to the days of Noah. Up until the day Noah entered the ark, the world went on as usual, and there was no reason for panic. However, on the day the flood began, the inhabitants of the earth quickly realized their predicament. The violent changes that took place on the earth destroyed all of them. The day overtook them as a thief, and the planet underwent legendary changes which no living creature outside the ark survived. Jesus stated it would be the same when he returns in the sky. He next reminded the disciples of the days of Lot:

> Luk 17:28 Likewise, **just as it was in the days of Lot**, people were eating, drinking, buying, selling, planting, building;
> Luk 17:29 but on the day Lot went out from Sodom, **fire and sulfur rained down from heaven and destroyed them all.**
> Luk 17:30 **It will be the same on the day the Son of Man is revealed [apokaluptetai].**

The destruction of Sodom and Gomorrah, as chronicled in Genesis chapter 19, resulted from the cities being pelted with supernatural fire and sulfur from the sky. Jesus then stated it will be "the same" when he returns; some type of destruction will take place on the earth at his lightning-quick revelation.

It should be very clear: in this portion of scripture, Jesus told his listeners that, when he appears in the sky like a lightning flash, the appearance will be followed by natural disasters on the earth similar to the flood and the destruction of Sodom by fire and sulfur from heaven. He clearly stated that the same conditions would be found on the earth when his appearance took place, and went into a fair amount of detail in the description. One should expect, therefore, that when the Son of Man is revealed in the future, and appears like lightning in the sky, the earth will experience similar types of destruction.

Both Noah's family and Lot and his two daughters escaped the destruction of their day, representing a righteous remnant that will completely escape the destruction that will take place on the earth at the time of the future three-stage event. On that day, the earth will experience incredible changes, and Earth's surviving inhabitants who do not escape via the catching-up event will be left behind: trapped in the midst of the devastation.

7.3 First Major Piece of Scriptural Evidence – The Black Sun and The Blood Red Moon

The placement of this three-stage event within the catastrophic events of the sixth seal in Revelation 6:12-14 is a conspicuous departure from the traditional interpretation of the seven seals of the scroll opened by the Lamb. The traditional interpretation, of course, states that the opening of the *first* seal and the appearance of the white horse and rider in Revelation 6:2 marks the beginning of what is commonly called the "tribulation period".

There are two major pieces of scriptural evidence, one within the description of the effects of the opening of the sixth seal, and one within the description of the reaction of the people on the earth to the sixth seal events, which require that the beginning of Daniel's 70th week be placed after the opening of the sixth seal. Revelation 6:12 includes the first of these major pieces of evidence, but also includes a description of the huge shaking of the earth that occurs after the opening of the sixth seal:

> Rev 6:12 Then I looked when the Lamb opened the sixth seal, **and a huge [megas] earthquake [seismos] took place;** . . .

The first occurrence after the opening of the seal is the major worldwide earthquake, which will occur at the moment of the resurrection of the dead in Christ and the changing of the bodies of believers into immortal ones. This conclusion is based on the pattern of earthquakes accompanying the resurrection of Jesus, the "many saints", and the two witnesses into immortal bodies continuing with the resurrection of the dead in Christ, as described in the previous chapter.

The final clause of verse 12 contains the first major clue that the events of the sixth seal must occur before the beginning of Daniel's 70th week, not within that seven-year period, or after it:

> Rev 6:12 . . .the sun became as **black as sackcloth** made of hair, and **the full moon** became **blood red**;

There are several verses in the Old Testament in which the prophets revealed that both the sun and the moon will withdraw their shining, implying that these heavenly bodies will somehow be shaded or covered relative to the earth, which could be accomplished by the presence of large amounts of volcanic ash in the atmosphere. However, there is but one prophecy in the Old Testament in which the prophet described the moon turning to blood, or a blood-red color. The prophecy is found in Joel chapter 2:

> Joe 2:31 The **sunlight will be turned to darkness** and **the moon to the color of blood,** before the day of the LORD comes—that great and terrible day!

There are only two other passages, both in the New Testament, in which the moon is described as turning to a blood-red color. The first is in Acts chapter 2, where Peter merely repeats the prophecy of Joel in his Feast of Pentecost message:

Act 2:20 The sun will be **changed** to darkness and **the moon to blood** <u>before the great and glorious day of the Lord comes</u>.

The only other reference to the moon turning blood-red is the present passage in Revelation chapter 6. The prophecy of Joel is fulfilled, therefore, at the opening of the sixth seal. What is key to understand is *when* Joel said this event would happen: "before the day of the Lord comes". Above, the "sudden destruction" that will introduce the day of the Lord was explored. Joel's prophecy reveals that, before the day of the Lord will occur, the moon will turn to a blood-red color. This disqualifies the notion that the day of the Lord will begin with the opening of the *first* seal, because the blood-red moon is part of the *sixth* seal events.

The beginning of Daniel's 70th week will occur with the strengthening of the covenant by the coming prince, according to Daniel 9:27. At that point, the Lord will turn his attention back to the salvation of Israel. Within Revelation, the turning of the Lord's attention back to Israel clearly begins with the sealing of 144,000 descendants of Jacob just after the events of the sixth seal, coinciding with the appearance of the two witnesses for a 42-month ministry. Therefore, it is quite possible that Daniel's 70th week and the day of the Lord's wrath begin at the same time. However, with the earth in such devastation after the events of the sixth seal, it seems that the confirmation of a covenant would not be high on anyone's agenda. Therefore, there may be a period of time between the beginning of the day of the Lord in Revelation 6:15-17 and the beginning of Daniel's 70th week in Revelation 7:2-8.

The moon will turn to a blood-red color before the day of the Lord begins. If the seven seals of Revelation chapter 6 are part of the 70th week of Daniel, as the traditional "pre-tribulation rapture" model holds, then the prophecy of Joel is fulfilled after the day of the Lord begins, and there is a contradiction between the passages in Joel and Revelation. But Joel's prophecy clearly states that the blood-red moon occurs *before* the day of the Lord begins. Therefore, the opening of the first *six* seals must also occur before the day of the Lord, not after.

This is a major clue that is not recognized in traditional prophetic models. The prophecy of Joel is very specific about the blood-red color of the moon, and this is exactly what is seen in the sixth seal. In addition, the prophecy of Joel is very specific that the moon turns to a blood-red color *before* the beginning of the day of the Lord. This requires that the first six seals be moved to a time before the beginning of the day of the Lord.

7.4 Natural Causes for a Blood-Red Moon

The sun could turn dark and the moon to the color of blood by supernatural means, such as the Lord commanding them to turn that color. However, the more plausible explanation will be some sort of natural phenomena. On Wednesday, October 27, 2004, during this writing, there was a lunar eclipse of the sun which provided an incredible view of an almost blood-red moon. During a lunar eclipse, the earth passes between the moon and the sun, so that the moon passes through the shadow cast by the earth when the sun shines upon it.

An article on the National Aeronautics and Space Administration (NASA) Internet site written about this particular lunar eclipse contained some interesting facts. According to this article, "The Blood Moon rises this year on Wednesday, Oct. 27th. At first it will seem pale and cold, as usual. And then . . .blood red." How interesting that the moon was called a "Blood Moon" with capital letters. The article continues by stating something extremely thought-provoking:

> Our planet casts a long shadow. It starts on the ground–Step outside at night. You're in Earth's shadow. Think about it!–and it stretches almost a million miles into space, far enough to reach the moon . . .That same red light plays across the moon when it's inside Earth's shadow. The exact color depends on what's floating around in Earth's atmosphere. **Following a volcanic eruption, for instance, dust and ash can turn global sunsets vivid red. The moon would glow vivid red, too.**[1] [emphasis added]

The article is pointing out that the reason the moon turns different colors during a lunar eclipse is due to the shadow the earth casts when the sun shines on it. A sunrise or sunset provides some amazing colors at times, depending on what is in the earth's atmosphere at the time. Therefore, with the sun shining on the earth and casting a shadow, and the moon passing through that shadow, whatever is in that shadow will cause the moon to appear that color.

The quote above states that when there are volcanic eruptions, the explosion of lava and ash into the air can cause not only the sunset to appear red globally, but also the moon. This is a powerful connection to what occurs within the description of the sixth seal. Volcanoes would almost certainly be part of a massive worldwide shaking of the earth, in which all mountains and islands move, due to the disturbance of the underlying magma. The gaseous pressure built up underneath the earth would cause an explosion of magma, rock, and ash up through the openings in volcanoes all over the world while the earth is shaking. The dust and ash from these explosions would cause the moon to appear a vivid, blood-red color even without a lunar eclipse. An earthquake resurrection of the dead in Christ at the sixth seal, in which the atmosphere filled with dust and ash from seismic and volcanic activity, would cause both a darkening of the sun and a blood-red moon.

7.5 Tsunamic Activity Accompanies Seismic and Volcanic Activity

The reality of global earthquakes and volcanoes would also include the threat of tsunami waves that would be capable of wiping out complete coastlines, devastating

[1] Phillips, Dr. Tony. "Total Lunar Eclipse", http://www.nasa.gov/vision/universe/watchtheskies/13oct_lunareclipse.html, accessed October 30, 2004.

islands, and more. A tsunami is a sea wave originating from large-scale ocean floor displacements associated with large earthquakes or exploding volcanic islands. When displacements of oceanic or continental plates occur along the fault lines separating the plates, earthquakes and volcanoes result. A tsunami can be just as destructive as the earthquake itself, especially around islands. The numerous islands dotting the expanse of the Pacific Ocean, including Japan, would be especially ripe for catastrophe and destruction in the wake of this event.

This was no more clearly evident than with what transpired on December 26, 2004. An extremely powerful earthquake, which hit 9.3 on the Richter Scale, struck six miles below the surface of the ocean floor in the Indian Ocean, about 155 miles southeast of the Indonesian island of Sumatra. Initially, this earthquake was estimated to be of 9.0 magnitude, but geologists at Northwestern University have announced that the quake was nearly three times stronger than initially thought, and was of 9.3 magnitude.[2] This qualified the earthquake as the second largest in recorded history, trailing only the May 22, 1960 earthquake of 9.5 magnitude in Chile.

The oceanic fault lines slammed into each other, generating nearly 500 mph tsunami waves hurdling toward the coastlines of Indonesia, Thailand, India, Sri Lanka, Somalia, and several other surrounding nations. As of the date of this writing, this event has thus far taken well over 200,000 lives, with thousands still declared "missing" and millions of survivors left homeless or ravaged by disease. The devastation from this event surpassed that of the 1883 eruption of the volcano Krakatoa, which took the lives of over 36,000, as well as the devastation of 1755 when tsunamis killed an estimated 60,000 in Portugal. Eyewitnesses described walls of water 20-30 feet high driving toward the coastlines on a beautifully clear and sunny day, leaving behind ruin as they slammed into the real estate.

In describing the conditions on the earth prior to his return, Jesus provided his disciples with a frightful picture. In one passage, Jesus described activity on the seas:

Luk 21:25 "And there will be signs in the sun and moon and stars, and on the earth nations will be in distress [sunoche], anxious [aporiai] over the roaring [echous] of the sea and the surging waves [salou].
Luk 21:26 People will be fainting [apopsuchonton anthropon] from fear and from the expectation of what is coming on the world, for the powers of the heavens will be shaken.

The nations of the earth will be in great distress, according to this passage, because of activity in the oceans. The massive earthquake activity and shifting of the oceanic plates will cause tsunamis on the oceans, roaring of the seas and surging waves. The Greek *salou*, as examined in a previous chapter, has its roots in *seio*, which means shaking or agitation. There will also be tremendous *echous*, or loud,

---

[2] Northwestern.edu. "Long Period Seismic Moment of the 2004 Sumatra Earthquake and Implications for the Slip Process and Tsunami Generation", http://www.earth.northwestern.edu/people/seth/research/sumatra2.html, accessed February 12, 2005.

reverberating sound, on the oceans. These descriptions match perfectly with what happens when earthquakes and volcanic eruptions cause tsunamic activity.

The Greek *sunoche* means to be completely consumed with something, such that it overtakes your entire being. They will be totally consumed with what is happening on the earth, specifically, what is happening on the oceans. The Greek *aporiai*, from *aporeo*, means to be left totally without options and to not know which way to turn. Combining these two words, humanity's focus will be completely consumed with what is happening in the oceans. People will be in utter disarray, in sheer panic over the surging waves, but knowing they are without defense against them. This is consistent with the fear of knowing that tsunami waves are heading toward a coastline with no defense against them but to flee to higher ground.

Because of this, people will be *apopsuchonton*, which is derived from two Greek words: *apo* and *psucho*. *Apo* is a preposition which simply means the separation of something, and *psucho* is a verb which means to grow cold by breathing, or to have breathing wane. While "fainting" is a serviceable translation into English, there may be more to what Jesus was trying to convey. Another possible interpretation is that people will cease to breathe, or their breath will be separated from them. Perhaps, as a figure of speech, their breath will be taken away from them, such as a state of shock. The modern expression is 'That took my breath away', meaning it was a profound feeling of shock or disruption. Jesus could have meant, therefore, that when people see the surging waves, and hear the resounding reverberation of the sea, they will be in an utter state of shock and panic with their breath metaphorically taken away from them, realizing that there is nothing that they can do. This is the only occurrence of the Greek *apopsuchoton* in the New Testament.

Worldwide earthquakes and volcanic eruptions would cause the effects described after the opening of the sixth seal, including the blood-red moon and the blackening of the sun from the volcanic ash. Tsunamis would also result from the shaking and shifting of the earth's crust, and mountains and islands, themselves a *result* of past seismic and volcanic activity, would also be moved. People on the earth will observe the activity taking place around them and realize they are in a desperate and helpless situation.

7.6 The Effects of a Massive Shifting of the Earth's Crust

After the Revelation 6:12 descriptions of the activities in the sun and the moon, the next verse describes what will appear to happen to the stars of the sky:

Rev 6:13 and the stars in the sky **fell to the earth** like a fig tree dropping its unripe figs when shaken by a fierce wind.

The question here arises as to whether the stars literally fall to the earth and strike it. For at least two reasons, this verse cannot mean that will happen:

1. One star hitting the earth would completely destroy the planet, since stars are many multiple times larger than the earth. In fact, if another star even came

close to the earth, its gravitational force would push the planet out of it place, making life impossible.

2. In describing the events of the third trumpet judgment, which will occur *after* the sixth seal events, the stars are still in the sky:

    Rev 8:12 Then the fourth angel blew his trumpet, and a third of the sun was struck, and a third of the moon, and **a third of the stars**, so that a third of them were darkened. And there was no light for a third of the day and for a third of the night likewise.

If the stars do not literally fall to the earth, then what is being described in Revelation 6:13? Perhaps the Greek *aster* for "stars" in this case simply means asteroids or meteors, rather than stars, and there will be a meteor or asteroid attack upon the earth and in the skies above the earth. Within the context of these three verses, it is clear that a massive shaking, and a major change, will be occurring on the earth at this time. Verse 12 describes a huge earthquake, and verse 14 reveals that every mountain and island are displaced from their locations:

    Rev 6:14 . . .and every mountain and island was **moved from its place**.

In order for mountains and islands to move in such a manner, there must be a shifting of the outer crust of the earth and breaking apart of the continental and oceanic plates. Mountains and mountain ranges are formed by being pushed up from below, and usually in a very messy manner, as rock and earth move under heat and pressure. As for islands, even though an island seems to be interconnected to the rest of the earth under the water, that earth is rarely solid rock. The subsurface is often molten magma, which can cause islands, or mountains in the sea, to rise or sink rather quickly. Under catastrophic conditions, such as an interrelated series of massive earthquakes extending from fault zone to fault zone, the magma under the surface would be extremely active. Volcanic eruptions would be frequent, and new mountain ranges could be formed while old ones disappear. Coastal areas, like western California, could disappear under the ocean, while other areas rise above the water.

Imagine the earth as a large baseball. Like the covering of a baseball, the earth has large seams in the form of continental and oceanic faults, except they are not neat and orderly like a baseball. The faults are under extreme pressure and are the location of the major earthquake faults and major volcanic activity. They are at odds with each other, bumping into each other like large bumper cars that cannot be controlled. Violent reactions within the crust of the earth, manifested in seismic and volcanic activity, are the result of the heat and pressure from the underlying magma.

From the perspective of a person on the earth looking up into the sky when such a violent shifting occurred, it may appear that the stars in the skies would be moving, shifting downward toward the horizon. In reality, however, the stars would remain stationary while the earth's outer crust was actually in motion. For John, describing the events of the sixth seal from the perspective of someone on the earth, the stars may have appeared to be falling to the earth at the horizon.

In confirmation of these ideas, the December 26, 2004 massive 9.3 earthquake in the Indian Ocean featured, in addition to the large waves, other startling side effects around the globe. Consider the following:

1. According to the United States Geological Survey, the island of Sumatra, and several other smaller surrounding islands, actually slid some 120 feet to the southwest when the India and Burma plates slammed into each other in the Indian Ocean.
2. According to geologist Ken Hudnut, "The earthquake **has changed the map.**" He also stated that the orbit of the earth on its axis may have actually **wobbled** "**due the massive amount of energy exerted and the sudden shift in mass.**"[3] [emphasis added]
3. This earthquake also sent shockwaves all over the planet, triggering earthquakes as far away as the Mt. Wrangell volcano in south-central Alaska,[4] and registering on seismic monitoring equipment as far away as Oklahoma.[5]
4. Scientists found that there was a slight polar shift from this earthquake. The "mean North pole" was shifted approximately 2.5 centimeters.[6]
5. Scientists also stated that the earthquake sped up the orbit of the earth on its axis, shortening the length of a day by less than three microseconds.[7] This brings brand new meaning to the Lord's statement that the days during Daniel's 70th week would be shortened:

    Mat 24:22 And if those days had not been cut short, no one would be saved. But for the sake of the elect those days will be cut short.

Is it possible that the shortening will be due to the massive amount of energy that will be expended during the events of the sixth seal, as well as the other earth changes during the trumpet and bowl judgments during that seven-year period?

---

[3] Channelnewsasia.com. "Deadly Quake Rattled Earth Orbit, Changed Map of Asia: Geophysicists", http://www.channelnewsasia.com/stories/afp_asiapacific/print/124431/1/.html, accessed December 28, 2004.
[4] Newkerala.com. "Periodic Tremors at volcano Mt. Wrangell in Arctic Region", http://news.newkerala.com/india-news/?action=fullnews&id=69158, accessed February 12, 2005.
[5] Oklahoma Geological Survey. "Earthquake Press Release 9:00pm CST Dec 26, Sunday", http://www.okgeosurvey1.gov/, accessed February 12, 2005.
[6] www.Physorg.com. "Earthquake Affects Earth's Rotation", http://www.physorg.com/printnews.php?newsid=2622, accessed January 15, 2005.
[7] Newsday.com. "Did Quake Trim Day Length?", http://www.newsday.com/news/health/ny-hsrang284098009dec28,0,5718787.story?coll=ny-health-headlines, accessed December 28, 2004.

6. The quake shook the entire surface of the earth, and weeks after the event, it was still trembling. So much water was displaced from the Bay of Bengal and the Andaman Sea that the worldwide sea level was raised .004 inches.[8]

7. The planet oscillated like a bell every 17 minutes after the quake, which was easily measured with new technology. In addition, the ground moved 0.4 inches everywhere on the planet's surface, though it wasn't discernible in most places. According to scientist Roger Bilham of the University of Colorado, "no point on Earth remained undisturbed."[9]

8. Since the massive earthquake, the peninsula on which the islands of Malaysia and Langkawi are situated have been slowly shifting westward rather than the normal shifting eastward.[10]

When the descriptions of the December 26, 2004 earthquake are compared to the description of the events after the opening of the sixth seal, the similarities are quite alarming. According to a scientist with the Indian government, "Because of the earthquake, the movement of the plates, the topography and the coastline [of the Andaman and Nicobar islands] has changed . . .There has been a northwest-southeast tilt."[11]

Just as the islands of Sumatra and Malaysia moved in response to this earthquake, and just as the entire planet shifted slightly, so the islands and mountains will move when the exponentially greater sixth seal events take place. Just as the earth wobbled slightly on its axis due to this earthquake, the earth will shift on its axis and possibly cause the stars to appear to fall toward the earth's horizon when the sixth seal events take place. Just as the length of a day shortened slightly due to this earthquake, so the days during Daniel's 70th week may be shortened considerably because of the sixth seal events.

In the final clause of the verse, John compared the falling of the stars to unripened figs flying off of a fig tree when a great wind blows. The Greek word for "unripe figs" is *olunthos*, found only in Revelation 6:13. It is referring to figs that grow on the tree during a season in which harvest is not timely, such as winter and summer. When spring and autumn arrive, these particular figs fall off the tree in an unripened state. Imagine a great wind blowing these unripe figs off the tree. They would fly off in every direction. This may be what is in view at the opening of the sixth seal from the perspective of a person on the earth due to all the shaking and movement occurring on the earth.

---

[8] CBS 2 – New York News. "Tsunami Quake Shook Entire Earth", http://cbsnewyork.com/topstories/topstories_story_139162220.html/resources_story PrintableView, accessed May 21, 2005.

[9] Ibid.

[10] Yahoo News. "Malaysia Moving West Since December's Tsunami Quake", http://news.yahoo.com/news?tmpl=story&u=/afp/20050701/sc_afp/malaysiaquake, accessed July 9, 2005.

[11] Yahoo India News. "Tsunami, Earthquake Reshapes, Tilts Andaman Islands", http://in.news.yahoo.com/050228/137/2jw4v.html, accessed March 4, 2005.

Consider what a survivor of the September 28, 2004 magnitude 6.0 earthquake, centered in Parkfield, California, observed about his surroundings:

'Things were **shaking so bad you couldn't tell where to go next**,' said Parkfield Vineyard owner Harry Miller, who grows 170 acres of wine grapes. '**Trees shaking like brooms**, and dust coming from everywhere.'[12] [emphasis added]

There are two interesting points within this statement in relation to the description of the events of the sixth seal. First, Mr. Miller described the shaking he experienced as being so bad that he couldn't tell where he was going. A huge worldwide shaking of the earth, which causes mountains and islands to move, would result in a far greater disorientation than with this relatively small and localized earthquake in California, perhaps even a disorientation on the order of the appearance that stars were falling toward the earth. Second, he stated that the trees were "shaking like brooms". This description is interesting in light of John's description of the figs falling off the fig tree in comparison to the stars falling to the earth.

7.7 Unimaginable Power Resulting in Worldwide Devastation

A violent shaking and disruption on the earth was prophesied over and over by the Old Testament prophets. Isaiah, Jeremiah, Haggai, Joel, Ezekiel, and others saw the future upheaval that will take place on this planet. One particular prophecy in Isaiah encapsulates what may be happening in Revelation chapter 6 at the opening of the sixth seal, or possibly at the pouring out of the seventh bowl judgment. Isaiah chapter 24 includes a description of a time when the Lord will judge the earth:

Isa 24:1 Look, the Lord is ready to **devastate the earth and leave it in ruins**; he will **mar its surface** and **scatter its inhabitants**.

Isa 24:3 **The earth will be completely devastated and thoroughly ransacked**. For the Lord has decreed this judgment.

Isa 24:19 The earth is **broken in pieces**, the earth is **ripped to shreds**, the earth **shakes violently**.

Isa 24:20 The earth **will stagger around like a drunk**; it will **sway back and forth like a hut in a windstorm**. Its sin will weigh it down, and it will fall and never get up again.

Clearly, there will come a day when the earth will experience incredible changes from its current state. It is prophesied several times, including the passage above from Isaiah. The events of the sixth seal are without question the first major stage of these changes.

---

[12] Yahoo News. "Strong Earthquake Shakes Central Calif.", http://story.news.yahoo.com/news?tmpl=story&e=2&u=/ap/20040929/ap_on_re_us/ calif_quake, accessed on September 28, 2004.

When God raised Jesus from the dead, he used massive power and immense strength:

> Eph 1:19 and what is the incomparable greatness of his power toward us who believe, as displayed in the **exercise of his immense strength**.
>
> Eph 1:20 This power he **exercised in Christ** **when he raised him from the dead** and seated him at his right hand in the heavenly realms

In the future, *all* of the righteous dead in Christ will be raised with this same power. If the power of the resurrection of the dead results in earthquakes, as has been shown to be a biblically repetitive and provable pattern in previous chapters, what will be the result when millions upon millions of the dead in Christ are all resurrected simultaneously all over the world? Will this worldwide resurrection of the dead, as well as the transformation of bodies into immortal ones, result in the devastating events described at the opening of the sixth seal? Further, does the link between this pattern to its effects in the sixth seal events point to a new revelation about the timing of the catching-up event? Can the claim be made that the three-stage resurrection, transformation, and catching-up event occurs very close to or during the sixth seal?

Life on earth is currently under the constraints of three spatial dimensions: length, height, and depth, as well as the fourth dimension space-time continuum. However, as shown in chapter 4, Jesus was able to enter into and out of the dimensions under which humanity is currently constrained while in his glorified resurrection body, moving through walls and vanishing from sight. These four dimensions were disturbed in such a way at the moment of Christ's resurrection that the surrounding earth quaked. The burst of nuclear energy when he was resurrected and changed into an immortal body not only caused an earthquake, but if the Shroud of Turin is Christ's shroud, it also caused the incredible images to be photographed onto the its surface. A repetition of this power at the future resurrection and transformation of the dead in Christ presents an ominous forecast for the earth.

7.8 Second Major Piece of Scriptural Evidence – "The Day of Their Great Wrath Has Come"

The second major piece of scriptural evidence proving that Daniel's 70th week cannot begin prior to the opening of the sixth seal is found in the reaction of the people remaining on the earth:

> Rev 6:15 Then the kings of the earth, the very important people, the generals, the rich, the powerful, and everyone, slave and free, hid themselves in the caves and among the rocks of the mountains.
>
> Rev 6:16 They said to the mountains and to the rocks, "Fall on us and hide us from the face of the one who is seated on the throne and from the wrath of the Lamb,
>
> Rev 6:17 because **the great day of their wrath has come**, and who is able to withstand it?"

According to those remaining on the earth, the great day of wrath will arrive after the events of the sixth seal. It could not be stated any more clearly than, "the great day of their wrath has come". This is the beginning of the day of the Lord, an incredible day of wrath that the prophets of the Old Testament saw and described over and over in great detail. Their statement provides further proof that the day of the Lord begins at this point or just after it, not at the opening of the first seal at the beginning of Revelation chapter 6.

The explanation offered by the traditional "pre-tribulation" interpretation to alleviate this problem is to separate the "tribulation period" into two types of wrath: first, the wrath of the Lamb in Revelation 6:1-14, and second, the wrath of God in the rest of the book. However, Revelation 6:16 states that the day of *their* wrath had come at the conclusion of the events of the sixth seal, not before. A pre-70th week of Daniel resurrection of the dead in Christ and catching up of believers, therefore, must occur after the opening of the first seal, not before.

The pronoun "their" preceding "wrath" in verse 17 is rendered in some translations with "his" using the Greek word *autou*, referring either to the Lamb or the one seated on the throne in the previous verse. However, the use of the Greek verb *auton* for "their" is well supported, and also makes the most grammatical sense. This is because the previous verse refers to two entities: the one seated on the throne and the Lamb. Since two entities are referred to, a plural pronoun is appropriate.

When one reads the first four seals of Revelation chapter 6, it is clear that these are symbolic representations of things taking place on the earth. There are not four horses riding around, at least, ones visible to the human eye, carrying out these judgments. Because of this, some scholars have concluded that *all* of the seven seal events are to be interpreted symbolically. However, recall the first rule of scripture interpretation:

Rule 1. When a prophetic verse or portion of prophetic scripture clearly makes sense with a literal interpretation, one should seek no other sense, but interpret it literally.

It clearly makes no logical sense to interpret a literal red horse roaming around with a rider who carries a huge sword. Nor does it make logical sense to interpret a literal black horse roaming around with a rider holding a yoke in his hand. The same can be said for the other two horses and riders. However, there is a shift at Revelation 6:9, with the opening of the fifth seal:

Rev 6:9 <u>Now</u> [kai] when the Lamb opened the fifth seal, I saw under the altar the souls of those who had been violently killed because of the word of God and because of the testimony they had given.

The translators of the NET Bible state that the first word of this verse signals this shift: "Here kaiv (kai) has been translated as "now" to indicate **the introduction of a new and somewhat different topic after the introduction of the four riders.**"[13]

---

[13] The NET Bible. Notes on Revelation chapter 6, verse 9, note 38.

[emphasis added] Therefore, from the fifth seal through the end of the chapter, there is no intellectual harm done to *literally* interpret the following:

1. An altar under which martyred souls abide.
2. The cry of the martyrs for the avenging of their blood.
3. The white robe they are given to wear and the word of confirmation and comfort.
4. A massive shaking of the earth at the opening of the sixth seal.
5. Changes in the appearance of the sun, moon, stars, and the heavens.
6. The effects of the earthshaking causes mountains and islands to move.
7. The physical and verbal response of those on the earth after the opening of the sixth seal.

The people certainly react to the events of the sixth seal as if they are literally happening on the earth, and so should the reader of the text. They will hide in the rocks and caves, and cry out for the rocks to fall on them for concealment from the wrath of God and the Lamb. No doubt, the devastating earthquakes and shifting of the earth's crust will result in a multitude of new caves and rocks among which people will be able to hide. Certain parts of the vision of John are clearly symbolic, and certain parts are clearly literal. Judging from the reaction of the inhabitants of the earth to the events of the sixth seal, what is described within the events of the sixth seal will literally happen.

7.9 Summary and Conclusion

Following are several important points to remember from this chapter:

*   If the resurrection of the dead in Christ is accompanied by worldwide earthquakes, in continuation of the pattern explored in previous chapters, then the events of the sixth seal match the description of what will happen on the earth just as the resurrection and catching-up event is taking place.
*   Both Jesus and Paul said the day of the Lord will be introduced by sudden destruction, and Jesus compared the days of his lightning-quick appearance in the sky to the destruction in the days of Noah and Lot.
*   Joel's prophecy of the sun turning to darkness and the moon to a blood-red color will be fulfilled within the sixth seal, and before the great and terrible day of the Lord will begin.
*   If Daniel's 70th week will begin with the opening of the first seal, and Revelation 6:12 is the fulfillment of Joel's prophecy of the blood red moon, then this event occurs after the day of the Lord has begun, not before, as Joel's prophecy demands.
*   The December 26, 2004 Indian Ocean 9.3 earthquake that triggered deadly tsunamis provided several startling confirmations of the effects to be felt during

the events of the sixth seal, including movement of islands, wobbling of the earth on its axis, and shortening of the length of a day.

- The proclamation of the inhabitants of the earth after the events of the sixth seal have taken place prove that the day of wrath–the day of the Lord–has begun just after the sixth seal is opened, not before. This stands in direct contradiction to the position that the opening of the first seal in Revelation 6:1 marks the beginning of the day of the Lord's wrath.

The term "Daniel's 70th week" has been used extensively in this book, and the time has come to briefly explore this most important prophecy. Even if the reader possesses a masterful understanding of Daniel's 70th week, there will almost certainly be ideas brought up that are unique to this prophetic model. One of those ideas is the crucial point in history at which Daniel's 69th week came to an end, and a gap of time between that week and the final 70th week.

- SECTION III -

UNDERSTANDING THE PROPHECY OF DANIEL'S 70 WEEKS

When I saw the wave of ground, I understood that it was a massive earthquake, and that the reverberation from the epicenter was coming toward us. I sat on the floor in the fetal position, eyes closed, waiting for the wave to reach our house. The thought of our house being swallowed under the earth ran through my mind. That thought was accompanied by a persistent, ferocious crunching sound...

Earthquake Resurrection Prophetic Model Timeline Progression

Weeks 1-69	Week 69 Ends; GAP Between Week 69 and Week 70									Week 70 Begins		
457BC - 27AD	27AD	31AD	31AD - PRESENT							FUTURE TIME		
			Opening of the First Five Seals - Birth Pains Begin									
			1	2	3	4	5	Sixth Seal				
Decree of Artaxerxes Longimanus; Weeks 1-69 of Daniel's 70 Weeks Prophecy	Transfer of the Priesthood of Melchizedek at Christ's Baptism	Christ's and the "Many Saints" Earthquake Resurrection	Christ's Ascension to the Right Hand of God	Spirit of Religious Domination in Christ's Name	Spirit of War and Bloodshed	Spirit of Financial Oppression	Spirit of Death, Disease, and Famine	Persecution and Death of Believers	Future Earthquake Resurrection of the Dead in Christ, Transformation and Catching Up	Confirmation / Strengthening of the Covenant	Sealing of the 144,000 Children of Israel	Enormous Group Before the Throne
Dan 9:24-25	Luk 3-4	Mat 27	Act 1, Rev 4-5			Rev 6:1-11			1 The 4, 1 Cor 15	Daniel 9:27		Rev 7
Ch. 8		Ch. 3-6	Ch. 10-11	Ch. 12	Ch. 13		Ch. 14		Ch. 4-5, 7		Ch. 9, 15, 16	

- CHAPTER EIGHT -

THE KEY TO UNDERSTANDING PROPHECY

Prophecy teachers often refer to a seven-year "tribulation period". Before continuing, it will be beneficial to gain an understanding of this period of seven years. Thus far, this seven-year period has been referred to as the 70th week of Daniel, an important prophecy in Daniel chapter 9 in which the angel Gabriel reveals the future of the Jews, Israel, and the city of Jerusalem.

How important is this prophecy to understanding the timing and structure of end-time events? Jesus himself made reference to it when explaining to his disciples what would happen in the last days:

> Mat 24:15 So when you see **'the abomination of desolation'**—spoken about by **Daniel the prophet**—standing in the holy place (let the reader understand),
> Mat 24:16 then those in Judea must flee to the mountains.

By this reference to Daniel in this passage, Jesus authenticated Daniel as being the author of the book, not someone who lived long after the events of which he prophesied. Many scholars have marveled so greatly at the accuracy of the prophecies in Daniel that they say it could not have been written until after the events prophesied therein took place. With Christ's endorsement, the validity of its authorship and prophetic content cannot be questioned.

8.1 The Abomination of Desolation – A Key Prophetic Event

But Jesus not only proved Daniel's authorship by this reference. He also revealed that the abomination of desolation would happen in the future. This is important because the actions of Antiochus IV Epiphanes seemingly fulfilled the visions that Daniel was given in chapters 8, 9, and 12 about the abomination of desolation by his desecration of the temple in sacrificing a pig to Zeus on the altar. Jesus' reference to the abomination of desolation after the actions of Antiochus IV Epiphanes must have perplexed his listeners well-versed in the Old Testament book of Daniel who thought the prophecy was fulfilled by Antiochus IV Epiphanes.

A closer look at the actions of Antiochus IV Epiphanes would be helpful, because they were a prophetic "type" of the actions surrounding the future abomination of desolation. Daniel's prophecy of the abomination of desolation will ultimately have dual fulfillment: first with Antiochus IV Epiphanes, and finally with the beast and false prophet during Daniel's 70th week. Dual application of a prophetic scripture to a later event as its fulfillment is found several times in the Bible.

Antiochus IV Epiphanes, whose name means "God's revelation" or "God made manifest", was a king in the Seleucid branch of the Grecian Empire. His reign included the region of Syria, Lebanon, Iraq, and Palestine. The first and second books of Maccabees, as well as Josephus' Antiquities of the Jews, provide excellent historical corroboration for Daniel's prophetic account of the invasion of Antiochus IV Epiphanes.

According to Josephus, Antiochus IV Epiphanes came to Jerusalem, though not for the first time, during the 153rd Olympiad. The Olympic games were dedicated in memory of the supreme Greek god Zeus, which began in approximately 776 BC and were held every four years. If Antiochus IV Epiphanes came in the 153rd Olympiad, this places the date between approximately 168-165 BC. He coveted the great amount of gold and riches located in the Jerusalem temple, and Josephus described the scene as such:

> So he left the temple bare, and took away the golden candlesticks, and the golden altar [of incense], and table [of shew-bread], and the altar [of burnt-offering]; and did not abstain from even the veils, which were made of fine linen and scarlet. He also emptied it of its secret treasures, and left nothing at all remaining; and by this means cast the Jews into great lamentation, for he forbade them to offer those daily sacrifices which they used to offer to God, according to the law.[1]

After wreaking additional havoc in the form of burning down buildings, killing city inhabitants, and taking approximately ten thousand prisoners, he built a citadel that overlooked the temple mount. He then forbade the sacrifices that were held on the altar of the outer court and took the following action:

> And when the king had built **an idol altar** upon God's altar, <u>he slew **swine** upon it,</u> and so offered a sacrifice neither according to the law, nor the Jewish religious worship in that country. He also compelled them to forsake the worship which they paid their own God, and to **adore those whom he took to be gods**; and **made them build temples**, and **raise idol altars in <u>every city and village</u>**, and **offer <u>swine</u> upon them every day.**[2] [emphasis added]

This passage from Josephus seems to directly fulfill the prophecy of Daniel chapter 11 about a king from one of Alexander the Great's four branches, the stopping of daily sacrifices, and the setup of the profane pig altar:

---

[1] Flavius Josephus. "Antiquities of the Jews", Book 12, Chapter 5.
[2] Ibid.

Dan 11:31 His forces will rise up and **profane the fortified sanctuary, stopping the daily sacrifice.** <u>In its place</u> they will set up **the abomination that causes desolation**.

In the Jewish view, the sacrifice of a pig on God's holy altar, an unclean animal according to the law of Moses, would be an abomination: the abomination of desolation prophesied by Daniel.

8.2 Gabriel's Prophecy of Seventy Weeks of Years

In order to understand the visions of Revelation, and the seven-year period of time commonly called the tribulation period, the prophecy of Daniel's 70 weeks must be understood. Daniel lived in Babylon for 70 years after being taken by king Nebuchadnezzar in the Babylonian exile. God gave him a series of visions about the future of the nation of Israel. Prior to the deportation to Babylon, God told Jeremiah that the nation of Israel would be in Babylonian captivity for 70 years:

Jer 25:11 This whole area will become a desolate wasteland. These nations will be subject to the king of Babylon **for seventy years.**

According to Jeremiah chapter 25, a servitude to the kings of Babylon would take place in the future, as well as a ransacking of Jerusalem. The actual servitude began in approximately 605 BC, the first year King Nebuchadnezzar came into power in Babylon. Over several years, the city of Jerusalem was torn down and devastated, lying in desolation:

Jer 39:8 The Babylonians **burned down the royal palace, the temple of the Lord,** and the people's homes and **tore down the wall of Jerusalem**.

II Chr 36:19 They burned down **the Lord's temple and tore down the wall of Jerusalem.** They **burned all its fortified buildings and destroyed all its valuable items.**

Daniel the prophet was taken into captivity at a young age, but remained faithful to the Lord and was delivered from certain death at the hands of Nebuchadnezzar. Near the end of the captivity, Daniel was fasting and praying to God during the time of the evening sacrifice. He read the sacred manuscripts of Jeremiah and understood from them that the Babylonian captivity was to last for 70 years. Now a prophet of approximately 80 years of age, Daniel was intensely praying for the sins of the priesthood and asking God if he was going to keep his promise about the 70 years. As he continued to pray in a weary state, the angel Gabriel appeared, informing him his prayer was heard, and gave him a vision about the future:

Dan 9:24 "**Seventy weeks** have been determined **concerning <u>your people</u>** and <u>**your holy city**</u> to finish the transgression, to bring sin to completion, to atone for iniquity, to bring in everlasting righteousness, to seal up the prophetic vision, and to anoint a most holy place.

> Dan 9:25 So know and understand: from **the going forth of the message to return and build Jerusalem <u>until</u> the anointed one [mashiyach], the prince**, there are **seven weeks and sixty-two weeks**. It will again be built, with plaza and moat, but in distressful times.
> Dan 9:26 Now **after the sixty-two weeks, the anointed one will be cut off and have nothing**. As for the city and the sanctuary, the people of the coming prince will destroy them. But his end will come speedily like a flood, until the end of the war that has been decreed; there will be desolations.
> Dan 9:27 He will confirm a covenant with many for <u>one week</u>. But in **the middle of that week** he will bring sacrifice and offering to a halt on **the wing of a desolating abomination**, until **the decreed end** is poured out on the one who makes desolate."

A "week" is a term used extensively throughout the Old Testament to refer to a period of seven years, but its first use can be found in the story of Jacob and Laban, when Jacob was working for him in order to receive Rachel as his wife, but instead was given Leah. Jacob worked seven years initially, all the time thinking that Rachel was the one for which he was working. At the end of the seven years, he found that Leah, instead of Rachel, was given to him because she was the firstborn daughter of Laban. Therefore, Jacob was forced to work a second seven years in order to obtain Rachel, fulfilling her bridal week. An English term to compare to the Hebrew week might be "decade", a period of ten years.

Gabriel's pronouncement to Daniel revealed that the end of the first 69 weeks, or 483 years, would be marked by the appearance of "the anointed one, the prince". It is key to remember that the end of the first 69 weeks was not marked by the cutting off of the anointed one in verse 26, a reference to the death of Christ on the cross, but rather the coming of the anointed one in verse 25. The cutting off of the anointed one was to take place *after* the 69th week had come to an end. Notice that verse 26 states "after the sixty-two weeks, the anointed one will be cut off". After the 62 weeks is also after the first seven, which are separated in verse 25. When the two are added together, the sum is 69 weeks, after which the anointed one was to be cut off.

Interestingly, the KJV renders the "anointed one, the prince" of verse 25 as "the Messiah, the Prince":

> Dan 9:25 Know therefore and understand, that from the going forth of the commandment to restore and to build Jerusalem **unto the Messiah the Prince** shall be seven weeks, and threescore and two weeks: the street shall be built again, and the wall, even in troublous times. (KJV)

The Hebrew word for "Messiah" in this translation is *mashiyach*, a word used 39 times in the Old Testament. Of those 39 occurrences, 37 times it is translated as "anointed" in the KJV, and only 2 times as "Messiah", both in this four-verse passage comprising the prophecy of Daniel's 70 weeks.

Why wouldn't the KJV translate these two occurrences as "Anointed One", or something similar, since all 37 other uses of *mashiyach* are translated with the word "anointed"? There is no doubt that these two occurrences in Daniel chapter 9 are referring to Jesus Christ, the Messiah of Israel. However, a correct translation from Hebrew to English is "Anointed One", or even "Christ", but not Messiah. Indeed, the Septuagint rendering of Daniel 9:25, as translated by Sir Lancelot C. L. Brenton, is as follows:

> Dan 9:25 And you shall know and understand, that from the going forth of the command for the answer and for the building of Jerusalem, **until Christ the Prince**, there shall be seven weeks, and sixty-two weeks; and then the time shall return, and the street shall be built, and the wall, and the times shall be exhausted. (LXX)

8.3 The Starting Point of the Seventy Weeks of Years

In Greek, the "Christ" means a christened or anointed person. The coming of the anointed one, the Christ, would mark the end of first 69 weeks. But which "coming"? Does this mean the birth of Jesus? The beginning of his ministry? The day on which he is declared king by the people at the triumphal entry into Jerusalem? The day on which he rose from the dead? In order to state the ending point of the 69th week with precision, the starting point of the 69 weeks must be sufficiently ascertained. According to Gabriel, the starting point of the first 69 weeks was "the message to return and build Jerusalem".

Since Jerusalem had been destroyed by the Babylonians, it had basically laid in ruin for many years. During the time of Ezra, Nehemiah, and Zerubbabel, the kings of Persia gave at least three recorded decrees allowing these men to return to Jerusalem and begin rebuilding. Please keep in mind that these dates are approximate and several are still debated by many scholars. However, the date ranges noted below are generally agreed upon by most scholars:

1. Decree of Persian King Cyrus in 539-538 BC recorded in Ezra 1:1-3 and confirmed by Persian King Darius in Ezra 6:1-5
2. Decree of Persian King Artaxerxes I Longimanus in 457-456 BC recorded in Ezra 7:11-26
3. Decree of Persian King Artaxerxes I Longimanus in 445 BC recorded in Nehemiah 2:1-8

Each of these decrees were given after the Babylonian captivity and the prophecy of the 70 weeks of Daniel. So, which decree is the one that marks the beginning of the 70 weeks? If the prophecy is to be fulfilled with accuracy, then one of these decrees must be the correct one.

1. The first decree was given by Persian King Cyrus to Zerubbabel in the first year of his reign, which was 539-538 BC. This commandment stated that the Jews were to be allowed to return to Jerusalem and begin rebuilding the temple that had been ransacked:

Ezr 1:1 In the first year of King Cyrus of Persia, in order to fulfill the LORD's message spoken through Jeremiah, the LORD stirred the mind of King Cyrus of Persia. He disseminated a proclamation throughout all his kingdom, announcing in a written edict the following:

Ezr 1:2 "So says King Cyrus of Persia: "'The LORD God of heaven has given me all the kingdoms of the earth. He has instructed me to build a temple for him in Jerusalem, which is in Judah.

Ezr 1:3 Anyone from his people among you (may his God be with him!) may go up to Jerusalem, which is in Judah, and may build the temple of the LORD God of Israel—he is the God who is in Jerusalem.

Counting off 483 years from 539-538 BC calculates to approximately 55 BC, which is definitely before Jesus Christ was even born, so this decree cannot be the one referred to in the 70 weeks prophecy. In addition, this decree referred only to the building of a temple, not to the rebuilding of Jerusalem.

2. The second decree was given by Persian King Artaxerxes I Longimanus in the seventh year of his reign, which began in approximately 464 BC. This decree was given to Ezra, the priestly scribe, in 457-456 BC, allowing Ezra and his men to return to Jerusalem and finish the work on the temple started by Zerubbabel:

    Ezr 7:12 "Artaxerxes, king of kings, to Ezra the priest, a scribe of the perfect law of the God of heaven.

    Ezr 7:13 I have now issued a decree that anyone in my kingdom from the people of Israel—even the priests and Levites—who wishes to do so **may go up with you to Jerusalem**.

    Ezr 7:14 You are authorized by the king and his seven **advisers to inquire concerning Judah and Jerusalem, according to the law of your God** which is in your possession,

The decree also mentions the institution of judges and court officials to oversee cases in the city of Jerusalem. In addition, according to the prayer of Ezra recorded in a later chapter during this rebuilding, God was allowing more than just a restoration of the temple:

Ezr 9:9 Although we are slaves, our God has not abandoned us in our servitude. He has extended kindness to us in the sight of the kings of Persia, in that he has **revived us to restore the temple of our God and to raise up its ruins** and to **give us a protective wall in Judah and Jerusalem**.

While the decree addresses the rebuilding of the temple, there is more going on in the restoration of the city of Jerusalem than just the rebuilding of the temple. Courts, judges and officials were being set up, and, according to Ezra, a protective wall was being raised around Jerusalem.

Counting off 69 weeks of seven years, or 483 years, from 457-456 BC calculates to an approximate date of 27-28 AD. If Jesus was born in the 4-3 BC time frame, which most scholars agree is the best supported date range for his birth, this coincides with the approximate time Jesus would have been baptized and began his ministry at the age of 30. This decree is an excellent candidate for the starting point of the first 69 weeks, placing the beginning of his ministry in 27-28 AD. When counting years that cross over the BC/AD point in the historic timeline, only one year is counted between 1 BC and 1 AD, not two.

3.   The third decree was also given by Persian King Artaxerxes I Longimanus, this time in the 20th year of his reign, which began sometime in 465-464 BC. This would place the decree in approximately 445-444 BC:

> Neh 2:7 I said to the king, "If the king is so inclined, let him give me letters for the governors of Trans-Euphrates that will enable me to travel safely until I reach Judah,
>
> Neh 2:8 and a letter for Asaph the keeper of the king's nature preserve, so that he will give me timber for beams for the gates of the fortress adjacent to the temple and for the wall of the city and for the home to which I go." So the king granted me these provisions, for the good hand of my God was on me.

Counting off 483 years from 445-444 BC calculates to an approximate date of 37-38 AD. This date is clearly after Jesus Christ was resurrected and ascended to heaven. This decree is not the starting point because the coming of the anointed one could not be several years after his ascension.

The decree of Artaxerxes I Longimanus in 457-456 BC, therefore, is the only acceptable fit for the starting point of the first 69 weeks. The first decree, given by Cyrus in 539-538 BC, occurred too early to even be considered, since 483 years after it would produce an ending point of the 69th week with a date before Jesus was born. The third decree, given by Artaxerxes I Longimanus in 445-444 BC, occurred too late to be considered, as it produces an ending point of the 69th week with a date after Jesus ascended to heaven.

8.4 The Ending Point of the First 69 Weeks of Years

Using this 457-456 BC date as an approximate starting point, what event in the 27-28 AD time frame in the life of Jesus marked the end of the first 69 weeks? Was it the baptism, triumphal entry, death, or resurrection of Jesus Christ, or some other event? Approximately 27-28 AD was the time Jesus was baptized and began his ministry. This is very strong corroboration for the 457-456 BC date being the correct starting point, and the year of the baptism of Jesus and the start of his ministry being the correct ending point, of the first 69 weeks.

The beginning of the ministry of Jesus Christ must therefore be examined in greater detail in order to defend the range from 457-456 BC to 27-28 AD as the 483 year period comprising the first 69 weeks. There are some very interesting clues in scripture that point to the beginning of Jesus' ministry as the arrival of the "Anointed One" and the end of the first 69 weeks.

1. Jesus was anointed by Holy Spirit at his baptism.

All four gospel writers record what took place at the baptism of Jesus by John the Baptist in the Jordan River. There can be no doubt from these passages that Jesus received an anointing from the Holy Spirit in a supernatural fashion at this event. Consider the descriptions in the gospels of Matthew and John:

Mat 3:16 After Jesus was baptized, just as he was coming up out of the water, the heavens opened and he saw **the Spirit of God descending like a dove and coming on him**.

Mat 3:17 And a voice from heaven said, "This is my one dear Son; in him I take great delight."

Joh 1:32 Then John testified, "I saw the Spirit descending like a dove from heaven, and it remained on him.

Joh 1:33 And I did not recognize him, but the one who sent me to baptize with water said to me, 'The one on whom you see **the Spirit descending and remaining**—this is the one who baptizes with the Holy Spirit.'

Notice that the Holy Spirit did not just light on him like a dove, then lift. According to the words of John the Baptist, the Holy Spirit descended, then remained upon Jesus at his baptism. After John the Baptist recalled what the Lord told him about the one who he would later see with a dove remaining on him, he remarked:

Joh 1:34 I have both seen and testified that **this man is the Chosen One of God**."

Was this the first time Jesus was anointed by the Holy Spirit? The Holy Spirit overshadowed Mary at the supernatural conception, and Luke recorded that Jesus had the favor of God on him as a young boy. But this anointing at his baptism was a special, public, supernatural anointing, followed by 40 days in the wilderness with Satan, and culminating with the beginning of his public ministry.

2. Jesus declared his baptism by John would fulfill all righteousness.

Matthew's gospel records the conversation between John the Baptist and Jesus as he approached him at the Jordan River:

Mat 3:13 Then Jesus came from Galilee to John to be baptized by him in the Jordan River.

Mat 3:14 But John tried to prevent him, saying, "I need to be baptized by you, and yet you come to me?"

Mat 3:15 So Jesus replied to him, "Let it happen now, for **it is right for us to fulfill all righteousness**." Then John yielded to him.

What did Jesus mean? Surely, not that his baptism would completely fulfill all righteousness, but instead that it was a part of the overall process in which all righteousness would be fulfilled. His death and resurrection would be essential parts of that process as well. The connection between this verse and the prophecy of Daniel's 70 weeks is striking. Looking at the purposes of Daniel's 70 weeks again, notice the following:

> Dan 9:24 "Seventy weeks have been determined concerning your people and your holy city to finish the transgression, to bring sin to completion, to atone for iniquity, **to bring in everlasting righteousness**, to seal up the prophetic vision, and to anoint a most holy place.

Jesus told John the Baptist that his baptism would help to fulfill all righteousness. As shown above, one of the six purposes of the prophecy of Daniel's 70 weeks was to "bring in everlasting righteousness". Through his death and resurrection, and ultimately his return to the earth to reign, this everlasting righteousness will be ultimately accomplished. The final week will conclude with his return to reign, but his baptism by John initiated the process of establishing everlasting righteousness.

3. Just after his baptism, Jesus was full of the Holy Spirit.

The gospel of Mark records that immediately after his baptism, the Holy Spirit led Jesus into the wilderness temptation:

> Mar 1:12 The Spirit **immediately** drove him into the wilderness.
> Mar 1:13 He was in the wilderness forty days, enduring temptations from Satan. He was with wild animals, and angels were ministering to his needs.

Luke's gospel records that Jesus was not only led by the Spirit into this temptation from Satan, but that he was full of the Holy Spirit:

> Luk 4:1 Then Jesus, **full of the Holy Spirit, returned from the Jordan River** and was led by the Spirit in the wilderness,
> Luk 4:2 where for forty days he endured temptations from the devil. He ate nothing during those days, and when they were completed, he was famished.

Therefore, before he went through the temptation, Jesus was full of the Holy Spirit. Since Mark records that he immediately left his baptism to go into the wilderness temptation, it is clear that Jesus received this powerful anointing of the Holy Spirit at his baptism.

4. The Holy Spirit was upon Jesus as he began his ministry.

Luke's gospel records that Jesus began his ministry at about the age of thirty. After his baptism and temptation, Jesus returned to Galilee to begin preaching:

> Luk 4:14 Then Jesus, **in the power of the Spirit**, returned to Galilee, and news about him spread throughout the surrounding countryside.

Jesus began his ministry in the power of the Holy Spirit, conveyed upon him at his baptism. The results were awesome, as spirits of infirmity were loosed from the people, and unclean spirits were cast out of those who were oppressed:

Act 10:37 you know what happened throughout Judea, **beginning from Galilee after the baptism that John announced**:

Act 10:38 with respect to Jesus from Nazareth, **that <u>God anointed him</u> with the Holy Spirit and with power**. He went around doing good and healing all who were oppressed by the devil, because God was with him.

These verses connect the baptism of John with the anointing of the Holy Spirit at his baptism and the beginning of his ministry in Galilee. This is powerful proof that the coming of the anointed one, prophesied by Gabriel through Daniel, occurred at the baptism of Jesus.

5. John the Baptist said Jesus was still coming in the future.

It is extremely interesting that, although Jesus had already been born, and was thirty years of age, John the Baptist declared that Jesus was still to come in the future. That somehow, because Jesus had not yet been revealed in earnest to Israel, he had not yet come. But that is exactly what is found in all four gospels, including John's gospel:

Joh 1:26 John answered them, "I baptize with water. Among you stands one whom you do not recognize,

Joh 1:27 who is **coming after me**. I am not worthy to untie the strap of his sandal!"

John the Baptist later clarified that the coming of Jesus he was referring to was not his birth, but his public appearance among the people, which beyond question began with his public baptism in the hands of John:

Joh 1:30 This is the one about whom I said, '**After me comes** a man who is greater than I am, because he existed before me.'

Joh 1:31 I did not recognize him, but I came baptizing with water **so that he could be revealed to Israel**."

This revelation to Israel referred to by John the Baptist clearly was not his birth, but his baptism. It is interesting that, though John the Baptist was conceived and born six months before Jesus, he said that Jesus existed before he did. This is proof of the eternal existence of Jesus Christ.

6. Jesus told the disciples they had been with him from "the beginning".

When Jesus had gathered his disciples together prior to the final Passover and his death, John's gospel records a lengthy discourse with them. During this private time with his disciples, he made a puzzling statement:

Joh 15:26 When the Advocate comes, whom I will send you from the Father— the Spirit of truth who goes out from the Father—he will testify about me,

Joh 15:27 and you also will testify, because **you have been with me from the beginning**.

The beginning he was referring to must have been the beginning of his ministry, rather than his birth or any time up until the beginning of his ministry. The disciples were called just after Jesus began his preaching in Galilee. He called Peter, Andrew, Philip, James, and John very early in his ministry, and they knew nothing about the man from Nazareth before their calling. Nathanael made an interesting proclamation about Jesus at the beginning of his ministry:

Joh 1:49 Nathanael answered him, "Rabbi, **you are the Son of God; you are the king of Israel!**"

This proclamation was a direct reference to a very famous Old Testament prophecy about the Messiah in the Psalms:

Psa 2:6 He says, "I myself have installed **my king on Zion**, my holy hill."

Psa 2:7 The king says, "I will tell you what the Lord decreed. He said to me: '**You are my son!** This very day I have become your father!

Note three key elements of the Nathanael's proclamation: (a) you are the Son of God, (b) you are a king, and (c) you are the king of Israel. Remember the prophetic vision given to Daniel:

Dan 9:25 So know and understand: from the going forth of the message to return and build Jerusalem until **the anointed one** [mashiyach], the **prince** [nagiyd], there are seven weeks and sixty-two weeks. It will again be built, with plaza and moat, but in distressful times.

The Hebrew *nagiyd* has a variety of translations in the Old Testament, with "captain", "ruler", and "prince" being the most common. Nathanael's proclamation that Jesus was the king of Israel is a direct reference to not only the Messianic prophecy in Psalm chapter 2, but also to the prophecy in Daniel chapter 9. Even more convincing proof that the baptism and early ministry of Jesus marked the ending point of the first 69 weeks is that Nathanael's proclamation came just after Jesus had been baptized and anointed by the Holy Spirit.

7. Jesus announced himself as the anointed one, and the exact date of his coming.

This is perhaps the most powerful connection of the time of Jesus' baptism and the beginning of his ministry to Daniel 9:25. Recall that, in Luke chapter 3, it is revealed that Jesus' ministry began when he was about 30 years old. After this, Luke continues a genealogy of Jesus Christ back to Adam, then records a 40-day temptation by Satan in the wilderness.

He then described his preaching and teaching in the Jewish synagogues with power and authority. When he came to his home town of Nazareth, where he grew up, he went into the synagogue on the Sabbath. When he stood up to read to the people, a very interesting passage was chosen. Picture Jesus rolling open that dusty scroll of Isaiah in the middle of the synagogue, with all the people gazing at him as he stated the following:

> Luk 4:18 "The Spirit of the Lord is upon me, because **he has anointed me** to proclaim good news to the poor. He has sent me to proclaim release to the captives and the regaining of sight to the blind, to set free those who are oppressed,
>
> Luk 4:19 to proclaim the year of the Lord's favor."

After reading the scroll, Jesus made an incredible announcement to the crowd on that day in the synagogue at Nazareth:

> Luk 4:20 Then he rolled up the scroll, gave it back to the attendant, and sat down. The eyes of everyone in the synagogue were fixed on him.
>
> Luk 4:21 Then he began to tell them, "**Today** this scripture has been **fulfilled even as you heard it being read**."

In this profound passage, Jesus revealed *the very day* of the coming of the anointed one. He stated that he was the anointed one with the Spirit of the Lord on him. Daniel 9:25 states that the coming of the anointed one would mark the end of 69 weeks, and in Luke 4:18-21, Jesus stated he was fulfilling the prophecy of the coming anointed one that very day. This passage corresponds exactly with the prophesied 483 years ending in the 27-28 AD time frame, and fits the description perfectly: the anointed one had come.

These seven points provide nearly irrefutable evidence that the arrival of the "anointed one" of Gabriel's vision to Daniel took place at the baptism of Jesus Christ and the subsequent start of his ministry 40 days after that. A three and one-half year ministry would place the crucifixion at the Passover of 31-32 AD.

8.5 Summary and Conclusion

In summarizing this chapter, the goals were to explain the importance of the prophecy of Daniel's 70 weeks, to identify its starting point, and to identify the ending point of the first 69 weeks. Important points to take from the discussion include:

- The abomination of desolation, referred to by Jesus in 31-32 AD as still to come in the future, will take place in the middle of the final seven years.
- The actions of Antiochus IV Epiphanes in 165-164 BC were a prophetic "type" of the future fulfillment of the abomination of desolation.
- The best candidate for the starting point of the 70 weeks was the decree of Artaxerxes I Longimanus in 457-456 BC, allowing Ezra to go to Jerusalem and rebuild it.
- The ending point of the first 69 weeks was the baptism of Jesus and the beginning of his ministry in approximately 27-28 AD. He was anointed by the Holy Spirit at his baptism and began his ministry in Nazareth of Galilee.

- There are many strong points of corroboration with the baptism of Jesus and the beginning of his ministry marking the end of the 69th week, including his anointing by the Holy Spirit, his emergence from the 40-day temptation full of the Holy Spirit, and the beginning of his ministry in the power of the Holy Spirit.
- Perhaps the most powerful passage of Biblical prophecy is found in Luke 4:16-21, in which Jesus read from the Isaiah scroll and announced that the anointed one had come and was sitting in their midst. This declaration fulfilled both the passage from Isaiah from which he read, and the prophecy of the coming of the anointed one in Daniel chapter 9.

This chapter dealt primarily with the identification of the first 69 weeks of the prophecy of Daniel, specifically its beginning and ending point. The next chapter will cover some interesting and important points about the future final week, Daniel's 70th week.

Just before it hit, I yelled at
everyone to brace themselves and
get ready for it. When it hit,
the ground came underneath the
house like a wave on the ocean,
but with a destructive eruptive
effect. It was the most
desperate and terrifying
feeling, to have no control over
where you are moving. As the
wave passed underneath, I was in
unbelief that I was still alive.

Earthquake Resurrection Prophetic Model Timeline Progression

	Weeks 1-69				Week 69 Ends; GAP Between Week 69 and Week 70						Week 70 Begins		
	457BC - 27AD	27AD	31AD	31AD	31AD - PRESENT						FUTURE TIME		
					Opening of the First Five Seals - Birth Pains Begin					Sixth Seal			
					1	2	3	4	5				
Event	Decree of Artaxerxes Longimanus, Weeks 1-69 of Daniel's 70 Week's Prophecy	Transfer of the Priesthood of Melchizedek at Christ's Baptism	Christ's the "Many Saints" Earthquake Resurrection	Christ's Ascension to the Right Hand of God	Spirit of Religious Deception in Christ's Name	Spirit of War and Bloodshed	Spirit of Financial Oppression	Spirit of Death, Disease, and Famine	Persecution and Death of Believers	Future Earthquake Resurrection of the Dead in Christ, Transformations and Catching Up	Confirmation / Strengthening of the Covenant	Sealing of the 144,000 Children of Israel	Enormous Group Before the Throne
Ref	Dan 9:24-25	Luk 3-4	Mat 27	Act 1; Rev 4-5	Rev 6:1-11					1 The 4; 1 Cor 15	Daniel 9:27	Rev 7	
Ref	Ch. 8	Ch. 3, 6	Ch. 10, 11		Ch. 12	Ch. 13			Ch. 14	Ch. 4, 5, 7	Ch. 9, 15, 16		

- CHAPTER NINE -

DANIEL'S 70TH WEEK: THE FINAL SEVEN YEARS

In the previous chapter, the first 69 weeks of Daniel's 70 weeks prophecy were examined. The final week will be explored in this chapter, as well as the gap between the 69th and 70th week after the coming of the anointed one and before the strengthening of the covenant with many.

If the 69 weeks concluded at the anointing of Jesus' baptism and beginning of ministry, then what about the final week, or seven years? Did the final week continue and end around 34-35 AD, or was the counting of weeks suspended at the end of the 69th week? Daniel's 70 weeks prophecy stated that after the 69 weeks were finished, the anointed one would be cut off, and the city of Jerusalem and the temple would be destroyed. History shows that both the crucifixion of Jesus and the destruction of Jerusalem and the temple did indeed occur after the end of the 69 weeks.

9.1 The Gap in the Seventy Weeks Prophecy

There are many ways to show that the 70 weeks, or 490 years, are not continuous from beginning to end, and that there must be a gap. First, examine again the verse which detailed the events within the final week, and the verse in which Jesus later made reference to them:

> Dan 9:27 He will confirm a covenant with many for <u>one week</u>. But **in the middle of that week** he will bring sacrifice and offering to a halt on the wing of **a desolating abomination**, until the decreed end is poured out on the one who makes desolate.

> Mat 24:15 So when you see 'the **abomination of desolation**'—<u>spoken about by Daniel the prophet</u>—standing in the holy place (let the reader understand), Mat 24:16 then those in Judea must flee to the mountains.

If the 69 weeks concluded at the time of the baptism of Jesus and the subsequent beginning of his ministry, then his declaration that the abomination of desolation was still in the future is absolute proof that there is a gap in the 70 weeks. This abomination of desolation will occur in the middle of that seven-year period, and according to Jesus in approximately 31 AD, this prophecy had not yet been fulfilled.

Daniel 9:27 states that "He" will confirm a covenant for the final week. It is clear that the "He" is not Jesus, because in Matthew chapter 24, Jesus stated that the abomination of desolation occurs in the future. If the first 69 weeks concluded at Jesus' baptismal anointing and beginning of his ministry in 27-28 AD, then the final week must be in the future. Approximately three and one-half years later, Jesus stated that the abomination of desolation would yet occur in the future.

Furthermore, this abomination of desolation is not only referenced in Daniel 9:27. The angel revealing the prophecy of the destiny of Israel over Daniel chapters 9-12 refers to the abomination of desolation at least two other times. In the final reference, the angel told Daniel that the prophecy would be applicable to the very end of time:

> Dan 12:8 I heard, but I did not understand. So I said, "Sir, what will happen after these things?"
>
> Dan 12:9 He said, "Go, Daniel. **For these matters are closed and sealed until the <u>time of the end</u>**.
>
> Dan 12:10 Many will be purified, made clean, and refined, but the wicked will go on being wicked. None of the wicked will understand, though the wise will understand.
>
> Dan 12:11 From the time that the daily sacrifice is removed and **the abomination that causes desolation** is set in place, there are 1,290 days.

There can be no doubt that the time of the end was not in 31-32 AD, since the current year is 2005 AD, nearly 2,000 years later, and the end has not yet come. Furthermore, both John's Revelation, written in approximately 95 AD, and Paul's second letter to the Thessalonians, reveal a more detailed picture of the abomination of desolation:

> Rev 13:15 The second beast was empowered to give life to **the image of the first beast** so that it could speak, and could cause all those who did not worship the image of the beast to be killed.

> II The 2:4 He opposes and exalts himself above every so-called god or object of worship, and as a result **he takes his seat in God's temple, displaying himself as God**.

This is the future prophetic abomination of desolation to which Jesus was referring, which will take place in a future temple. Since John saw this in approximately 95 AD, and declared it would happen in the future, there was at least a gap of over 60 years from when Jesus declared the abomination was to come in the future in approximately 31 AD until its mention by John in Revelation chapter 13. Again, since this event still has not happened, the gap has lasted nearly 2,000 years.

Therefore, because the abomination of desolation has not yet occurred, it can be conclusively stated that there is a gap between the 69th and 70th weeks of Gabriel's vision to Daniel, and that gap has so far lasted at least to the present. The apostle

Paul confirmed that Israel was experiencing a partial blindness when he wrote his epistle to the Romans, and that this partial blindness would continue until the full number of Gentiles had come into the new covenant:

> Rom 11:25 For I do not want you to be ignorant of this mystery, brothers and sisters, so that you may not be conceited: A partial hardening has happened to Israel **until the full number of the Gentiles has come in**.

When the full number of Gentiles has been grafted into the new covenant, God will, as he promised, turn his attention back to re-grafting the Jewish people, which will be discussed in chapter 16. This is the gap of time until Daniel's people and holy city Jerusalem will experience the final seven years of the prophecy.

9.2 The Final Seven Years

The final week of seven years, or Daniel's 70th week, can be found within the Revelation chronology, but is difficult to pinpoint. According to Daniel 9:27, a covenant will be confirmed or made strong by "the coming prince". Yet, other than Daniel 9:27, neither Daniel nor Revelation directly refer to this period as one continuous seven-year unit. Interestingly, however, a three and one-half year period is referred to many times and in a variety of ways in Revelation:

> Rev 11:2 But do not measure the outer courtyard of the temple; leave it out, because it has been given to the Gentiles, and they will trample on the holy city for **forty-two months**.
> Rev 11:3 And I will grant my two witnesses authority to prophesy for **1,260 days**, dressed in sackcloth.

> Rev 12:6 and she fled into the wilderness where a place had been prepared for her by God, so she could be taken care of for **1,260 days**.
> Rev 12:14 But the woman was given the two wings of a giant eagle so that she could fly out into the wilderness, to the place God prepared for her, where she is taken care of—away from the presence of the serpent—for **a time, times, and half a time**.

> Rev 13:5 The beast was given a mouth speaking proud words and blasphemies, and he was permitted to exercise ruling authority for **forty-two months**.

From Revelation 13:5 above, it is clear that the beast is given power to rule for 42 months. Therefore, the end of the 70th week of Daniel is clearly demarcated within Revelation. The ruling authority of the beast comes to an end when he is cast into the lake of fire when Jesus Christ returns to the earth:

> Rev 19:20 Now **the beast was seized**, and along with him the false prophet who had performed the signs on his behalf—signs by which he deceived those who had received the mark of the beast and those who worshiped his image. Both of them were **thrown alive into the lake of fire** burning with sulfur.

Since the end of the 42-month beast reign is also the end of the full seven-year period, Daniel's 70th week, then it can be positively stated that this event described in Revelation 19:20 marks the end of the 70th week of Daniel.

9.3 The Confirmation of the Covenant

It is revealed in Daniel 9:27 that the final week of seven years will begin with the confirmation of a covenant by the coming prince. Many believe this will be the creation of a new covenant or treaty which will make the beginning of the final seven years obvious to everyone who has a general knowledge of Biblical prophecy. However, this may not be the way the covenant is confirmed. Review the verse again:

> Dan 9:27 He will **confirm [gabar] a covenant** with many **for one week**. But in the middle of that week he will bring sacrifices and offerings to a halt. On the wing of abominations will come one who destroys, until the decreed end is poured out on the one who destroys."

The coming prince will confirm a covenant that could already be in existence prior to the final seven years. The Hebrew *gabar* is a primitive verb that primarily means "to give strength to" or "to make strong". This means that the covenant being referred to is in a weak or unstable condition, and the coming prince will make it stronger.

This is extremely interesting in light of the relatively recent "covenant" or agreement between the nation of Israel and the Palestinian Liberation Organization led by Yasser Arafat called The Oslo Peace Accords. Keep in mind that the 70 weeks of Daniel's prophecy concern the Jews and the holy city of Jerusalem. This fact makes the 1993 Oslo Peace Accords, involving the nation of Israel and the dividing of the land for a Palestinian state, a very good candidate for the covenant or treaty that is in need of strengthening. These Accords have lost much credibility since the famous handshake between Yasser Arafat and Yitzhak Rabin on September 13, 1993, but George W. Bush, in the opening years of his 2001 presidency, made it clear that peace in the Middle East one of his most important agenda items. As of the date of this writing, both Arafat and Rabin have passed away. Perhaps, in the future, someone will be installed into power who will attempt to strengthen this peace agreement between the Israelis and Palestinians.

But what about the length of the years and the different references to a period of three and one-half years? It is clear from these passages that one year is 360 days each, not 365.25 as it is currently, during this final seven year period. That equates to 36.75 days shorter over seven years. There are a number of reasons why this could be the case, including the earthquakes and activity referred to in Revelation 6:12-14 explored in previous chapters. Jesus prophesied that this would be the case during this period of history:

> Mar 13:20 And if the Lord had not cut short those days, no one would be saved. But because of the elect, whom he chose, **he has cut them short**.

9.4 The Final Seven Years Within Revelation

The key question, therefore, is how to discern whether each of the seven references to three and one-half years throughout Daniel and Revelation are the same three and one-half years. There are references to 1,260 days, 42 months, and time, times, and half a time, all of which are a different way of referring to a period of three and one-half years. While the two witnesses are allowed to prophesy for 1,260 days (Revelation 11:3), it is not clear from a cursory reading whether this three and one-half year period is different from the 42 months in which the beast is allowed to be in power (Revelation 13:5). But there is absolute proof, when comparing Revelation chapters 9, 11, and 13, that the 1,260 days during which the two witnesses prophesy are completely separate from the 42 months of the reign of the beast.

First, it is revealed that the two witnesses prophesy 1,260 days, then are killed by the beast who comes out of the abyss:

> Rev 11:7 When they have completed their testimony, the beast that comes up from the abyss will make war on them and conquer them and kill them.

After the two witnesses are resurrected from the dead, the scripture states that "the second woe" has just passed:

> Rev 11:14 The **second woe** has come and gone; **the third is coming** quickly.

What is the second woe? Revelation chapter 9 reveals that the second woe is the sixth trumpet judgment, when four angels are released from under the Euphrates River:

> Rev 9:12 The **first woe** has passed, but **two woes** are still coming after these things!
> Rev 9:13 Then the sixth angel blew his trumpet, and I heard a single voice coming from the horns on the golden altar that is before God,

The first woe had passed, which was an attack of locust-like creatures from the abyss. The second woe, therefore, comes to completion at the end of the prophesy of the two witnesses, which lasts 1,260 days. If the sixth trumpet marks the end of 1,263.5 days (allowing three and one-half days for the two witnesses to lie dead in the streets of Jerusalem), then more time is needed to at least unleash the seventh trumpet and the seven bowls of judgment, as well as to allow the initiation of the mark of the beast and the image of the beast during final 42 months.

Because of the clue of the second woe passing just after the death and resurrection of the two witnesses, it can be confidently stated that Revelation refers to two distinct periods of 42 months each. The first 42 months feature, among many other events, the ministry of two witnesses, while the final 42 months feature the rise of the beast to power. It is also clear that the final week of Daniel's 70 weeks will feature 2,520 days and years that contain only 360 days each. Forty-two months containing 1,260 days, both of which are referenced in Revelation, computes to a month of 30 days each.

9.5 The Work of Sir Robert Anderson

But does this also mean that the first 483 years would also have to be computed using a 360 day year? Not necessarily. Again, remember that Jesus stated that the days during this final period of prophecy would be cut short:

Mar 13:20 And if the Lord had not cut short those days, no one would be saved. But because of the elect, whom he chose, **he has cut them short.**

In order to be cut short, the days will have to be longer prior to that point. Assuming that the earth continues to orbit the sun at a rate of approximately 365.25 days until the final week of seven years begins, then a move to a 360-day orbit around the sun would indeed cut short those days. The period during the first 69 weeks, or 483 years, were not operating under a 360-day orbit around the sun, but rather under a 365.25-day orbit. The final seven years without a doubt, however, operate under a 360-day orbit around the sun because both Daniel and Revelation refer to both the first and second halves of the final week as 1,260 days.

A hallmark of Bible prophecy for over one hundred years has been the work of Sir Robert Anderson in his book The Coming Prince, written in 1895. Anderson squashed the criticism in his day by those who claimed Daniel was not an authentic book of prophecy, and is famous for attempting to calculate the precise day on which the 70 weeks prophecy began and the precise day on which the first 69 weeks ended. However, to do so, Anderson claimed that a 360-day per year calendar should be used for *all* of the 70 weeks, because that is God's "prophetic year". Anderson converted the years to days and calculated the end of the 69th week to take place on the same day of Jesus' triumphal entry into Jerusalem.

However, many scholars have noted problems and inconsistencies with the work of Robert Anderson, all of which are too detailed to attempt to explain in this book. Jesus stated the days during that period will be cut short. In order to be "cut short", the previous rendering of time before the cutting short must logically be longer. Since the 70th week definitely consists of 360-day years, and the time before it must be longer in order to be cut short, the use of a 365.25 day year fits perfectly. This is a worthy explanation for the use of normal 365.25-day solar years during the first 483 years, but 360-day "cut short" solar years during the final 7 years.

9.6 The Purpose of the 70th Week of Daniel

Traditional prophetic models hold that the "tribulation" is a seven-year time period in which many millions or perhaps billions of people will realize the catching-up event has taken place, and will have missed it. These models hold that this group, made up of both Jews and Gentiles, will have to give their lives and be beheaded in order to be saved and enter the 1,000 year period during which Christ rules the earth. However, Daniel 9:24 makes it clear what the purpose of the 70 weeks, which includes that final week, concerns:

> Dan 9:24 "Seventy weeks have been determined **concerning your people and your holy city** to put an end to rebellion, to bring sin to completion, to atone for iniquity, to bring in perpetual righteousness, to seal up the prophetic vision, and to anoint a most holy place.

Note the emphasized portion above states that all 70 weeks, or 490 years, are concerning Daniel's people, and the holy city Jerusalem. This does not mean, however, that Gentiles will be completely ignored, but rather that the focus of God's attention will be on the salvation of the Jews and bringing to fulfillment the six purposes of the prophecy of Daniel's 70 weeks.

The key is to understand that all 70 weeks pertain to the Jews and Jerusalem. There have been, so far, almost 2,000 years in the gap between the 69th and 70th weeks during which time the Gentiles have been grafted into the new covenant. But the Word is clear that God will turn his attention back to the Jews, and their partial blindness will come to an end. This will come to an end when the full number of Gentiles have been grafted into the new covenant according to the apostle Paul:

> Rom 11:25 For I do not want you to be ignorant of this mystery, brothers and sisters, so that you may not be conceited: A partial hardening has happened to Israel **until the full number of the Gentiles has come in**.
> Rom 11:26 And so all Israel will be saved, as it is written: "The Deliverer will come out of Zion; he will remove ungodliness from Jacob.

This is a key passage that the student of Bible prophecy must grasp. God will turn his attention back to Israel, which will begin with the sealing of the 144,000 Jewish men just after the completion of the sixth seal events and before the trumpet judgments begin. But what is the implication of "the full number of Gentiles" coming into the covenant? Once the partial hardening of Israel concludes, may there be no further Gentiles grafted into the covenant? Once the removal of the restraining force–a force restraining the embodiment of the spirit of antichrist–has taken place, those left behind are sent a strong delusion, and they will believe a lie:

> II The 2:9 The arrival of the lawless one will be by Satan's working with all kinds of miracles and signs and false wonders,
> II The 2:10 and with every kind of evil deception directed against those who are perishing, because they found no place in their hearts for the truth so as to be saved.
> II The 2:11 **Consequently God sends on them a deluding influence so that they will believe what is false**.

The two witnesses minister in the Jewish city of Jerusalem, not in Washington D.C. or New York City. Uniting all these scriptures, it seems clear that the ultimate purpose of the final week of the prophecy will be a re-grafting of the children of Israel back into the covenant olive tree, not to evangelize the rest of the world. Revelation indicates several times that humanity refuses to repent, and it seems that this strong deluding influence is the reason–they will believe to be true what is actually false.

149

9.7 Summary and Conclusion

The goal of this chapter was to continue the exploration of Daniel's 70th week. There has been a gap in the 70 weeks between the 69th and 70th weeks that has lasted nearly 2,000 years. After this long discussion, it is clear that the seven-year period to come in the future is not so simple a concept to explain. The key points to take from the discussion include:

- The final week of seven years includes two separate periods of 42 months or 1,260 days.
- The final week of seven years has exactly 2,520 days, meaning a 360-day orbit around the sun will be in place.
- The final week of seven years will begin with the strengthening of a covenant by the coming prince, called the beast in Revelation, and ends when the 1,260 days of the beast's ruling authority ends at Jesus Christ's return.
- The 1993 Oslo Peace Accords, which dealt with the peace between the Jews and Palestinians and the partitioning of God's chosen land of Israel, is an interesting candidate for a treaty or covenant that could be strengthened by the coming prince of the final week of Daniel's 70 weeks.
- A key clue to the presence of two distinct periods of 1,260 days within Revelation chapters 9 and 11 is a reference to the second woe, the sixth trumpet judgment, which will end just after the death of the two witnesses in Jerusalem.
- The final week of seven years will feature God's primary focus on the salvation of the Jews and Jerusalem.

In previous chapters, the three-stage event involving the resurrection of the dead, the transformation of the bodies of believers, and the catching up of all believers was presented within the events of the sixth seal. It is now time to explore the events that immediately precede the opening of the seals in Revelation chapters 4 and 5, then move into the opening of the seals in Revelation chapter 6. What will be explored in the next two chapters will challenge almost every single prophetic model in existence.

- SECTION IV -

REVELATION: FROM THE ASCENSION TO THE CATCHING UP

A wonderful sense of relief swept over me as I realized I was still breathing and unharmed. I slowly lifted myself up at the sliding glass door so I could look out and assess the damage in my backyard. While everyone in the house was shaken mentally, the inside of the house itself was in surprisingly decent shape. As I turned to look out the sliding glass door, I saw huge gaping cracks in the earth where green grass formally resided. But the mangled scene that was formally my backyard was a pleasant site compared to the next wave that was quickly approaching...

Earthquake Resurrection Prophetic Model Timeline Progression

Weeks 1-69	Week 69 Ends; GAP Between Week 69 and Week 70					Week 70 Begins
457BC - 27AD	27AD	31AD		31AD - PRESENT	FUTURE TIME	

Decree of Artaxerxes Longimanus; Weeks 1-69 of Daniel's 70 Week's Prophecy	Transfer of the Priesthood of Melchizedek at Christ's Baptism	Christ's and the "Many Saints'" Earthquake Resurrection	Christ's Ascension to the Right Hand of God	Opening of the First Five Seals - Birth Pains Begin					Sixth Seal			

Opening of the First Five Seals - Birth Pains Begin:

1	2	3	4	5
Spirit of Religious Domination in Christ's Name	Spirit of War and Bloodshed	Spirit of Financial Oppression	Spirit of Death, Disease and Famine	Persecution and Death of Believers

Sixth Seal:

Future Earthquake Resurrection of the Dead in Christ, Transformation and Catching Up	Confirmation / Strengthening of the Covenant	Sealing of the 144,000 Children of Israel	Enormous Group Before the Throne

Scripture References:

Dan 9:24-25	Luk 3-4	Mat 27	Act 1; Rev 4-5	Rev 6:1-11	1 The 4; 1 Cor 15	Daniel 9:27	Rev 7
Ch. 5	Ch. 3, 6		Ch. 10, 11	Ch. 12 / Ch. 13 / Ch. 14	Ch. 4, 5, 7		Ch. 9, 15, 16

- CHAPTER TEN -

THE SETTING FOR THE HEREAFTER

With the foundation and background of the model now past, it is time to reexamine the traditional interpretation of Revelation chapters 4 through 7 with this emerging prophetic model in mind. This reexamination will begin with an exploration of the throne room scene described in Revelation chapter 4. First, an examination of how Jesus introduced the vision of the future to John will be presented, followed by an exploration of the identity of the 24 elders in connection with the transfer of the priesthood of Aaron to the priesthood of Melchizedek.

10.1 Introduction to the Vision

In the first sentence of Revelation chapter 1, John revealed the subject of the entire letter: the revelation of Jesus Christ. Too often, this book is viewed as one of the doom of mankind and the end of the world. While the details of the seven-year wrath of God on this earth are described in harrowing detail, the overall theme in the first verse is the true name of the book:

Rev 1:1 **The revelation of Jesus Christ**, which God gave him to show his servants what must happen very soon. He made it clear by sending his angel to his servant John,

The Greek word for "revelation" is *apokalupsis*, from which the English word apocalypse is derived. This word does not mean the end of the world, as it is so often used in popular books, television shows, and motion pictures. The word simply means "revelation", a revelation of Jesus Christ. This prophetic model will arrange what must take place before the glorious *apokalupsis* of Jesus Christ for the second time on earth. Daniel's 70th week will involve God's judgment on an earth soaked with the blood of the innocent, whose cry for vengeance is dramatically answered by the righteous judge on the throne:

Rev 16:5 Now I heard the angel of the waters saying: "You are just—the one who is and who was, the Holy One—**because you have passed these judgments,**

Rev 16:6 **because they poured out the blood of your saints and prophets**, so you have given them blood to drink. They got what they deserved!"

Rev 16:7 Then I heard the altar reply, "Yes, Lord God, the All-Powerful, **your judgments are true and just!**"

Not only was the letter a revelation of Jesus Christ as King of Kings, but a testimony of what things he saw while on the isle of Patmos. John said about himself, speaking in the third person:

Rev 1:2 who then testified to **everything that he saw** concerning the word of God and the testimony about Jesus Christ.

Later in Revelation chapter 1, John is introduced to the risen Savior, but only after he described himself as being "in the Spirit on the Lord's Day". It is likely that, at this point, John either fell into an exalted trance, or left his physical body and was in the spirit, similar to the experience of Paul described in II Corinthians chapter 12. In that account, Paul could not tell whether he went to paradise in his physical body, or whether his spirit was taken while his body remained on the earth.

John, however, stated that he was in the spirit when he heard a voice he described as being "like a trumpet" speaking to him. After John turned around to see the "son of man" speaking to him, Jesus continued to speak to John uninterrupted from Revelation 1:17 through the end of chapter 3. Each of the separate letters to the seven churches of Asia are the spoken words of Jesus to John. Therefore, the discourse must be viewed as occurring in one sitting, as John was first introduced in the spirit to Jesus Christ in his exalted risen state.

Twice in chapter 1, John is admonished to write about what he was being shown. First, Jesus told him to record what he is shown:

Rev 1:11 saying: "Write in a book **what you see** and send it to the seven churches—to Ephesus, Smyrna, Pergamum, Thyatira, Sardis, Philadelphia, and Laodicea."

Later, he is told again to write about what he sees: about what currently is happening, and what is to happen afterward:

Rev 1:19 Therefore write what you saw, **what is**, and **what will be after these things**.

Still in the spirit, John began recording the words of Jesus as he spoke the letters to the seven churches. These letters, brimming with symbolism and references to the Old Testament, were written to address specific issues at these churches. However, the admonitions, warnings, and promises to each church are also applicable to every church throughout history and today.

10.2 Revelation Chapter Four – The Throne Room Setting

Jesus concluded his dictation of the final letter to the Laodicean church at the end of chapter 3, and finally ceased speaking. Perhaps John, under the inspiration of the Holy Spirit, came out of the spirit state and was given time to record what Jesus had just spoken to the seven churches. Perhaps he needed time to recoup and gather strength, similar to Daniel who, after being given visions of the future, described his status:

> Dan 8:27 I, Daniel, was **exhausted and sick for days**. Then I got up and again carried out the king's business. But I was astonished at the vision, and there was no one to explain it.

Whether John experienced such a physical reaction is not known. There is an indication that John did come back into a normal state, at least briefly, because he stated that he was again "in the spirit" at another time. In order to *again* be in the spirit, logic requires that he came out of the spirit state at some point. But before he was again in the spirit, he heard something familiar:

> Rev 4:1 After these things I looked, and there was a door standing open in heaven! **And the first voice I had heard speaking to me like a trumpet** said: "<u>Come up here</u> so that I can show you <u>what must happen after these things</u>."

The voice belonged to Jesus Christ, as John was referring to the voice he first heard in Revelation chapter 1. Recall that in chapter 1, John was to write what would happen "after these things", or events of the future. Now, just after Jesus finished the letters to the seven churches, he told him it was time to show him these future events. Immediately after John received the command to come up to the door in the sky, he was in the spirit again:

> Rev 4:2 Immediately I was in the Spirit, and a throne was standing in heaven with someone seated on it!

Jesus gave him a command to come up to heaven, through this door in the sky, so that he could be shown what was going to happen in the future. Before he was shown those things which were to happen in the future, however, John was shown what the "here" in the command "Come up here" was.

This is a key point. The description of the setting in which John was going to be shown events of the future (the "here") should not be confused with the events of the future themselves (the "what must happen after"). John was immediately taken up to the heavens which was the "here" to which Jesus was referring. The "here" in the command to "Come up here" is described in Revelation chapters 4 and 5, while the things to happen afterward which John was to be shown are described in Revelation chapters 6 through the end of the book. Revelation chapters 4 and 5 do not contain events that will happen in the future, but rather events that have already happened in the past. This will become clear in this chapter and the chapters to follow.

10.3 The Twenty-four Elders and Four Living Creatures

The throne room scene of Revelation chapters 4 and 5 is exquisite and majestic. Isaiah experienced a similar vision of this throne room as recorded in Isaiah chapter 5. Both Isaiah and John described a throne and mysterious, six-winged living creatures. Ezekiel also saw four living creatures, but the living creatures witnessed by Ezekiel were not in the throne room of heaven, and their descriptions do not match the descriptions of the living creatures witnessed by Isaiah and John.

Before the throne was a group of 24 figures described as "elders", or *presbuteros* in Greek:

> Rev 4:4 In a circle around the throne were twenty-four other thrones, and seated on those thrones were twenty-four elders. They were dressed in white clothing and had golden crowns on their heads.

Who were these elders and what do they represent? Because they were sitting on thrones, many believe that twelve of them must be the twelve apostles because of Jesus' promise that they would sit on thrones and judge the twelve tribes of Israel:

> Mat 19:28 Jesus said to them, "I tell you the truth: **In the age when all things are renewed**, when the Son of Man sits on his glorious throne, you who have followed me will also **sit on twelve thrones, judging the twelve tribes of Israel.**

> Luk 22:30 that you may eat and drink at my table **in my kingdom,** and you will **sit on thrones judging the twelve tribes of Israel.**

Because the twelve apostles would be considered members of the "dead in Christ", those who hold to this interpretation believe that the three-stage resurrection, transformation, and catching-up event must have already occurred by this point in Revelation chapter 4. As for the other twelve, the most frequent interpretation is that they are twelve sons of Jacob, resulting in twelve under the old covenant and twelve under the new covenant.

There are at least three points that provide sufficient doubt as to the validity of this interpretation about the identity of the 24 elders:

1. The twelve apostles will judge during the age when all things are renewed, or the kingdom age. This is clear from the two verses above. Jesus told the disciples that they would indeed sit on thrones and judge the twelve tribes of Israel. However, this will be during the 1,000-year period when Satan is incarcerated while Christ reigns from Jerusalem after the battle in the valley of Megiddo. This is what Jesus referred to as the "age in which all things are renewed", and he clarified it in Luke by stating it was "in my kingdom". The scene described in Revelation chapter 4 featuring the 24 elders is neither taking place during the 1,000-year period following Armageddon on earth, nor is there any mention of judgment taking place. In fact, it clearly takes place before the events of Armageddon and judgment.

2. There are at least three verses that reveal those who had sinned under the old covenant had their sins forgiven by the sacrifice of Jesus Christ on the cross. This is contrary to the belief that the 24 elders will consist of twelve representatives of the old covenant who will judge the words and deeds of people who lived under the first covenant:
    Rom 3:25 God publicly displayed him at his death as the mercy seat accessible through faith. This was to demonstrate his righteousness, **because God in his forbearance <u>had passed over the sins previously committed</u>**.

    Heb 11:40 For God had provided something better for us, so that **they [the old covenant heroes of faith] would be made perfect <u>together with us</u>**.

    Heb 9:15 And so he is the mediator of a new covenant, so that those who are called may receive the eternal inheritance he has promised, since he **died to set them free from the violations <u>committed under the first covenant</u>**.

    These three verses make it clear that the righteous individuals who lived under the first covenant, before Christ's sacrifice on the cross, were set free from the violations they committed under that covenant. There is no need, therefore, for judgment of those under the first covenant by the 24 elders.

3. The twelve apostles are identified in Revelation chapter 21:
    Rev 21:14 The wall of the city has twelve foundations, and on them are **the twelve names of the twelve apostles of the Lamb**.

    If the twelve apostles are referred to as a specific group in Revelation chapter 21, why would they be referred to as part of the 24 elders in previous chapter? The twelve apostles and the 24 elders are referred to separately as different groups because they are just that: different. If the 24 elders consisted partially of the twelve apostles, then why not refer to them as such? And why refer to the twelve apostles in one part of Revelation as the twelve apostles but as 24 elders in another part?

    If the 24 elders are not made up of the twelve apostles, then the belief that the three-stage resurrection, transformation, and catching-up event must have *already occurred* by this point in Revelation chapter 4 must be re-evaluated. Is there a better interpretation of this group of 24 elders?

10.4 Identification of the Twenty-four Elders

Following one of the rules of scripture interpretation established at the beginning of this book, the Bible is a book of patterns and parallels. Putting this rule into action, there is an interesting pattern involving 24 men in the old covenant Levitical priesthood. From this pattern, an understanding as to the identity of the 24 elders will emerge.

It is recorded in I Chronicles chapter 24 that David established 24 divisions of the priesthood under Aaron's sons Eleazar and Ithamar:

I Chr 24:4 The descendants of Eleazar had more leaders than the descendants of Ithamar, so they divided them up accordingly; the descendants of Eleazar had **sixteen leaders**, while the descendants of Ithamar had **eight**.

I Chr 24:5 They divided them by lots, for there were **officials of the holy place** and **officials designated by God** among the descendants of both Eleazar and Ithamar.

These 24 men were to carry out the priestly duties in support of the high priest in the new temple that was to be built in Jerusalem by David's son, Solomon. These duties can be understood by a thorough reading of I Chronicles chapters 24 through 27. As will be discussed later in this chapter, the Levitical priesthood and the temple was a pattern of what is in heaven. But scripture is clear that this priesthood was replaced with a new and better priesthood:

Heb 7:11 So if perfection had in fact been possible through **the Levitical priesthood**—for on that basis the people received the law—**what further need would there have been for another priest to arise, said to be in the order of Melchizedek and not in Aaron's order**?

Heb 7:15 And this is even clearer if another priest arises in the likeness of Melchizedek,

Heb 7:16 who has become a priest not by a legal regulation about physical descent but by the power of an indestructible life.

Heb 7:22 accordingly Jesus has become the guarantee of **a better covenant**.

Heb 8:6 But **now Jesus has obtained a superior ministry**, since the covenant that he mediates is also better and is enacted on better promises.

Heb 8:7 For if that first covenant had been faultless, no one would have looked for a second one.

Notice how the priesthood of Jesus is contrasted with the Levitical priesthood? The remainder of Hebrews makes it clear that the activities carried out under Levitical priesthood were only able to temporarily cover up the sins of the people, and for this reason the first covenant priesthood was weak. The priesthood of the order of Melchizedek, over which Jesus is high priest, is better because one offering covered the sins under the old covenant as well as the sins of the future:

Heb 9:15 And so he is the mediator of a new covenant, so that those who are called may receive the eternal inheritance he has promised, since he died **to set them free from the violations committed under the first covenant**.

Heb 7:24 but he holds his priesthood permanently since he lives forever.

Heb 7:25 So he is able to **save completely those who come to God through him**, because he **always lives to intercede for them**.

10.5 The Transfer of the Priesthood to the Order of Melchizedek

But when did this transfer and replacement of the Levitical priesthood take place? In a previous chapter, powerful evidence was explored, showing that the beginning of Jesus' ministry just after his baptism was the fulfillment of the coming of the prophesied "anointed one". This event marked the transfer of the Levitical priesthood to the priesthood over which Jesus became the high priest, the priesthood after the order of Melchizedek:

> Heb 5:9 And by being perfected in this way, he became the source of eternal salvation to all who obey him,
> Heb 5:10 and he was designated by God **as high priest in the order of Melchizedek**.

Under the Levitical priesthood, a Levite had to be thirty years of age before he could become a priest. There are no less than seven verses in Numbers chapter 4 that make this clear. Luke chapter 4 states that John the Baptist was six months older than Jesus Christ, as he was born to Elizabeth and Zechariah just before Jesus was born. Speaking to Mary, the angel Gabriel said the following:

> Luk 1:36 "And look, your relative Elizabeth has also become pregnant with a son in her old age—although she was called barren, she is now in her sixth month!

Mary was told that she was going to become pregnant by the overshadowing of the Holy Spirit, and that Elizabeth was already six months pregnant with John the Baptist. Later in Luke, it is revealed that Jesus was about 30 years of age when he went to the Jordan River to be baptized by John:

> Luk 3:23 So Jesus, when he began his ministry, was **about thirty years old**. He was the son (as was supposed) of Joseph, the son of Heli,

If Jesus was about 30 years old, and John was six months older, then John was also at least 30 years old. Therefore, Jesus began his public ministry at the age of 30, the same age that is required in the law of Moses for a Levite to become a priest. But that priesthood was passed on from Levitical father to Levitical son, and that is where John the Baptist comes into the story.

John the Baptist was born to parents Elizabeth and Zechariah, and Luke revealed that Zechariah was a priest at the temple, and Elizabeth was a daughter of Aaron:

> Luk 1:5 During the reign of Herod king of Judea, there lived a priest named Zechariah who belonged to **the priestly division of <u>Abijah</u>**, and he had a wife named Elizabeth, who was **a descendant of Aaron**.

There is usually an important reason for seemingly insignificant facts such as these to be included in the narrative of the Bible. Without question, Elizabeth was in the lineage of Aaron, a Levite. But what about Zechariah? He was of "the course of Abijah". Recall that the sons of Eleazar and Ithamar made up the 24 courses of the priesthood. One of the sons of Eleazar and Ithamar, the sons of Aaron, was Abijah:

I Chr 24:6 The scribe Shemaiah son of Nethanel, a Levite, wrote down their names before the king, the officials, Zadok the priest, Ahimelech son of Abiathar, and the leaders of the priestly and Levite families. One family was drawn by lot from Eleazar, and then the next from Ithamar.
I Chr 24:10 the seventh to Hakkoz, the **eighth to <u>Abijah</u>,**
I Chr 24:19 This was the order in which they carried out their assigned responsibilities when they entered the Lord's temple, according to the regulations given them by **their ancestor <u>Aaron</u>,** just as the Lord God of Israel had instructed him.

Both Zechariah and Elizabeth were of the house and lineage of Aaron. Therefore, John the Baptist, supernaturally brought forth from the barren womb of Elizabeth, was a true priest of the lineage of his forefathers Levi and Aaron.

As Zechariah was engaged in the priestly function of burning incense on the golden altar in the temple, the angel Gabriel appeared to him on the right side of the altar. The angel comforted him, told him he was going to have a son, and told him to name him John. He was told his son would prepare the people for the arrival of the Lord among them.

As John the Baptist began preaching and teaching, the people wondered if he was actually Elijah, but John said he was not. Instead, he said he fulfilled the prophecy of Isaiah, quoted earlier, that he was the voice of one crying in the wilderness. John began his ministry at the Jordan River, in the wilderness area around Betharaba. The priests ministering at the temple as John ministered in the wilderness were corrupt and illegitimate, made clear in Malachi, the final book of the Old Testament.

Yet John was a true priest and over 30 years of age. As such, he was called to minister in the wilderness and baptize at the Jordan River because he was to prepare the way for the transfer of the priesthood from the order of Aaron to the order of Melchizedek. He was to introduce the new high priest, Jesus Christ, and transfer the priesthood after the order of Aaron to Jesus Christ after the order of Melchizedek. This is the critical point of the ministry of John the Baptist:

Mat 3:13 Then Jesus came from Galilee to John to be baptized by him in the Jordan River.
Mat 3:14 But John tried to prevent him, saying, "I need to be baptized by you, and yet you come to me?"
Mat 3:15 So Jesus replied to him, "Let it happen now, for it is right for us to fulfill all righteousness." Then John yielded to him.

For Jesus Christ to become a priest after the order of Melchizedek, and for it to succeed the Levitical priesthood, there had to be a transfer of the priesthood. For a transfer to take place, a member of both parties must be present. In this case, a member of both the former Levitical priesthood and the new Melchizedekan priesthood were present at the baptism. Notice that Jesus stated the baptism had to take place "now" in order for righteousness to be fulfilled.

The transfer of the priesthood took place in a most extraordinary fashion, after the pattern given to Moses. Under the Levitical priesthood, God set forth the example for the transfer of the priesthood from father to son with Moses, Aaron, and Aaron's sons. The consecration ceremony, among other things, included the following:

Lev 8:6 So Moses brought **Aaron and his sons** forward and **washed them with water**.

Lev 8:10 Then Moses took the anointing oil and anointed the tabernacle and everything in it, and so consecrated them.

Lev 8:12 He then **poured some of the anointing oil on the head of Aaron and anointed him to consecrate him**.

All of these elements were present in the baptism of Jesus. First, the Father and his Son were present. Second, he was submerged in water by a member of the legitimate priestly line, John the Baptist. Third, as he came up out of the water, the Holy Spirit of anointing came down in the form of a dove and landed on him:

Mat 3:16 After Jesus was baptized, just as he was **coming up out of the water**, the heavens opened and he saw the **Spirit of God descending like a dove and coming on him**.

Mat 3:17 And a voice from heaven said, "This is **my one dear Son**; in him I take great delight."

The consecration of Jesus at his baptism included the washing of water in the Jordan River by a legitimate priest of the Levitical priesthood, the anointing of the Holy Spirit in the form of a dove, and the presence and approval of the Father. This is a perfect parallel of the consecration ceremony under the Levitical priesthood. Jesus Christ was thereby set apart and anointed as the high priest of the new priesthood at his baptism in the Jordan River, the time and place of the transfer of the priesthood from Aaron's order to the order of Melchizedek.

10.6 A Pattern of the Heavenly Temple

The temple and the Levitical priesthood on earth was a pattern of the temple and priesthood in heaven. Moses was instructed to build a pattern of what was in heaven:

Heb 8:5 The place where they serve is **a sketch and shadow of the heavenly sanctuary**, just as Moses was warned by God as he was about to complete the tabernacle. For he says, "See that you make everything according to the design shown to you on the mountain."

Heb 9:23 So it was necessary for **the sketches of the things in heaven** to be purified with these sacrifices, but the heavenly things themselves required better sacrifices than these.

Heb 9:24 For Christ did not enter a sanctuary made with hands—the **representation** of the true sanctuary—but into heaven itself, and he appears now in God's presence for us.

This is a key point. Because the Levitical priesthood had 24 orders of the priesthood, and was a pattern of what is in heaven, it follows that the 24 elders are a heavenly parallel of the priestly order of the 24 descendants of Eleazar and Ithamar. They serve the Melchizedekan priesthood of the high priest of heaven, Jesus Christ:

I Pet 3:21 . . . through the resurrection of Jesus Christ,

I Pet 3:22 who went into heaven and is at the right hand of God with <u>angels and authorities and powers</u> **subject to him.**

Heb 5:9 And by being perfected in this way, he became the source of eternal salvation to all who obey him,

Heb 5:10 and **he was designated by God as <u>high priest in the order of Melchizedek</u>.**

Peter wrote that there are different levels of angelic beings who are currently serving Jesus Christ as he performs the duties of the high priest of heaven at God's right hand. These angelic beings include the 24 elders around the throne, and the four living creatures.

Hebrews states that heavenly tabernacle items had to be purified with blood, just as the earthly tabernacle, which Moses and his helpers crafted, were purified with blood. However, a better sacrifice than the blood of bulls and goats was required to purify the heavenly temple. The sacrifice of Jesus Christ for sin accomplished this purification:

Heb 9:23 So it was necessary for the sketches of the things in heaven to be purified with these sacrifices, **but <u>the heavenly things themselves required better sacrifices than these</u>.**

Heb 9:24 For Christ did not enter a sanctuary made with hands—the representation of the true sanctuary—but **into heaven itself,** and he appears now in God's presence for us.

Heb 9:25 And he did not enter to offer himself again and again, the way the high priest enters the sanctuary year after year with blood that is not his own,

Based on Hebrews chapters 6 through 13, the heavenly temple, the true tabernacle with all the original items after which the earthly tabernacle was patterned, was not accessible until Jesus' sacrifice accomplished the purification. Jesus was described as the forerunner, opening the way for all believers to be able to enter the holy place:

Heb 6:19 We have this hope as an anchor for the soul, sure and steadfast, which reaches inside **behind the curtain,**

Heb 6:20 **where Jesus our forerunner entered on our behalf,** since he became a priest forever in the order of Melchizedek.

This heavenly temple is clearly referred to several times within Revelation, along with the golden altar of incense and the ark of the covenant:

Rev 8:3 Another angel holding a golden censer came and was stationed at the altar. A large amount of **incense** was given to him to offer up, with the prayers of all the saints, on **the golden altar** that is before **the throne**.

Rev 11:19 Then **the temple of God in heaven** was opened and **the ark of his covenant** was visible **within his temple**. And there were flashes of lightning, roaring, crashes of thunder, an earthquake, and a great hailstorm.

The altar of incense, the ark of the covenant, and the Mercy Seat were located in the Most Holy Place under the Levitical priesthood:

Heb 9:3 And after the second curtain there was a tent called **the holy of holies**.

Heb 9:4 It contained **the golden altar of incense and the ark of the covenant** covered entirely with gold. In this ark were the golden urn containing the manna, Aaron's rod that budded, and the stone tablets of the covenant.

Heb 9:5 And above the ark were the cherubim of glory overshadowing **the mercy seat**. Now is not the time to speak of these things in detail.

Because Revelation refers to these temple furnishings in heaven, it is clear that a temple and the elements of the Most Holy Place are present in heaven. The golden altar of incense has the prayers of the saints offered upon it. The ark of the covenant was visible in heaven, and the Mercy Seat, God's throne, is also present.

If the heavenly tabernacle is truly a representation of the earthly Levitical priesthood, then there are also 24 "sons of the high priest" in heaven who represent the sons of Eleazar and Ithamar. The 24 elders are that heavenly angelic representation, serving the high priest Jesus Christ.

As explored above, the transfer of the Levitical priesthood to the Melchizedekan priesthood took place before Jesus' sacrifice on the cross and ascension to heaven. Therefore, the 24 elders may have been in place since the time of that event marking the transfer on earth, Jesus' baptism by John the Baptist. The appearance of the Lamb of God before the throne in Revelation chapter 5, therefore, becomes even more dramatic when viewed in this light. In addition, the physical and verbal reaction of the elders to his appearance as the perfect Lamb sacrificed for all humanity is illuminated.

10.7 The Twenty-four Elders Contrasted with the Vast Throng

Is there more evidence that the 24 elders represent an angelic order of the heavenly Melchizedekan priesthood? Other than a conversation with John that will subsequently be explored in depth, the 24 elders are consistently shown before the throne worshipping God. Recall that this throne is in the Most Holy Place, along with the golden altar of incense and the ark of the covenant, consistent with the view that the elders are also present in the temple. There is also an important passage in Revelation chapter 19 that reveals interesting facts about the 24 elders:

Rev 19:1 After these things I heard what sounded like **the loud voice of a vast throng in heaven**, saying, "Hallelujah! Salvation and glory and power belong to our God,

Rev 19:2 because his judgments are true and just. For he has judged the great prostitute who corrupted the earth with her sexual immorality, and has avenged the blood of his servants poured out by her own hands!"

Rev 19:3 Then a second time **the crowd** shouted, "Hallelujah!" The smoke rises from her forever and ever.

Rev 19:4 **The twenty-four elders** and **the four living creatures** threw themselves to the ground and worshiped God, who was seated on the throne, saying: "Amen! Hallelujah!"

This passage provides an important distinction between the vast throng in heaven and the 24 elders and the four living creatures. If the future three-stage event has taken place by this point in the chronology of Revelation, chapter 19, then this vast throng is that group in heaven, rejoicing for the judgment that has been poured out. The crowd is identified for a second time in verse 3, but, the 24 elders and the four living creatures are identified separately from this vast throng, and their exclamations are separately announced from them. They agreed with the statements of the vast throng by saying "Amen!", which means they were not part of the group that uttered them.

If the crowd is a group of human beings in heaven, then the 24 elders cannot be human beings, or representative of human beings, based on this passage. Each group is identified separately, and their statements are separately rendered in the text. Furthermore, the 24 elders are consistently grouped with the four living creatures, which without question are not human. If the 24 elders are representatives of the caught-up, living believers in heaven, then why are they singled out and made separate from the vast throng of believers in this passage?

10.8 Summary and Conclusion

Some of the key points to remember from this chapter include:

- The *apokalupsis* is a revelation of Jesus Christ, not merely a description of doom and gloom during Daniel's 70th week.
- In Revelation chapter 1, John was commanded to write what he saw in the spirit about what was currently taking place, and what was to happen afterward.
- In Revelation chapter 4, John was told to "Come up here" and be shown what was to happen afterward. The "here" in the command to "Come up here" is described in Revelation chapters 4 and 5, while what would happen afterward is described in Revelation chapters 6 through 22.
- Jesus Christ is the high priest of the priesthood after the order of Melchizedek.

- The earthly temple and the items in it were patterned after the heavenly temple, and the Levitical priesthood had 24 divisions of priests who were traced to the sons of Aaron, a Levite.
- The dramatic transfer of the Levitical priesthood to the Melchizedekan priesthood was accomplished at the baptism of Jesus by John the Baptist, a descendant of the priestly line of Aaron and Levi.
- The 24 elders are a heavenly angelic representative of the 24 divisions of the earthly Levitical priesthood.
- The vast throng in heaven and the 24 elders are identified as two separate groups in Revelation chapter 19.

The content covered in this chapter was necessary to understand the setting as John was invited to see what was going to happen afterward. This will continue in the next chapter, as Revelation chapter 5 will be carefully examined in light of what has been presented thus far. The chapters to follow will shed new light on the timing and overall structure of Revelation chapters 4 through 7.

The second wave of ground I saw
in the distance was even higher
than the first wave. I would
estimate their height at eight
to ten feet. That feeling of
relief about still being alive
was replaced with a new sense of
desperation. There was no way
that I could keep surviving
these intense shockwaves. My
eyes were glued on the
approaching wave, and I found
myself unable to tear them away
from the awesome sight...

Earthquake Resurrection Prophetic Model Timeline Progression

Weeks 1-69	**Week 69 Ends; GAP Between Week 69 and Week 70**	**Week 70 Begins**

Time Period	Event	Scripture	Chapter
457BC - 27AD	Decree of Artaxerxes Longimanus; Weeks 1-69 of Daniel's 70 Week Prophecy	Dan 9:24-25	Ch. 8
27AD	Transfer of the Priesthood of Melchizedek at Christ's Baptism	Luk 3-4	Ch. 8
31AD	Christ's and the "Many Saints" Earthquake Resurrection	Mat 27	Ch. 3-6
31AD	Christ's Ascension to the Right Hand of God	Act 1; Rev 4-5	Ch. 10, 11
31AD - PRESENT — Opening of the First Five Seals – Birth Pains Begin	1 — Spirit of Religious Domination in Christ's Name	Rev 6:1-11	Ch. 12
	2 — Spirit of War and Bloodshed		Ch. 13
	3 — Spirit of Financial Oppression		
	4 — Spirit of Death, Disease, and Famine		Ch. 14
	5 — Persecution and Death of Believers		
	Sixth Seal — Future Earthquake Resurrection of the Dead in Christ, Transformation and Catching Up	1 The 4; 1 Cor 15	Ch. 4, 5, 7
FUTURE TIME	Confirmation / Strengthening of the Covenant	Daniel 9:27	Ch. 9, 15, 16
	Sealing of the 144,000 Children of Israel	Rev 7	
	Enumerable Group Before the Throne		

- CHAPTER ELEVEN -

THE ASCENT TO THE RIGHT HAND OF GOD

Revelation chapters 4 through 7 should be viewed together as one continuous story, not as broken and separate chapters. The chapter breaks do not necessitate a gap in time. Revelation chapter 5 features the introduction of a seven-sealed scroll held in God's right hand. Before the contents of the scroll are revealed, a dramatic description of the appearance of the Lamb in heaven is provided. This chapter will focus on that dramatic appearance.

11.1 The Ascension of Christ

While there are numerous verses in the Old Testament which mention God's right hand, there is but one in which the Lord is prophesied to sit at the right hand of God. Peter quoted this same verse on the day when the baptism in the fire of the Holy Spirit was unleashed:

> Psa 110:1 Here is the Lord's proclamation to my lord: "Sit down at **my right hand** until I make your enemies your footstool!"

> Act 2:34 For David did not ascend into heaven, but he himself says, '**The Lord said to my lord, "Sit at my right hand**
> Act 2:35 **until I make your enemies a footstool for your feet.**"'

Just before his crucifixion, Jesus himself declared to Caiaphas the high priest that he would be at the Father's right hand after his death:

> Mat 26:64 Jesus said to him, "You have said it yourself. But I tell you, from **now on you will see the Son of Man sitting at the right hand** of the Power and coming on the clouds of heaven."

Christ's ascension to heaven was an incredible supernatural event that took place on the Mount of Olives 40 days after his resurrection from the dead. The disciples were privileged to see it with their own eyes. It was described by Luke in Acts chapter 1, at the conclusion of the 40-day period in which he appeared to the disciples:

Act 1:9 After he had said this, while they were watching, **he was lifted up** and a cloud hid him from their sight.

Act 1:10 As they were still **staring into the sky while he was going,** suddenly two men in white clothing stood near them

Act 1:11 and said, "Men of Galilee, why do you stand here looking up into the sky? **This same Jesus who has been taken up from you into heaven** will come back in **the same way you saw him go into heaven."**

In the final chapter of Mark, more detail is added to the ascension event, specially, exactly where he went when he arrived in heaven:

Mar 16:19 After the Lord Jesus had spoken to them, he was taken up into heaven and **sat down at the right hand of God.**

11.2 Who Will Open the Scroll?

Revelation chapter 5 opens with a description of the throne and a seven-sealed scroll. Note where this scroll is located with respect to God:

Rev 5:1 Then I saw in **the right hand** of the one who was seated on the throne a scroll written on the front and back and sealed with seven seals.

After the scroll is described in God's right hand, the search began for someone to open the scroll:

Rev 5:2 And I saw a powerful angel proclaiming in a loud voice: "Who is worthy to open the scroll and to break its seals?"

Rev 5:3 But **no one in heaven or on earth or under the earth was able** to open the scroll or look into it.

This is a perplexing passage if viewed as occurring in the future. If Jesus Christ had already ascended to the throne and been in heaven for nearly 2,000 years, then why would he not be already seated on the right hand of God, ready to take the scroll? Why would the angel have to call throughout heaven and earth to find him, the only one worthy to open the scroll? Was Jesus playing a game of Hide and Seek?

According to scripture, when Jesus ascended to heaven, he sat down at the right hand of God, as Mark described in the verse above. In fact, as Stephen was being stoned to death, he said he actually saw Jesus at God's right hand:

Act 7:55 But Stephen, full of the Holy Spirit, looked intently toward heaven and saw the glory of God, and **Jesus standing at the right hand of God.**

Act 7:56 "Look!" he said. "I see the heavens opened, and **the Son of Man standing at the right hand of God!"**

As discussed above, Jesus told Caiaphas the high priest that he would be sitting at the right hand of power in heaven. In addition, in several of their letters, both Paul and Peter proclaim that Jesus Christ is currently at the right hand of God, interceding for prayers:

Rom 8:34 Who is the one who will condemn? **Christ** is the one who died (and more than that, he was raised), who **is at the right hand of God**, and who also is interceding for us.

Col 3:1 Therefore, if you have been raised with Christ, keep seeking the things above, **where Christ is, seated at the right hand of God**.

I Pet 3:22 **who went into heaven and is at the right hand of God** with angels and authorities and powers subject to him.

Therefore, according to these verses, Jesus should be at God's right hand to open the seven-sealed scroll. But he is not there in Revelation chapter 5. The call for someone to open the sealed scroll becomes even more perplexing when one considers the following passage from Hebrews:

Heb 10:12 But when this priest had offered one sacrifice for sins for all time, **he sat down at the right hand of God**,

Heb 10:13 **where he is now waiting** until his enemies are made a footstool for his feet.

This is a key point. Not only did Christ sit down at the right hand of God after his death, resurrection, and ascension, but he must remain there until his enemies are made a footstool for his feet. Now consider Revelation chapter 5 in this light. If what is described in this chapter takes place in the future, then where is Jesus, and why is he not seated at God's right hand? Why is there a call throughout the universe for him? Where is Jesus hiding?

The clear answer is that the scene at the opening of Revelation chapter 5 does not take place in the future. In the vision that John was being shown, Jesus had not yet arrived at the throne from the earth. Rather than a description of the throne room scene *after* the future resurrection, transformation, and catching-up event, this is a vision of the scene at God's throne just after the ascension of Jesus Christ and just before he took his seat at the right hand of God.

11.3 The Lamb Ascends to the Throne

If the call throughout the universe for someone to open the scroll is perplexing, then the verse that follows is doubly so. In response to the angel's cry for someone to take the seven-sealed scroll, which went unanswered, John began weeping:

Rev 5:4 So I began **weeping bitterly** because no one was found who was worthy to open the scroll or to look into it.

The Greek indicates John was weeping greatly and profusely. At this point in his life, John had known of Jesus Christ for approximately 60 years. He was the beloved disciple, watching Jesus die as he hung on the cross. He ran to the tomb to see if Jesus truly had been resurrected from the dead. He wrote the Gospel of John and was called the disciple whom Jesus loved. He had a three and one-half year vault of memories upon which to draw during the time Jesus Christ was among them. Now, he was exiled on the Isle of Patmos, where he was visited by Jesus Christ himself in a vision:

> Rev 1:17 When I saw him I fell down at his feet as though I were dead, but he placed his right hand on me and said: "Do not be afraid! I am the first and the last,
>
> Rev 1:18 and the one who lives! **I was dead, but look, now I am alive—** forever and ever—and I hold the keys of death and of Hades!

Suddenly, in Revelation chapters 4 and 5, John saw the awesome throne room scene, but Jesus was not present at the right hand of God as was declared by Stephen, Paul, and Peter in the verses cited above. When John saw the vision, why wouldn't his memories of Jesus Christ come into play? Wouldn't John cry out something on the order of, "I know the One who is worthy to open the scroll!! It's Jesus Christ! He died on the cross and rose from the dead. He walked among us for 40 days after his resurrection. As a matter of fact, I just saw him while I was on the Isle of Patmos!", instead of weeping bitterly?

In order for this scene to make logical sense, it must be a vision of the throne room just before Jesus' ascension to the throne to take his prophesied place at the right hand of God, where the seven-sealed scroll resided. Note that John was not literally taken to this time in history, but that he was given a vision of this time in history. In a dramatic fashion, the Lamb who had been brutally slain appeared in the middle of the throne room:

> Rev 5:5 Then one of the elders said to me, "Stop weeping! Look, the Lion of the tribe of Judah, the root of David, has conquered; thus he can open the scroll and its seven seals."
>
> Rev 5:6 Then I saw standing in the middle of the throne and of the four living creatures, and in the middle of the elders, **a Lamb that appeared to have been killed.** He had seven horns and seven eyes, which are the seven spirits of God sent out into all the earth.

The first action taken by the Lamb after his appearance in the heavenly throne room is critically important. He proceeded to the right hand of the throne of God and took the scroll out the right hand of God:

> Rev 5:7 Then he came and **took the scroll from <u>the right hand</u>** of the one who was seated on the throne,

Perhaps John's bitter weeping was because his memories were not active in the visionary state. Or, perhaps he was weeping because he knew that Jesus was supposed to be at the right hand of the Father, but not realizing this was a vision of the past right before Jesus arrived, and seeing Jesus was not there, he became troubled. Maybe John simply wept because Jesus was not present to open the seals to set in motion the consummation of history that would lead to his return to the earth. All of these are speculation, because the text does not definitively state the reason

John was weeping other than that there was no one present to open the scroll. The visionary scene within which John found himself was the heavenly throne room scene just prior to the first century ascension of Jesus Christ, just before he took his seat at the right hand of God.

11.4 The Reaction to His Ascension and Appearance

After the appearance of the Lamb in the throne room, note the reaction of the 24 elders, as well as the four living creatures:

> Rev 5:8 and when he had taken the scroll, the four living creatures and the twenty-four elders threw themselves to the ground before the Lamb. Each of them had a harp and **golden bowls full of incense (which are the prayers of the saints)**.

There are two important clues within the description of the reaction of the 24 elders and the four living creatures which shed light upon whether these entities are human beings. The first clue is that the 24 elders were holding golden bowls, full of incense. This incense is further described as being the prayers of the saints. The prayers of the saints are heard by Jesus Christ, according to the New Testament.

The 24 elders, if they are a symbolic representative of saints, would not be holding golden bowls which contain their own prayers. However, if the 24 elders represent an angelic order of priests, it would make perfect sense for them to be holding the golden bowls with the prayers of the saints. As these prayers reach the throne, they are offered up as incense before the throne, where Jesus Christ intercedes before the Father for the saints based on their prayers.

The scene in Revelation chapter 5, therefore, is a description of the first appearance of the high priest of heaven after his ascension to sit in intercession for the prayers of the saints. The 24 elders were holding golden bowls before the throne in preparation for their offering of the incense upon the altar.

The second important clue is found within the song that is sung by the 24 elders and the four living creatures. This song is key in eliminating the possibility that they are human beings or representative of human beings. There is an important difference between the KJV, which is dependent on the Textus Receptus, and the NET, as well as several other translations:

> Rev 5:9 They were singing a new song: "You are worthy to take the scroll and to open its seals because you were killed, and at the cost of your own blood you have purchased for God **persons** from every tribe, language, people, and nation.
> Rev 5:10 You have appointed **them [autous]** as a kingdom and priests to serve our God, and **they** will reign on the earth."

Compare this rendition, noting the words in bold and underline, to the KJV below:

Rev 5:9 And they sung a new song, saying, Thou art worthy to take the book, and to open the seals thereof: for thou wast slain, and hast redeemed **us** to God by thy blood out of every kindred, and tongue, and people, and nation;
Rev 5:10 And hast made **us** unto our God kings and priests: and **we** shall reign on the earth.

The passage above in the KJV is the main reason for the traditional interpretation that the 24 elders are representative of human believers in heaven. The KJV uses the pronouns "us" and "we", while the NET and the vast majority of other translations use "them" and "they", including the NIV, NASB and ASV. According to the translation notes supplied with the NET, "The vast majority of witnesses have *aujtouv*" (*autous*, "them") here, while the Textus Receptus reads *hJma*'" (*Jhmas*, "us") with insignificant support . . .*There is __no question__ that the original text read aujtouv" here.*"[1] [emphasis added]

According to the NET translators, there is no question that the original manuscript contained *autous*, the Greek pronoun "they". Furthermore, Revelation 5:8 states that the 24 elders and the four living creatures are worshipping the Lamb, and verse 9 states "they" are singing the song to the Lamb. If the KJV rendition of "us" and "we" is correct, then the four living creatures also claimed to be members of the redeemed, purchased by the blood of Jesus Christ. In addition, they claimed to be part of the kingdom of priests that will reign on earth. It is quite clear that the four living creatures are not human beings: on this point, there is 100% agreement among scholars. Therefore, it makes no logical sense for the four living creatures to be singing this song, using the pronouns "us" and "we". Angelic beings were not redeemed by the blood of Jesus Christ, but they rejoice in heaven when a person is redeemed, and they greatly desire to know about the gospel of salvation:

I Pet 1:12 They were shown that they were serving not themselves but you, in regard to the things now announced to you through those who proclaimed **the gospel** to you by the Holy Spirit sent from heaven—**things angels long to catch a glimpse of.**

This means that the 24 elders and the four living creatures were not singing about themselves, as rendered by the KJV, but about the redeemed that the Lamb had purchased with his own blood. It is powerful evidence against the notion that the 24 elders are human beings or representatives of them, as well as proof that Revelation chapter 5 is a description of the appearance of the Lamb in the heavenly throne room for the first time after his violent death and victorious resurrection. Carefully study the original Greek language in Revelation 5:8-10 to ascertain the validity of what has been proposed in this section. The reader will discover that the information presented above is accurate. There are several good programs on the Internet that can be downloaded free of charge that include the original Greek language that was translated into English.

---

[1] The NET Bible. Notes on Revelation chapter 5, verse 10, note 31.

11.5 A New Song?

In verse 9, the song of the 24 elders and the four living creatures is described as a "new song". The Greek word for "new" is *kainos*, and is used to describe something that is particularly fresh, recent, and unused.[2] If this song, in John's vision, were being sung 2,000 or more years after Jesus' death and resurrection, then why would it be described as "new"? The content of the song would denote something had just happened such that it would be labeled new. But the redemption of Jesus Christ on the cross and his purchase of the saints on earth took place at a certain time in the past. The song would not be called "new" unless the actions of the Lamb, as described in the song, had just taken place. Why call it "new", if it had occurred over 2,000 years ago?

If the song is being sung at a time in the future, after the catching up of believers for example, then the 24 elders and the four living creatures would have waited at least 2,000 years to sing the "new" song. But if the redemption of mankind and the establishment of the royal priesthood took place nearly 2,000 years ago and Jesus ascended about 43 days after his death, why would they wait so long to sing this new song?

The royal priesthood was established when Jesus Christ ratified the new covenant by shedding his blood once and for all. If the new song is sung at least 2,000 years after the establishment of the new covenant, then that would make the establishment of the kingdom of priests referred to in the song a "new" event. But this cannot be the case. The New Testament writers made it clear that the establishment of the priesthood of the believer took place upon the establishment of the new covenant:

> I Pet 2:9 But **you are** a chosen race, **a royal priesthood**, a holy nation, a people of his own, so that you may proclaim the virtues of the one who called you out of darkness into his marvelous light.

> Rev 1:6 and **has appointed us as a kingdom, as priests** serving his God and Father—to him be the glory and the power for ever and ever! Amen.

At the time Peter wrote his first epistle, he declared that believers are a royal priesthood. John declared the same at the opening of Revelation, written in approximately 95 AD. The proper interpretation of this new song, therefore, is that it was sung in celebration of the new covenant that had been established at the death and resurrection of Christ nearly 2,000 years ago, not in the future. The content of the song was that Jesus had purchased mankind with his blood and made believers a kingdom of priests, all of which occurred in approximately 31-32 AD. The 24 elders and the four living creatures, upon the appearance of the Lamb and his procession to God's right hand, sang the new song in celebration of these awesome acts.

Such an interpretation provides more proof that what John saw in the vision beginning in Revelation chapter 4 was:

---

[2] Thayer's Greek Definitions

1.   The throne room scene just before Jesus' ascension to the throne,
2.   The appearance of Jesus in the middle of the throne room after his ascension,
3.   His procession to God's right hand to take the seven-sealed scroll, and
4.   The reaction of the 24 elders and the four living creatures to his appearance at that particular time.

Take note that John was not seeing the actual events as they took place, but that he was shown a vision of the events which took place in the past relative to his lifetime.

Revelation chapter 5 closes with a harmonic praise to the slain Lamb and the resurrected and conquering Lion of Judah. Worthy is that Lamb and Lion of all praise and adoration for what he accomplished.

11.6 Summary and Conclusion

The key points to take from this chapter are as follows:

- The ascension of Jesus from the earth to heaven is described in Acts chapter 1.
- According to the Psalmist, Stephen, and the apostles Peter and Paul, Jesus was seated at the right hand of God, and will remain there until the time all things are restored, as the prophets foretold.
- The seven-sealed scroll was at the right hand of the one seated on the throne.
- If the Revelation chapter 5 scene will take place just after the catching up of believers, as the traditional prophetic models suggest, it is perplexing that a search for Jesus was necessary. He should have been seated at the right hand of God, or with the caught-up group of believers.
- According to Paul in Hebrews, Jesus is now seated at the right hand of God, and is waiting there until his enemies are made a footstool for his feet.
- The vision of Revelation chapters 4 and 5 must have been a vision of the throne room just before, and just after, the ascension to the right hand of God.
- In the Revelation chapter 5 description of John's vision, the first act performed by the Lamb after his appearance in the middle of the throne was to proceed to the right hand of God and take the seven-sealed scroll.
- The 24 elders, if humans or representative of them, would not be holding their own prayers in golden bowls before the high priest of heaven. Rather, the 24 elders are angelic beings presenting the prayers of human beings to the Lord at the altar of incense.
- The song of the 24 elders and the four living creatures is key in understanding that the 24 elders are not humans or their representatives. The KJV rendition of "us" and "we" in the song is not a reliable translation.
- The song of the 24 elders and the four living creatures is described as a "new song". If John's vision was a vision of the future just after the catching-up event, then the contents of the song should not have been new. However, if in response

to the Lamb's appearance in heaven just after his death, resurrection, and ascension to the throne, the contents of the song would most assuredly be new.

- The establishment of the kingdom of priests took place at the time of the redemption provided by Jesus. For the "new song" to be sung 2,000 years after the redemptive act of crucifixion took place makes no logical sense. Rather, the song was sung just as Jesus made his dramatic appearance in heaven after his ascension.

In the chapters to follow, the opening of the seven-sealed book of history will be examined in depth. The events that would take place from the opening of the first seal until the future resurrection, transformation, and catching-up event, and the beginning of Daniel's 70th week, unfold in Revelation chapter 6.

The wave of ground possessed a majestic quality, flowing with uniformity underneath the immediate top of the soil, but leaving destruction and havoc in its wake. At the peak of the wave as it rolled, clumps of grass and soil split apart and flew into the air as if an explosion had taken place underneath. This was happening in a split second, yet it seemed like I was watching it happen in slow motion. Majestic indeed, yet horrific knowing that those explosions would soon be below me.

Earthquake Resurrection Prophetic Model Timeline Progression

Weeks 1-69			Week 69 Ends; GAP Between Week 69 and Week 70			Week 70 Begins
457BC - 27AD	27AD	31AD	31AD - PRESENT			FUTURE TIME
			Opening of the First Five Seals - Birth Pains Begin			
			1 / 2 / 3 / 4 / 5	Sixth Seal		
Decree of Artaxerxes Longimanus, Weeks 1-69 of Daniel's 70 Weeks Prophecy	Transfer of the Priesthood of Melchizedek at Christ's Baptism	Christ's and the "Many Saints" Earthquake Resurrection	Christ's Ascension to the Right Hand of God	Spirit of Religious Domination in Christ's Name	Spirit of War and Bloodshed	Spirit of Financial Oppression	Spirit of Death, Disease, and Famine	Persecution and Death of Believers	Future Earthquake Resurrection of the Dead in Christ, Transformation and Catching Up	Confirmation / Strengthening of the Covenant	Sealing of the 144,000 Children of Israel	Enormous Group Before the Throne
Dan 9:24-25	Luk 3:4	Mat 27	Act 1 Rev 4-5	Rev 6:1-11	1 The 4; 1 Cor 15	Daniel 9:27	Rev 7
Ch. 6	Ch. 3, 6	Ch. 10, 11	Ch. 12	Ch. 13	Ch. 14	Ch. 4, 5, 7	Ch. 9, 15, 16

- CHAPTER TWELVE -

THE FIRST SEAL: RELIGIOUS DOMINATION IN CHRIST'S NAME

As explained in the previous chapter, if one were sitting in front of the original manuscript of Revelation that was penned by John, it would be one continuous letter, and Revelation chapters 4 through 6 would run together as one continuous vision. However, with the chapter breaks in the English translations of the Bible, many have been inclined to treat each chapter separately, as if thousands of years pass in between them. But, as Revelation chapter 6 opens, the Lamb was simply opening the first seal of the scroll that he just took out of the right hand of the Father at the end of Revelation chapter 5. Thousands of years did not pass between his sitting down at the right hand of God, his taking of the scroll, and his opening of the first seal. Treat what is described in Revelation chapter 4 through the beginning of chapter 6 as one continuous vision.

With that in mind, recall what was just viewed in Revelation chapter 5. The Lamb that was slain had ascended to the throne, which resulted in rejoicing by the angelic beings in heaven. The Lamb then proceeded to the right hand of God to take the scroll.

12.1 The Four Horses and Riders of the First Four Seals

The opening of the seals represents the unlocking and progression of future events, from a first century perspective. The events symbolized within the seals were future and prophetic as John saw them in the first century. Do not assume that the events are only future and prophetic from a modern-day perspective. As John saw them unfolding in his vision, they would have been future, or "what will happen after", events from his perspective.

The colored horses in Zechariah chapters 1 and 6 are interesting, and may be related to the horses of the four seals. Two overall traits of the Zechariah horses that are similar to the traits of the horses of the first four seals emerge, and reveal clues about their identity and mission:

Zec 6:4 Then I asked the angelic messenger who was speaking with me, "What are these, sir?"

> Zcc 6:5 The messenger replied, "These are **the four spirits of heaven** that have been **presenting themselves [yatsab]** before the Lord of all the earth.

> Zec 6:7 All these strong ones are scattering; they have **sought permission to go and walk about [halak]** over the earth." The Lord had said, "Go! Walk about over the earth!" So they are doing so.

There are several interesting things of which to take note in this passage. First, the horses were symbols of spirits that roam the earth, presenting themselves before the Lord. Second, there were four spirits, which could be synonymous with the four riders of Revelation chapter 6. Third, these spirits were presenting themselves before the Lord and seeking permission to walk about in the earth. This is similar language to the angelic "sons of God" and Satan who presented themselves before the Lord and were walking in and through the earth, as described in Job chapter 1:

> Job 1:6 Now the day came when the sons of God came to **present themselves [yatsab]** before the Lord—and Satan also came among them.
> Job 1:7 The Lord said to Satan, "Where have you come from?" And Satan answered the Lord, "From roving about on the earth, and from **walking up and down [halak]** in it."

These Job and Zechariah passages taken together may shed some light on the identity of the four spirits of Zechariah, symbolized by horses in his vision. These four horses are symbolic representations of evil spirits which are given permission by the Lord to carry out judgments on the earth. The idea of the Lord giving permission to spirits to wreak havoc in the lives of believers is confusing. However, the devil is described as the god of this present evil age and, in addition to possessing his own kingdom, has been granted temporary limited control over all the kingdoms of the world:

> Luk 4:5 Then **the devil** led him up to a high place and showed him in a flash **all the kingdoms of the world**.
> Luk 4:6 And he said to him, "To you I will grant **this whole realm**—and **the glory that goes along with it**, for it has been **relinquished to me**, and I can give it to anyone I wish.

> Mat 12:26 So if **Satan** casts out Satan, he is divided against himself. How then will **his kingdom** stand?

The Satanic kingdom consists of a hierarchical realm of evil spirits against whom humanity struggles:

> Eph 6:12 For our struggle is not against flesh and blood, but against the **rulers**, against the **powers**, against the **world rulers of this darkness**, against the **spiritual forces of evil in the heavens**.

These are the same evil spirits at work within the symbolism of the first four seals of Revelation chapter 6. They are unseen enemies that continuously oppress and deceive the human race, carrying out the prophetic agenda of the devil in the earth. That agenda includes temptation, lies, oppression, possession, thievery, destruction, condemnation, accusation, and slavery: a wide array of deception in an attempt to eternally damn every soul on the earth.

12.2 The Symbolism of the First Seal

The opening of the first seal brings forth what is symbolized as a white horse with an infamous rider:

> Rev 6:1 I looked on when the Lamb opened one of the seven seals, and I heard one of the four living creatures saying with a thunderous voice, "Come!"
> Rev 6:2 So I looked, and here came **a white horse**! The one who rode it had a bow, and he **was given [edothe]** a crown [stephanos], and as a conqueror [nikon] he rode out to conquer [nikesei].

The symbols of the first seal are:

1. a white horse
2. a bow
3. a victor's wreath crown
4. a mission to conquer or dominate

Within the New Testament, the color white is always used in either a positive or neutral manner. *Leukos* in Greek, within Revelation alone, is used in many descriptions, including the hair on Jesus' head, the clothing of the overcomer, the clothing of the 24 elders, the robes of the martyrs, the horse and the cloud on which the Son of Man will return, the horses of the armies of heaven, and the throne on which God judges. With all these positive people and things associated with white, it would certainly make sense to interpret this horse as a symbol of something positive going forth into the earth. Some interpret the white horse and rider as the progress of the gospel and the kingdom of heaven on earth.

However, there are several reasons why the symbolism of this horse should be interpreted in a negative rather than a positive light. First, as will be shown, the other three horses and riders all represent negative events on the earth. To interpret this seal as a positive conquering of the people would be inconsistent with the other three horses and riders. The analysis of the Zechariah horses as evil spirits above bolsters this view.

Second, the red horse rider and the pale green horse rider are both granted permission or given their authority to wreak havoc. Similarly, the white horse was given a crown, a symbol of earthly conquering authority. The Greek word for "given" in this verse, *edothe*, is also used in describing the authority given to two of the other three horses and riders. As with the horses in the passage from Zechariah, to be "given" or "granted" authority means that the Lord gave them permission to carry out their acts.

Third, the similarities between the white horse riders of Revelation chapters 6 and 19 are few. While crowns are associated with both riders, the chapter 19 rider has many crowns, and the Greek word is *diadema* for royal diadem crowns. In contrast, the chapter 6 rider has one crown, and the Greek word is *stephanos* for a victor's wreath crown. The rider in chapter 19 is clearly Jesus Christ, while the rider in chapter 6 is a deceptive spiritual representation of him.

Fourth, Jesus predicted his name would be used for false pretenses after he was gone and before the end of the age:

Mat 24:5 For many will come **in my name**, saying, 'I am the Christ,' and they will mislead many.

Fifth, Jesus did not advocate the use of force or a conquering spirit when he instructed the disciples to preach the gospel. It is a choice that all men make of their own free will. In contrast, the white horse rider is bent on being a *nikon* in Greek, or conqueror. When Jesus first sent his disciples into the cities of Israel, he gave the following instructions:

Mat 10:14 And if anyone will not welcome you or listen to your message, shake the dust off your feet as you leave that house or that town.

Luk 10:10 But whenever you enter a town and the people do not welcome you, go into its streets and say,
Luk 10:11 'Even the dust of your town that clings to our feet we wipe off against you. Nevertheless know this: The kingdom of God has come.'

This is not the spirit of force or domination, but of preaching the truth to whomever will hear. It involves the free choice of the listener, not a forced decision.

For these reasons, this first horse and rider symbolizes an evil conquering spirit going forth into the earth using a religious system and the name of Christ (a white horse) with conquest and domination of the masses as the goal. The symbols of the bow and the crown are further representations of a spirit of conquering and domination.

The rider of the white horse should not be interpreted as an actual human being, such as the future Antichrist, any more than the riders of the second, third, and fourth horses should be interpreted as actual human beings. Both the horses *and* their riders are symbolic of an evil presence sent forth into the earth to carry out an evil prophetic agenda.

12.3 Interpreting the Symbolism: A Spirit of Religious Domination

A study of history from the first century to the present shows indisputable evidence of this conquering, dominating spirit in the earth, using religion to dominate and even brainwash the masses. Any religion, organization, hierarchy, or denomination that uses the name of Jesus Christ, Christianity, or the gospel to force, coerce, or brainwash its adherents is being led by the spirit of religious domination symbolized within the first seal.

In contrast to the true believing "church" that began in the first century, the Roman Empire offered a strange combination of Greek and Roman god and goddess worship along with worship of the Imperial leaders of the Empire, including Nero and Domitian. These leaders were known as Pontifex Maximus, the monarchical leader of both the political and religious realms, and any rejection of their worship along with the pagan gods resulted in crucifixions, roastings, impalings, beheadings, and some of the most excruciating, mind-numbing torture that can be imagined.

When Constantine revolted against Rome and took his power to Byzantium, later renamed Constantinople, it marked a split in the Roman Empire. His Edict of Toleration brought to an end the severe persecution of Christians and instituted freedom of religion, but also served to incorporate the worship of Greek and Roman gods into Christianity. Later, Theodosius made Catholic Christianity the state religion:

> We order those who follow this doctrine to receive the title of Catholic Christians, but others we judge to be mad and raving and worthy of incurring the disgrace of heretical teaching, nor are their assemblies to receive the name of churches. They are to be punished not only by Divine retribution but also by our own measures, which we have decided in accordance with Divine inspiration.[1]

The result of this edict was forced conversions of pagans, causing churches to be filled with false converts. In response to the split of the Roman Empire from Rome by Constantine and others from the Western branch, the bishops of Rome established the papal hierarchy, a hierarchy which featured an earthly priesthood with bishops, cardinals, priests, and other ministers, with the Pontifex Maximus at the head, the Pope. While believers are without a doubt members of a royal priesthood, it is a spiritual priesthood rather than a physical, earthly priesthood. Believers worship in spirit and truth, offer the sacrifice of praise, have bodies which are the temple of God within which the Holy Spirit dwells, and offer prayers as incense on the altar of heaven.

Though this spirit of domination in the name of Christianity applies to any religion, organization, hierarchy, or denomination who would use the gospel to force, coerce, or brainwash its adherents, the most powerful example is the Roman Catholic Church through the papal system. The Catholic Church is the largest and most powerful religious order on the earth today, and the modern Protestant denominations have branched out of it.

The history of the Roman Catholic Church has reverberated through the centuries and its influences are still felt today in modern denominations, despite the Protestant Reformation. Its persecution of underground Christianity during the Inquisitions in

---

[1] Ehler, Sidney Z. and John B. Morrall, translators and editors, (1954). *Church and State Through the Centuries*, London.

Spain, Germany, Holland, France, and Italy, the crusades against Islam, and the persecutions of the Reformation in the 16th and 17th centuries, all reveal the fruit of the spirit of domination that permeates through the history of the papacy. As will be shown from history, as well as from their own statements, the papal system has dominated the religious world ever since its foundation and has required submission and obedience from the universal corporate church to its decrees as if they were uttered by Jesus Christ himself.

The following sections contain quotations from popes or Catholic authorities throughout the centuries. This is a very small sampling of thousands of incredible statements made throughout history and recorded in books. These quotations will establish the brainwashing and cult-like dominance that was forced on the people through the papacy in the name of Christianity. Beyond a cursory explanation of the setting in which these quotations were given, there will not be abundant commentary on them. The quotations will speak for themselves. Where bold and underline font appears below, emphasis has been added.

12.4 Domination Over Heads of State

We desire to show the world that **we can give or take away at our will** kingdoms, duchies, earldoms, in a word, **the possession of all men**; for we can bind and loose.[2]

- Pope Gregory VII (1073-1085) in the Roman Synod of 1080.

By the authority which God has given us in the person of St. Peter, we declare you king, and **<u>we order the people</u>** to render you, in this capacity, **homage and obedience**. We, however, shall expect you to **subscribe to all our desires** as a return for the imperial crown[3]

- Pope Innocent III (1198-1216) in declaring Otho of Saxony to be the king of Germany.

The First See **is judged by no one**. It is the right of the Roman Pontiff himself alone to judge . . .those who hold the highest civil office in a state . . .
There is **neither appeal nor recourse** against a decision or decree of the Roman Pontiff.[4]

- The Code of Canon Law

---

[2] von Dollinger, J. H. Ignaz (1869), *The Pope and the Council,* pp. 87-89. London.
[3] Cormenin. *History of the Popes,* p. 243, as cited in R.W. Thompson (1876) *The Papacy and the Civil Power,* p. 459. New York.
[4] Coriden, James, A., Thomas J. Green, Donald E. Heintschel, eds. (1985). *The Code of Canon Law,* Canons 1404, 1405, and 333, sec. 3, pp. 951, 271. Paulist Press.

> The crown is the symbol of the **sovereignty of the papacy** . . .The tiara is adorned with pearls and precious gems and is inscribed in Latin, which translates as: 'To the **infallible** Vicar of Christ; To **the Supreme Governor of the world on earth**; To the **father of Nations and Kings**.[5]

- A description of the tiara of Pope Pius IX (1846-1878), who convened the Vatican I Council in 1869 and pronounced papal infallibility as a dogma of the Catholic Church.

12.5 Domination Through Violence Against Dissenters

> I glorify you for having maintained **your authority by putting to death those wandering sheep who refuse to enter the fold**; and . . .congratulate you upon having opened the kingdom of heaven to the people submitted to your rule.

> A king need not fear to command massacres, when these will **retain his subjects in obedience, or cause them to submit** to the faith of Christ; and **God will reward him in this world, and in eternal life, for these murders**.[6]

- Pope Nicholas I (858-867) when encouraging the King of Bulgaria to force Roman Catholicism on his subjects.

> We hear that you forbid torture as contrary to the laws of your land. But **no state law can override canon law, our law**. Therefore **I command you** at once to submit those men to torture.[7]

- Pope Clement V (1305-1314) to King Edward II of England due to a revolt against papal power.

> Know that the interests of the Holy See, and those of your crown, make it a duty to exterminate the Hussites. Remember that these impious persons **dare proclaim principles of equality**; they maintain that all Christians are brethren, and that God has not given to privileged men the right of ruling the nations; they hold that Christ came on earth to abolish slavery; they call the people to liberty, that is to the annihilation of kings and priests.
> While there is still time, then, turn your forces against Bohemia; burn, massacre, make deserts everywhere, **for nothing could be**

---

[5] Our Sunday Visitor, August 22, 1993, pp. 10-11.
[6] Cormenin. *History of the Popes*, p. 243, as cited in R.W. Thompson (1876) *The Papacy and the Civil Power*, p. 244. New York.
[7] Durant, Will (1950). *The Story of Civilization*, vol. IV, p. 680. Simon and Schuster.

more agreeable to God, or more useful to the cause of kings, than **the extermination of the Hussites.**[8]
- Pope Martin V (1417-1431), who commanded the King of Poland to massacre the Hussites, a group who resisted the papacy in honor of Jan Hus, a martyr.

12.6   Domination Through Declaration of Papal Infallibility and Authority

It is not enough for the people only to know that the Pope is the head of the Church . . .they must also understand that **their own faith and religious life flow from him**; that in him is the bond which unites Catholics to one another, and the power which strengthens and the light which guides them; **that he is the dispenser of spiritual graces**, the giver of the benefits of religion, the upholder of justice, and the protector of the oppressed.[9]

- La Civilta Cattolica, or The Catholic Civilization, a journal in which Roman Catholic doctrine has been published for over 150 years.

The Roman Pontiff, when he speaks ex cathedra—that is, when in the exercise of his office as pastor and teacher of all Christians he defines, by virtue of his supreme Apostolic authority, a doctrine of faith or morals to be held by the whole Church—is, by reason of the Divine assistance promised to him in blessed Peter, **possessed of that infallibility** with which the Divine Redeemer wished His Church to be endowed in defining doctrines of faith and morals[10]

- Vatican I Council, 1869-1870.

The Pope, Bishop of Rome and Peter's successor, 'is the perpetual and visible source and foundation of the unity both of the bishops and of the whole company of the faithful. For the Roman Pontiff, by reason of his office as Vicar of Christ, and as pastor of the entire Church has full, supreme, and universal power over the whole Church, **a power which he can always exercise unhindered.**'

The Roman Pontiff, head of the college of bishops, enjoys this **infallibility in virtue of his office,** when, as supreme pastor and teacher of all the faithful—who confirms his brethren in the faith—

---

[8] Cormenin. *History of the Popes*, pp. 116-117, as cited in R.W. Thompson (1876) *The Papacy and the Civil Power*, p. 553. New York.

[9] La Civilta Cattolica, 1867, vol. Xii, p. 86.

[10] "The Catholic Encyclopedia", http://www.newadvent.org/cathen/07790a.htm#IIIB, accessed July 1, 2004.

he proclaims by a definitive act a doctrine pertaining to faith or morals . . .The infallibility promised to the Church is also present in the body of bishops when, together with Peter's successor, they exercise the supreme Magisterium, above all in an Ecumenical Council. When the Church through its supreme Magisterium proposes a doctrine "for belief as being divinely revealed," and as the teaching of Christ, **the definitions "must be adhered to with the obedience of faith." This infallibility extends as far as the deposit of divine Revelation itself.** [11]

- Vatican II Council, 1962-1965, Canons 882 and 891.

12.7 Domination Through Required Submission of Intellect and Will

Each individual must receive the faith and law from the Church . . .**with unquestioning submission and obedience of the intellect and the will . . .We have no right to ask reasons of the church,** any more than of Almighty God . . .We are to take with **unquestioning docility whatever instruction the Church gives us.** [12]

- The Catholic World, in 1871, the time of the Vatican I Council.

From which **totally false idea** of social government they do not fear to foster that **erroneous opinion, most fatal in its effects** on the Catholic Church and the salvation of souls, called by Our Predecessor, Gregory XVI, **an "insanity",** . . .that **"liberty of conscience and worship is each man's personal right,** which ought to be legally proclaimed and asserted in every rightly constituted society; and that a right resides in the citizens to an absolute liberty, which should be restrained by no authority whether ecclesiastical or civil, whereby they may be able openly and publicly to manifest and declare any of their ideas whatever, either by word of mouth, by the press, or in any other way." [13]

- Pope Pius IX (1846-1878), Quanta Cura, or "Condemning Current Errors", speaking out <u>against</u> freedom of worship and conscience.

---

[11] "Office for the Catechism",
http://www.usccb.org/catechism/text/pt1sect2chpt3art9p4.htm, accessed July 1, 2004.
[12] "The Catholic World", August 1871, vol. xiii, pp. 580-589.
[13] "The Encyclical Letter of Pope Pius IX,"
http://www.ewtn.com/library/ENCYC/P9QUANTA.HTM, accessed July 1, 2004.

Fear, then, our wrath and the thunders of our vengeance; for **Jesus Christ has appointed us with his own mouth absolute judges of all men**; and kings themselves are submitted to our authority.[14]

- Pope Nicholas I (858-867).

Through his great efforts and incomprehensible stealth he introduced into Spain prohibited books that he brought from far away places where they give protection to the ungodly . . .He firmly believes that God, by means of the Scriptures, **communicates to the laity just the same as He communicates to the priest.**[15]

- Read at the sentencing of Julian Hernandez during the Spanish Inquisition in 1560, who was burned at the stake for smuggling Bibles into Spain from Germany, and, apparently, for believing that God communicates to regular people in addition to Catholic priests.

Man can obtain a knowledge of God's Word from the Catholic Church and through its duly constituted channels.
When he has once mastered this principle of divine authority, the inquirer is **prepared to accept whatever the divine church teaches** on faith, morals and the means of grace.[16]

- The Convert's Catechism of Catholic Doctrine.

12.8 Domination Through Declaring Salvation Only Through the Church

Basing itself on Scripture and Tradition, the Council teaches that **the Church**, a pilgrim now on earth, **is necessary for salvation . . .**Hence, **they could not be saved who, knowing that the Catholic Church was founded as necessary by God through Christ, would refuse either to enter it, or to remain in it.**[17]

- Vatican II Council, 1962-1965, Canon 846.

If any one **denieth**, either that sacramental confession was instituted, or is necessary to salvation, of divine right; or saith, that

---

[14] Cormenin. *History of the Popes*, p. 243, as cited in R.W. Thompson (1876) *The Papacy and the Civil Power*, p. 369. New York.

[15] Martinez, Emilio (1909) *Recuerdos de Antano*, p. 390. CLIE.

[16] Geierman, Peter (1977). *The Convert's Catechism of Catholic Doctrine*, pp. 25-27. Tan Books and Publishers, Inc.

[17] "Catechism of the Catholic Church", http://www.usccb.org/catechism/text/pt1sect2chpt3art9p3.htm, accessed July 2, 2004.

> the manner of confessing secretly to a priest alone, which the Church hath ever observed from the beginning, and doth observe, is alien from the institution and command of Christ, and is a human invention; **let him be anathema.**[18]

- The Council of Trent, 14th Session, Canons Concerning the Most Holy Sacrament of Penance, Canon VI. The "Anathemas" [Curses] of the Council of Trent were created in response to the Protestant Reformation, from 1545-1563.

> If any one saith, that, after the grace of Justification has been received, to every penitent sinner the guilt is remitted, and the debt of eternal punishment is blotted out in such wise, that there remains not any debt of temporal punishment to be discharged either in this world, or in the next in Purgatory, before the entrance to the kingdom of heaven can be opened (to him); **let him be anathema.**[19]

- The Council of Trent, 6th Session, Canons Concerning Justification, Canon XXX, 1545-1563.

12.9 A Spiritual Force At Work

Many other quotations were omitted from the sections above in the interest of conciseness and length. While pondering the information above, remember that what is symbolized in the first four seals is the granting of permission in the spirit world to carry out the events within the seals. A spirit of religious domination in the name of Christ was unleashed to conquer the people and dominate their minds, and the acts are carried out in the lives of the people on the earth.

Any group that would attempt to place curses on people who disagree with their views, whether those views are absolutely correct or not, is bent on mind control, conquest, and domination, as signified in the first seal white horse and rider. There weren't only a few anathema curses, but many hundreds of them established throughout Roman Catholic Church history. The New Testament contains three anathemas, but these do not contradict the whole of scripture, and they were penned by Paul, an apostle and eyewitness of the resurrection of Jesus Christ:

> Gal 1:8 But even if we (or an angel from heaven) should preach a gospel contrary to the one we preached to you, let him be condemned to hell [anathema]!
> Gal 1:9 As we have said before, and now I say again, if any one is preaching to you a gospel contrary to what you received, let him be condemned to hell [anathema]!

---

[18] The Council of Trent, http://history.hanover.edu/texts/trent/ct14.html, accessed on July 2, 2004.
[19] The Council of Trent, http://history.hanover.edu/texts/trent/ct06.html, accessed on July 2, 2004.

I Cor 16:22 Let anyone who has no love for the Lord be accursed [anathema]. Our Lord, come!

Any organization that would go outside of the inspired Word of God to attempt to instill fear and bondage into the hearts of people by cursing them to eternal damnation, again, whether the views associated with the curses are absolutely sound or not, is practicing nothing more than mind control. The concept is very similar to that used by popular cults, including Sun Myung Moon's Unification Church, Jehovah's Witnesses, The Church of Jesus Christ of Latter Day Saints (Mormons), and many others.

While the bulk of this chapter has focused on the Roman Catholic Church, there are many other groups who have either in the past used, or are currently using, the name of Jesus Christ to dominate their adherents. The goal was not to denigrate the Catholic faith, but to use some of its history as an example of what the first seal symbolizes. Again, any religion, organization, hierarchy, or denomination that uses the name of Jesus Christ, Christianity, or the gospel to force, coerce, or brainwash its adherents is being led by the spirit of religious domination symbolized within the first seal. The Catholic Church has changed greatly from the early periods of murderous conquest and inquisition, but that time of bloodshed was very real to those who were engulfed within it.

12.10 Jesus' Contrasting Style: A Miracle of Restraint

With this background of the history of the Roman Catholic Church in mind, consider the contrasting style Jesus Christ possessed while he was on the earth. During the temptation in the wilderness, Satan offered Jesus a chance to show off his power in three ways:

1.   Show the power to turn stones into bread, a temptation made even more palpable given the fact that Jesus had not eaten for 40 consecutive days.
2.   Worship the devil, and Jesus could take over the power of the world's kingdoms while in their fallen state. Because Jesus had not yet died to cleanse the world of sin and provide a way to the Father, giving in to this temptation would have ruined God's plan of redemption.
3.   Prove that God and the angels will supernaturally protect him by jumping off the top of a tall building.

Jesus answered these temptations using only the Word of God, knowing that yielding to the temptations would be a sin, and Jesus would no longer be the sinless sacrificial Lamb of God. Victory over the devil during this 40-day temptation was a miracle: a miracle of self-control.

This type of restraint was evident throughout the ministry of Jesus. Why didn't he just crush the Roman Empire like the disciples wanted him to? Why didn't he just heal all the diseases in the world with his power to heal? Why didn't he bring fire down from heaven on his enemies? All these things were possible. Instead, he allowed people to come to him in humility and receive from him. A measure of faith healed a cowering woman who strained to just touch the hem of his garment. Lepers came to him, crying out for mercy from a distance in their decrepit state. A paralyzed man was lowered through a roof to him because the crowd was too large to reach him. A Roman centurion with incredible faith came to him asking him to heal his sick servant, and Jesus honored his faith and humility. A demon possessed man approached him after Jesus and his disciples arrived on the Gentile shores of Gadara and received an amazing deliverance of thousands of demons.

Jesus never forced or imposed himself on these people. He never coerced, tricked, or brainwashed anyone into believing in his teaching. He clearly taught that no one could come to the Father except through him, yet stressed no one could come to him unless the Father drew them to him. He never made his teachings, his ways, or his ideas a compulsory requirement. Humanity's free will to choose was in no clearer display than during the ministry of Jesus. How much less compulsory could Jesus become than to declare that, in order to follow him, a person had to pick up their cross every day? Picking up the cross meant, to the Jews of his day, the cross of crucifixion upon which many of their contemporaries had died. Jesus didn't try to manipulate anyone into following him, but instead, made his listeners realize that to follow him would be a sacrifice.

In contrast, the Roman Catholic Church made their religion the official religion of the state and prerequisite for salvation. They forced people to turn from different versions of Christianity or face excommunication and death. They burned "heretics" on stakes and murdered entire villages who dared to question their authority to impose their will. They granted kings the authority to kill people, and promised them that God would reward them in heaven for it. All of this was accomplished using the name of Christ, claiming dominant authority over the masses with Christ as the justification for their actions.

In the modern climate of tolerance, the Roman Catholic Church no longer unseats heads of state or commissions troops on crusades of murderous bloodshed. Today's Roman Catholic Church is one of tolerance and ecumenical cooperation with other faiths and denominations in an effort to heal wounds of the past. For example, according to their catechism:

> The plan of salvation also includes those who acknowledge the Creator, in the first place amongst whom are the Muslims; these profess to hold the faith of Abraham, and together with us they adore the one, merciful God, mankind's judge on the last day.[20]

Modern attempts to reach out to Muslims by the Roman Catholic Church resulted in the current Pope John Paul II kissing the Qu'ran in front of the world at the Vatican on May 14, 1999.[21] It is the ultimate in irony that the pope, who claims to be

---

[20] Ibid.

[21] "The Kiss and the Blood", http://www.traditioninaction.org/HotTopics/a001ht.htm, accessed July 2, 2004.

the Son of God's vicar on earth, would kiss a book that states the Lord God doesn't even have a Son. Many other attempts to reconcile with other faiths around the world could be explored.

12.11 Summary and Conclusion

A spirit is at work, symbolized by a white horse with a bow and a crown, going out into the earth to conquer and dominate using Christ's name. That spirit began its domination on earth in the first century after Jesus Christ finished his work on the cross and ascended to God's right hand, and still works today in many different fashions and within many different religious orders. That spirit also recognizes the times in which we live, and has adapted to those changing times in order to continue his mission of dominance. Remember these key points:

- Jesus took the scroll at the end of Revelation chapter 5 and began to open the first seal at the beginning of Revelation chapter 6.
- Keep in mind the perspective of John and the readers of the Revelation letter when considering future and prophetic events. The events described within the seal were future when viewed from their perspective.
- The white horse and rider of the first seal represent a religious spirit of domination and conquest, using Christianity and the name of Jesus Christ to dominate the people.
- The best example of domination of the people through the name of Jesus Christ from the first century to the present is the Roman Catholic Church.
- Any religion, organization, hierarchy, or denomination that uses the name of Jesus Christ, Christianity, or the gospel to force, coerce, or brainwash people is being led by the spirit of religious domination symbolized within the first seal.
- Christ's example was not one of force, coercion, or brainwashing, but one of allowing humanity to come to him of their own free will in humility and faith.
- The white horse and rider symbolized within the first seal began its domination on earth in the first century and continues to the present day.

The interpretation that has been presented in this chapter, though sensitive, is in agreement both with history and with the chronological progress from the beginning of Revelation, through chapters 4 and 5. The second, third, and fourth seals, and their comparison to the description Jesus provided in Matthew chapter 24 and Luke chapter 21, will be explored in the next chapter.

When I was a teenager, I was at home alone one day when a strong storm came through the city. I went to the basement as the tornado sirens went off, and soon the storm was directly over our the house. The sound was incredible: it sounded like a freight train was rushing by the basement windows for about 20-30 seconds, then calm. When I went outside, I found broken windows everywhere and a yard full of softball to baseball-sized hail. That 20-30 second time frame of sound was similar to the sound heard as the massive first aftershock of the original earthquake was approaching. This time, I didn't roll up in a ball and wait, but I tightly shut my eyes, tensed every muscle in my body, and waited for its fury to pass...

Earthquake Resurrection Prophetic Model Timeline Progression

Weeks 1-69				Week 69 Ends; GAP Between Week 69 and Week 70						Week 70 Begins		
457BC - 27AD	27AD	31AD	31AD	**31AD - PRESENT**					Sixth Seal	**FUTURE TIME**		
				Opening of the First Five Seals - Birth Pains Begin								
				1	2	3	4	5		Confirmation / Strengthening of the Covenant	Sealing of the 144,000 Children of Israel	Enormous Group Before the Thrust
Decree of Artaxerxes Longimanus, Weeks 1-69 of Daniel's 70 Weeks Prophecy	Transfer of the Priesthood of Melchizedek at Christ's Baptism	Christ's and the "Many Saints" Earthquake Resurrection	Christ's Ascension to the Right Hand of God	Spirit of Religious Domination in Christ's Name	Spirit of War and Bloodshed	Spirit of Financial Oppression	Spirit of Death, Disease, and Famine	Persecution and Death of Believers	Future Earthquake Resurrection of the Dead in Christ, Transformation and Catching Up			
Dan 9:24-25	Luk 3-4	Mat 27	Act 1; Rev 4-5		Rev 6:1-11				1 The 4; 1 Cor 15	Daniel 9:27	Rev 7	
Ch. 8		Ch. 3, 6	Ch. 10, 11	Ch. 12	Ch. 13			Ch 14	Ch. 4, 5, 7		Ch. 9, 15, 16	

- CHAPTER THIRTEEN -

THE SEALS CONTINUE: BIRTH PAINS BEFORE THE END

The first through fifth seals should be viewed as being opened by the Son of God in heaven at approximately the same time early in the first century. They should be seen as overlapping each other and continuous throughout history, not as consecutive with one ending and another beginning. The events symbolized within each of the first five seals began in the first century, overlapping and continuing until at least the opening of the sixth seal.

13.1 The Symbolism of the Second Seal

After the Lamb opened the first seal, the second seal was opened:
Rev 6:3 Then when the Lamb opened the second seal, I heard the second living creature saying, "Come!"
Rev 6:4 And another horse, **fiery red [purros]**, came out, and the one who rode it **was granted [edothe] permission** to take peace from the earth, so that people would **butcher one another [sphaxousin]**, and he was given [edothe] a huge sword.

The symbols of the second seal are:

1. a fiery red horse
2. a twofold mission to (a) take peace from the earth, and (b) cause people to brutally murder each other
3. a large sword

A fiery red horse conjures up certain negative images, such as hellfire and bloodshed. In keeping with these images, the spirit symbolized by this horse takes peace from the earth and causes people on earth to kill each other. The rider is "granted" authority to take peace. Who is doing the granting? God in his sovereign wisdom and justice granted these spirits the authority to do what they have done and are still doing. Recall the discussion in the previous chapter regarding the four spirits, symbolized by horses, that roamed the earth and presented themselves before the Lord.

The Greek word for "red" is *purros*, and is an adjective found in very few other places in the New Testament. Its root word is *pur*, meaning "burn" in Greek, which is why the NET used the word "fiery" to further describe its color. It is used to describe the dragon, Satan, in Revelation chapter 12, and in Matthew chapter 16, Jesus used a similar word to describe the sky as red when you can see a storm coming. The root word, and several different variations of it, are found in several different places in the New Testament to describe fire or something hot.

The first of the twofold mission of this spirit is to take peace from the earth. This deceptive power has no doubt resulted in the violence that we have seen in numerous wars throughout the centuries, beginning in the first century. The history books are full of these wars, so a rehash of history is not warranted in this book. But not only the normal kind of violence and murder that takes place in territorial wars is in play within this seal, but a special type of demonized violence that causes people to viciously torture and murder.

13.2 Interpreting the Symbolism: A Spirit of Violence, Torture, and Bloodshed

The more common Greek verb for "kill" in the New Testament is *apokteino*, used 82 times in the New Testament. The root Greek word for "butcher" in verse 4, however, is *sphazo*, a verb used to describe the act of slaughtering animals for sacrifice or food. It means to put to death in an extremely violent and merciless manner, but even more than that, without a conscience for the act. That is the context of this verb: to kill human beings with violence and without conscience. This verb is used sparingly throughout the New Testament, appearing only ten times in I John and Revelation. Among those uses are the following:

I Joh 3:12 not like Cain who was of the evil one and **brutally murdered [esphaxen] his brother.** And why did he **murder [esphaxen]** him? Because his deeds were evil, but his brother's were righteous.

Rev 5:6 Then I saw standing in the middle of the throne and of the four living creatures, and in the middle of the elders, **a Lamb that appeared to have been killed [esphagmenon].** He had seven horns and seven eyes, which are the seven spirits of God sent out into all the earth.

Rev 6:9 Now when the Lamb opened the fifth seal, I saw under the altar the souls of **those who had been violently killed [esphagmenon]** because of the word of God and because of the testimony they had given.

Rev 18:24 The blood of the saints and prophets was found in her, along with **the blood of all those who had been killed [esphagmenon]** on the earth."

This type of senseless, violent killing was definitely seen under the brutal rule of Nero in the first century, and continued throughout the rules of many of the Roman Emperors, including Domitian and Diocletian. Again, the history books are full of accounts detailing ways in which Christians were killed for sport, without conscience, so a detailed account in this book isn't necessary. This type of murder continued throughout the centuries, seen in the crusades by papal rule in Rome, the inquisitions, the Muslim conquests, and in response to the Protestant revolt beginning in the 16th century. In addition, wars of "ethnic cleansing" in Europe, Asia, and other parts of the world have raged for centuries, and many still do today.

This spirit of violence continues its work in modern times. The 20th century was, by the account of some historians, the most violent century in the history of the world. In fact, some theorize that more human beings were killed in wars or by murder during the 20th century than during the previous 19 centuries combined. While this may be hard to believe and even harder to prove, remember that there were two large "world wars" during that century which took millions of lives each. Indeed, the Holocaust was an attempt to completely wipe out the population of Jews in Europe.

Violence against Christians over the 20th century, and at the present, goes largely unnoticed by the major media outlets. The public at large is carefully manipulated to see on television only what those in the upper echelon of the massive media companies dictate it will see. The stories of violence in countries such as Burma, Bangladesh, Sudan, Somalia, Indonesia, China, Pakistan, and many others will not be seen on such networks as NBC, CBS, ABC, CNN, or FOX. One must frequent faithful Internet sites such as Persecution.org[1] to be aware of the intolerance for Christianity outside of the United States, and the brutality and torture being suffered by Christians. These are Christians who don't have large, comfortable churches with padded pews, basketball courts, bookstores, or coffee shops.

But the spirit symbolized in the second seal red horse also had a mission to take peace from the earth. The same type of imperialistic pursuit of kingdoms and territories is not seen today outside of the United States current campaign in Iraq, using war to try to establish peace. The wars fought in this age of tolerance are fought for "democracy", to depose evil dictators, and to provide a type of pseudo-freedom for the people under their rule. As a result of these "goals", wars have become big business today. Large and small defense companies alike now make big profits, and keep the economies of the world moving from the billions of dollars generated by war machines, artillery, equipment, and intelligence. This is a subtle way that this spirit has taken peace from the earth: perpetual war for perpetual pseudo-peace.

The type of violence described in the second seal was prophesied by Jesus Christ. He described them as the beginning of the birth pains:

> Mat 24:6 You will hear of **wars and rumors of wars**. Make sure that you are not alarmed, for this must happen, but **the end is still to come**.

---

[1] "Persecution.org, an International Christian Concern", http://www.persecution.org/, accessed July 3, 2004.

Mat 24:7 For **nation [ethnos] will rise up in arms against nation [ethnos]**, and **kingdom [basileia] against kingdom [basileia]**. And there will be famines and earthquakes in various places.
Mat 24:8 All these things are **the beginning of birth pains**.
Mat 24:9 "Then they will hand you over to be **persecuted and will kill you**. You will be **hated by all the nations** because of my name.

The symbol of the huge sword of the red horse rider further solidifies the interpretation that has been presented above. In the Old Testament, the sword was routinely used as a metaphor for war and violence. The sword symbolized the threat of invading armies against the Israelites. Similarly, the sword of the second seal symbolizes the use of force and violence to kill humanity throughout the centuries.

13.3 The Symbolism of the Third Seal

John heard the third living creature call out, and the Lamb opened the third seal:
Rev 6:5 Then when the Lamb opened the third seal I heard the third living creature saying, "Come!" So I looked, and here came a black [melas] horse! The one who rode it had **a balance scale [zugon]** in his hand.
Rev 6:6 Then I heard something like a voice from among the four living creatures saying, "A quart [choinikes] of wheat will cost a day's pay [denariou] and three quarts [choinikes] of barley will cost a day's pay [denariou]. But do not damage the olive oil and the wine!"

The symbols of the third seal are:

4. a black horse
5. a *zugon*, or yoke, in his hand
6. an oppressive declaration and command concerning food and money

The color of the horse was black, or *melas* in Greek. Two other verses in the New Testament use the English word "black", and in both cases the color is used in a more neutral manner, one to describe hair and one to describe the sun. Because black is the opposite of light and white, black rightly has been associated with darkness and evil. This is the case with the symbolism of this horse.
The object this rider held in his hand must be explored. Almost every translation and paraphrase of the Bible examined in preparation of this book rendered the Greek noun *zugos* as a pair of balances, or a balance scale. The noun *zugos* has other meanings, but the reason provided for translating it as a balance scale is the language of the verse that follows, which speaks of grain and barley. The common interpretation has been that food will be measured out and scarce, and rationing necessary. Therefore what the rider held must be a balance scale for measuring wheat and other grains.

However, the primary definition of *zugos* or *zugon* in the Septuagint Old Testament, and the Greek New Testament, is a yoke that is used to bind two or more cattle together for plowing. According to both Strong's Notes and Thayer's Greek Definitions, the metaphorical meaning of the word is burden or bondage, and was often used in the Old Testament to describe the burdensome Mosaic laws. In fact, *zugos* comes from the root word *zeugnumi*, which means to join or bind together. Nevertheless, in the Septuagint Greek translation of the Old Testament, the noun *zugos* was translated many times as a balance scale, including the following verses:

Lev 19:35 You shall not act unrighteously in judgment, in measures and weights **and scales [zugoi]**.

Pro 11:1 False **balances [zugoi]** are an abomination before the Lord, but a just weight is acceptable unto Him.

Isa 40:12 Who has measured the water in His hand, and the heaven with a span, and all the earth in a handful? Who has weighed the mountains in scales, and the forests in a **balance [zugo]**?

What about the New Testament Greek? There are several verses in the New Testament in which this noun is found. In each case, however, *zugon* was translated as "yoke", and the context is one of slavery, burden, or oppression:

Mat 11:29 Take **my yoke [zugon]** on you and learn from me, because I am gentle and humble in heart, and you will find rest for your souls.
Mat 11:30 For **my yoke [zugos] is easy to bear**, and my load is not hard to carry."

Act 15:10 So now why are you putting God to the test **by placing on the neck of the disciples a yoke [zugon] that neither our ancestors nor we have been able to bear**?

Gal 5:1 For freedom Christ has set us free. Stand firm, then, and do not be subject again to **the yoke [zugo] of slavery**.

I Tim 6:1 Those who are under **the yoke [zugon] as slaves** must regard their own masters as deserving of full respect. This will prevent the name of God and Christian teaching from being discredited.

Jesus explained his yoke or burden is easy to bear. The disciples in Acts described the prescriptions of the law of Moses as a proverbial yoke around their necks. In both Galatians and I Timothy, Paul referred to the yoke of slavery. These verses provide guidance about the meaning of the *zugon* in the hand of the black horse rider: a symbolism of a certain kind of bondage and oppression. The traditional interpretation that the *zugon* must be a balance scale representing famine and rationing of food is weakened by the fact that the fourth seal specifically mentions famine. Why would the third and fourth seals both specifically refer to famine?

Finally, the message of the voice that emerges from among the four living creatures, who are showing John the symbolism of the first four seals, provided clarification for what kind of bondage and oppression the yoke was meant to represent. A comparison of first century and 21st century wages aside, the first part of the message is a declaration meaning "a day's wage will buy one person a day's ration of food." This declaration symbolizes either a rise in the price of food, commodities, or necessities of life, or a decline in the value of the currency. The second part of the message was a command that indicates olive oil and wine would not be immune to the price and wage controls.

13.4   Interpreting the Symbolism: A Spirit of Financial Bondage and Oppression

The meaning of the symbolism of the third seal, combining all the ingredients above, is a spirit of financial bondage and oppression that was sent out into the earth. It would be very difficult, given the lack of information in this seal, to make definitive conclusions about what type of financial oppression is being referred to. Some possibilities based on the message that emerged from among the four living creatures include:

- heavy taxation of income by a government,
- interest (usury) charged on debt,
- price controls on the necessities of life, such as food,
- inflation and hyperinflation in the price of goods,
- efforts by a government to exercise control over worker wages,
- scarcity of the necessities of life due to controls on production,
- efforts by a government to exercise control over the value of currencies,
- efforts by a government to expand or contract the supply of money, and
- government and its citizens indebted to creditors in order to purchase goods.

History is full of examples of all of these types economic controls. As the Roman Empire began to flourish in the first and second century, problems started to surface, especially harsh and excessive taxation. According to G. Edward Griffin's landmark work The Creature From Jekyll Island: A Second Look at the Federal Reserve, some of these problems caused the eventual disintegration of the Roman Empire:

> Especially in the later Empire, debasement of the coinage became a deliberate state policy. **Every imaginable means** for plundering the people was devised. In addition to taxation, coins were clipped, reduced, diluted, and plated. Favored groups were given franchises for state-endorsed monopolies . . .and, amidst constantly

rising prices in terms of constantly expanding money, speculation and dishonesty became rampant.[2] [emphasis added]

In response, the Roman Emperor Diocletian issued a proclamation to fix the prices of goods and services. The proclamation stated in part:

Who is of so hardened a heart and so untouched by a feeling of humanity that he can be unaware, nay that he has not noticed, that in the sale of wares which are exchanged in the market, or dealt with in the daily business of the cities, an exorbitant tendency in prices has held spread to such an extent that the unbridled desire of plundering is held in check neither by abundance nor by seasons of plenty . . . Inasmuch as there is seen only a mad desire without control, to pay no heed to the needs of the many . . .it seems good to us, as we look into the future, to us who are the fathers of the people, that justice intervene to settle matters impartially.[3]

The price controls did not work, and only led to more severe problems for the Roman Empire. Eventually, money became extinct due to the currency manipulation that followed, and the Roman Empire slipped into obscurity.[4] Since the fall of the Roman Empire, there have been many similar examples of experimentation with money and goods. Some prospered, as with the Byzantine Empire led by Constantine, but many have failed. The brunt of the failures has always been borne by the common person in the form of lost wealth, scarcity of goods, oppressive taxation, or insurmountable debt.

Perhaps the greatest success story since the fall of the Roman Empire has been the United States of America. In its infancy, in accordance with its Constitution, the monetary system was backed by silver and gold, whose value was set by Congress. Since the early 1900's, the privately-held Federal Reserve banking system has created a financial engine that has produced the most amazing technological revolution in the history of the world. Not only the United States of America, but almost all countries of the world are indebted to a central banking system such as the Federal Reserve. Including future obligations such as Social Security and Medicare, it is estimated that the United States is in debt to the Federal Reserve and the American people to the tune of over $40 trillion.

The incredible boom in productivity since the Great Depression has been built upon expansion of the money supply, debt, and taxation, and has resulted in both rising wages and inflation for all. Expansion of the money supply is accomplished in

---

[2] Griffin, G. Edward (1998). *The Creature From Jekyll Island: A Second Look at the Federal Reserve*, p. 150. Westlake Village, California: American Media.

[3] Groseclose, Elgin (1976). *Money and Man: A Survey of Monetary Experience*, 4th ed. Oklahoma: University of Oklahoma Press.

[4] Griffin, G. Edward (1998). *The Creature From Jekyll Island: A Second Look at the Federal Reserve*, p. 151. Westlake Village, California: American Media.

two main ways: (1) printing more money, and (2) the fractional reserve banking system. The United States Constitution was amended in 1913 to make the taxation of income a law of the land, and is the main source of revenue for the government to pay its debts to the Federal Reserve as well as to purchase goods and services for the public.

Gradually, the currency on which the financial universe currently runs, the United States dollar, was taken off a gold standard, and now is no longer backed by any actual physical commodity. Expansion of the money supply greatly outpaced the mining and production of silver and gold, so the original laws of the Republic were amended several times until the currency became a fiat currency. The result is that the paper money used as a medium of exchange in the United States is worth nothing more than the paper on which it is printed. It cannot be traded in for gold or silver, as was the case before the laws were changed. It is a debt note to the Federal Reserve, and every single United States note has this printed across the top.

Unfortunately, history has shown that fiat currencies, which have no commodity backing them, have always devalued to the paper or metal out of which they were created. Does this mean the same fate will befall the United States and other countries who have no commodity backing their currency? It is difficult to tell, but many experts in finance and economics believe it will. The decision makers are constantly tweaking the money supply and interest rates in order to keep that from happening. But the citizenry of any country in severe debt to an international banking conglomerate such as the Federal Reserve, and with huge trade deficits, is in danger of massive loss of wealth and financial meltdown. As has been the case throughout history, if that meltdown occurs, the citizenry will bear the consequences in the form of loss of wealth, hyperinflation, unbearable taxation, and scarcity of goods. Consider what Thomas Jefferson, one of the Founding Fathers of the United States Republic, said about excessive indebtedness prior to the establishment of the Federal Reserve:

> We must not let our rulers load us with perpetual debt. We must make our election between economy and liberty or profusion and servitude.
>
> If we run into such debt, as that we must be taxed in our meat and in our drink, in our necessaries and our comforts, in our labors and our amusements, for our calling and our creeds...[we will] have no time to think, no means of calling our miss-managers to account, but be glad to obtain subsistence by hiring ourselves to rivet their **chains on the necks** of our fellow-sufferers...And this is the tendency of all human governments.
>
> A departure from principle in one instance becomes a precedent for [another]...till the bulk of society is reduced to be **mere automatons of misery**...And the fore-horse of this frightful team is public debt. Taxation follows that, and in its train **wretchedness and oppression**.[5] [emphasis added]

---

[5] Letter of Thomas Jefferson to Samuel Kercheval, Monticello, July 12, 1816.

Chains on the neck and mere automatons of misery: a perfect picture of the oppressive yoke around the neck of a beast of burden, and a poignant representation of what is currently seen in the United States. From the first century until the present, a spirit has been at work to wreak havoc on the financial systems of the world. Injustice, oppression, and inequity are the goals, and the tools have been governments who have implemented unsound economic controls and unjust taxation through their laws. That spirit is symbolized by the black horse and rider, holding a yoke in his hand to symbolize bondage and oppression of the people.

13.5 The Symbolism of the Fourth Seal

John heard the fourth and final living creature call out, and the Lamb opened the fourth seal:

Rev 6:7 Then when the Lamb opened the fourth seal I heard the voice of the fourth living creature saying, "Come!"

Rev 6:8 So I looked and here came a **pale green [chloros]** horse! The name of the one who rode it was **Death [Thanatos]**, and **Hades followed** right behind. They were **given [edothe] authority** over a fourth of the earth, to kill its population with the **sword, famine,** and **disease**, and by the **wild animals of the earth**.

The symbols of the fourth seal are:

1. a pale green horse
2. a rider with the name Death
3. a follower of the rider named Hades, or the Underworld
4. authority to kill one fourth of the earth's population with four different types of physical oppression

Similar to the first seal rider and the third seal rider, this fourth seal rider is "given" authority to perform his oppressive acts. The pale green color of the horse brings to mind sickness and death. In agreement with that image, the name of the rider of this horse is "Death", or *Thanatos*. This is the common Greek word for death, used over 100 times in the New Testament. In this case, however, the capitalization of the word gives it a personification. In Greek mythology, Thanatos was a god who personified death, and he dwelt in the underworld with his twin brother Hypnos, or "Sleep". Hades was the Greek god of the underworld, son of the Titans Cronus and Rhea, brother of Zeus and Poseidon, who ruled the upperworld and the sea, respectively. Hades was assisted by Charon the ferryman of the River Styx, the hound Cerberus, and by Hypnos and Thanatos. Hades was not well liked in Greek mythology, neither by the gods nor by the people who worshipped the gods.

Death and hades, however, are also described throughout the New Testament as realities. Death and hades are used repeatedly to describe death of the mortal body, and hell, the place of eternal punishment and torment, created for the devil and his angels. Paul addressed both death and hades just after describing the new bodies believers will be given at the resurrection of the dead:

> I Cor 15:54 Now when this perishable puts on the imperishable, and this mortal puts on immortality, then the saying that is written will happen, "**Death [Thanatos]** has been swallowed up in victory."
>
> I Cor 15:55 "Where, O **death [thanatos]**, is your victory? Where, O **death [hades]**, is your sting?"

In Revelation chapter 20, both death and hades are described as being cast into the lake of fire. This is also the final destination of Satan, the beast, the false prophet, and all those whose names are not found written in the book of life:

> Rev 20:13 The sea gave up the dead that were in it, and **Death [Thanatos] and Hades** gave up the dead that were in them, and each one was judged according to his deeds.
>
> Rev 20:14 Then **Death [Thanatos] and Hades were thrown into the lake of fire**. This is the second death—the lake of fire.

These two personifications were granted permission to kill a quarter of the earth's population by four oppressive methods. These exact same four methods are described in Ezekiel chapter 14, yet in that case, they are described as the Lord's "four terrible judgments":

> Eze 14:21 "For this is what the Sovereign Lord says: How much worse will it be when I send <u>my four terrible judgments</u>—**sword, famine, wild animals, and plague**—against Jerusalem to kill both man and beast!

The passage in Ezekiel, combined with Revelation 6:8, reveals an interesting consideration. First, the passage in Revelation states that Death and Hades are "given" the authority that they possess. They didn't possess it on their own, but it had to be given to them. Second, the passage in Ezekiel reveals that these four oppressive methods of death are the Lord's own four terrible judgments. In a vision given to Jeremiah, the Lord told the prophet that he himself was bringing devastation on the people of Israel:

> Jer 24:10 **I will bring <u>war</u>, <u>starvation</u>, and <u>disease</u> on them** until they are completely destroyed from the land I gave them and their ancestors.'"

Note the three things that the Lord said he would bring: war, starvation, and disease. These three things are also embodied in the symbolism of the seals, as shown above, and the Lord permitted them. In the case of the fourth seal, God, in his wisdom, has granted the permission of these evil spirits to exact these judgments during the period extending from Christ's ascension until the present. This is evident with the red horse, and again with the pale green horse.

13.6 Interpreting the Symbolism: A Spirit of Death, Disease, and Famine

The meaning of the symbolism of the fourth seal pale green horse is a spirit of death that was sent out into the earth to torment and oppress one-fourth of the living population. This spirit was granted its authority to kill with the sword, with famine, with diseases, and with beasts of the earth. History, of course, is full of examples of these kinds of things occurring both before and after the incarnation of Christ on earth. However, this was a specific granting of authority at the opening of the fourth seal, just after the ascension of Jesus Christ to God's right hand. Since that time, this spirit of death has been restricted to being able to kill a quarter of the population with the Lord's four terrible judgments.

It would be impossible to try to quantify the number of deaths due to these judgments versus the deaths from other causes. One must consider which forms of death might fall into the categories of violence, famine, disease/pestilence/plague, and beasts of the earth. Each method will be briefly examined below in order to determine whether it is possible that this has taken place.

The first method of judgment, the sword, was discussed within the second seal red horse. It symbolizes war and violence throughout the Bible, but its mention within the fourth seal may represent a general spirit of violence and murder in the earth outside of wars. Who can argue that a spirit of murder, suicide, and homicide, has pervaded over the nations to the point that crime rates continue to rise all around the world?

The second method of judgment, famine or hunger, is another way this spirit of death has authority to kill one-fourth of the population. It would not be fruitful to document every case of famine throughout the last twenty centuries. However, there is no doubt that famine has been a major killer of humanity on every populated continent, especially more recently in Africa and Asia in such countries as Cambodia, Thailand, Bangladesh, Ethiopia, Zimbabwe, Russia, Sudan, Somalia, India, and many others. Throughout history, famine has resulted from many conditions, such as poor weather, drought, natural disasters, and war.

The third method of judgment, disease, is actually "death" or *thanatos* in Greek. So why is it translated as "disease" in the NET? According the Greek lexicon by Bauer, Danker, Arndt, and Gingrich, *thanatos* can refer to a specific type of death in certain circumstances, such as disease.[6] The scripture states Death and Hades have the authority "to kill its population", so to state they would kill people with death would be quite redundant. Therefore, a specific type of death must be in view.

Disease, plague, and pestilence have resulted in much devastation on the earth. History is full of examples, such as the Black Death of the 14th century, the Spanish influenza of 1918 which killed anywhere from 30 to 50 million people, and the Asian and Hong Kong influenzas of 1957 and 1968. These plagues took many millions of lives over the centuries, and there are many more worldwide epidemic and pandemic examples that could be explored.

---

[6] Bauer, Danker, Arndt, and Gingrich (2000). *A Greek-English Lexicon of the New Testament and Other Early Christian Literature*, 3rd edition, 443 s.v. 3.

However, the most potent of the diseases is seen in our current world. Think about the number of deaths from lung cancer, breast and prostate cancer, lymphoma, and leukemia every hour, every day, every month, every year. These diseases also take the lives of countless victims every year. In contrast to how cancer is commonly portrayed, a mysterious disease of unknown origin, cancer is a result of the build-up of free radical cells in the body due to a combination of poor nutrition and diet, stress, and a severe lack of certain vitamins and minerals in the diet.

While cancer is solid evidence of this spirit of death killing through disease, it doesn't grab the headlines like some of the other plagues and pestilence around the globe. Much time could be spent analyzing the devastation caused by viruses and diseases currently wreaking havoc and death around the planet such as Severe Acute Respiratory Syndrome (SARS), Lyme disease, the Ebola virus, West Nile virus, anthrax, malaria, and many others. Whether some of these diseases are man-made, as some of the evidence suggests, is another question. Whatever their origin, the fact remains that millions are being killed by these oppressive diseases and plagues.

The fourth method of judgment, the beasts of the earth, may have the most stealth interpretation of the four. There are many examples of wild beasts killing humans throughout the centuries, including grisly accounts in Fox's Book of Martyrs in which Christians under the persecutions of the Roman Empire were killed by lions, bulls, and other wild animals. The fourth seal rider was given authority to kill with "beasts", but what is meant by this? Perhaps what took place under the Roman Empire, and later in other parts of the world, is part of what John saw in his vision.

Without a doubt, however, the most convincing candidate for death being dealt to humanity through the wild beasts of the earth is the bacteria that are present in the cattle and pigs from which humanity gets the majority of the meat and dairy products it consumes. Cattle and pigs provide products such as milk, cheese, and a host of fresh cut and processed meats. While pasteurization helps to eliminate some bacteria, it does not eliminate all of them. Researchers have discovered a link between the milk and meat consumed by humans, which contain bacterium such as paratuberculosis, and the following diseases:

- Inflammatory bowel disease (Crohn's disease)
- Irritable bowel disease
- Tuberculosis (in many parts of the body)
- Brain disease (Parkinson's disease)
- Alzheimer's disease
- Mycobacterial skin disease (leprosy)
- Lupus
- Rheumatoid arthritis
- Diabetes

Little do trusting consumers of milk, ice cream, and various other dairy products know that the smooth and delicious tasting products they consume in innocence are the clandestine purveyor of bacteria that wreak deadly havoc on their bodies. Other beast-borne plagues and diseases include the avian influenza that has infected millions of chickens in Asia recently. According to a September 14, 2004 article, Asia is facing a horrible avian influenza outbreak. The World Health Organization stated, "This outbreak is historically unprecedented. Its infectious agents don't respect international boundaries."[7] In addition, the aforementioned debilitating Lyme disease is transmitted by ticks, and malaria by mosquitoes.

Perhaps this deeper meaning of the "beasts of the earth" has merit. Indeed, these tiny, microscopic bacterial agents are unseen to the human eye and attack humans invisibly. To assume that the beasts of the earth are only larger animals that attack may be too narrow a focus. There are billions of germs and viruses that have the ability to kill humans, including viruses that have been genetically engineered by human beings as biological weapons. Jesus Christ prophesied that these types of diseases and pestilence would occur prior to his return:

> Luk 21:11 There will be great earthquakes, and famines and **plagues in various places**, and there will be terrifying sights and great signs from heaven.

An important point to remember with the first four seals is that evil spirits and demonic powers work through human beings. While given the authority to oppress and kill humanity, they use humanity to carry out their tasks of evil. However, it still remains that human beings have the free will to choose whether or not they will carry out the acts which the evil spirits devise.

13.7 Summary and Conclusion

Consider these interpretations within the framework of the other chapters within Revelation, as well as within the framework of other scriptures. In the famous discourse on the Mount of Olives just before his arrest, Jesus prophesied of the events that would occur throughout history, and they are embodied within the first five seals of Revelation chapter 6. This will be examined thoroughly later in this book. Some of the important points to remember from this chapter include:

- The first four seals should be seen as overlapping each other and continuous throughout the centuries, not as consecutive with one ending and another beginning.
- The second seal red horse symbolizes a spirit of violence, torture, and bloodshed given authority to cause men to violently kill each other and to take peace from the earth.
- The third seal black horse symbolizes a spirit of financial bondage and oppression through a myriad of means. The rider of the horse holds a *zugon*, or yoke of oppression, rather than a balance scale.

---

[7] "Asia Faces Bird Flu Crisis of Unprecedented Scale", http://story.news.yahoo.com/news?tmpl=story&u=/nm/20040914/hl_nm/birdflu_chi na_who_dc_1, accessed on September 14, 2004.

- The fourth seal pale horse symbolizes a spirit of death, disease, and famine given authority to kill by murderous violence, famine, disease and plague, and beasts of the earth.
- Evil spirits always operate through human beings, and human beings struggle against evil spirits, not other humans. While God may have granted the authority to these evil spirits to influence humanity, it still remains that human beings possess the free will to choose whether or not they will carry out the acts.

The next chapter is an extremely important one, in which the importance of the laws against shedding of innocent blood will be explored. God established laws in the first covenant for the what the people were to do in cases of an intentional murder, an accidental death, and an unsolved death. Throughout history, the blood of the innocent has been shed. There will come a point in the future when the cup of God's wrath is full due to the blood of the innocent and martyrs of Christ shed on the earth.

After the initial quake and
first aftershock, I began to
realize that I could actually
survive these shocks if there
were more. But that was a mixed
blessing, because the short time
that the waves came through and
passed underneath were almost
too excruciating and frightening
to bear. The terror in seeing
the inescapable horror was so
great that I felt I might be
better off dead than going
through it. Still standing at
the glass door, my eyes opened,
hoping it was over. But it
wasn't...

Earthquake Resurrection Prophetic Model Timeline Progression

Weeks 1-69				Week 69 Ends; GAP Between Week 69 and Week 70							Week 70 Begins		
457BC - 27AD	27AD	31AD	31AD	31AD - PRESENT							FUTURE TIME		
				Opening of the First Five Seals - Birth Pains Begin					Sixth Seal				
				1	2	3	4	5					
Decree of Artaxerxes Longimanus; Weeks 1-69 of Daniel's 70 Weeks Prophecy	Transfer of the Priesthood of Melchizedek at Christ's Baptism	Christ and the "Many Saints" Earthquake Resurrection	Christ's Ascension to the Right Hand of God	Spirit of Religious Domination in Christ's Name	Spirit of War and Bloodshed	Spirit of Financial Oppression	Spirit of Death, Disease, and Famine	Persecution and Death of Believers	Future Earthquake Resurrection of the Dead in Christ, Transformation and Catching Up	Confirmation / Strengthening of the Covenant	Sealing of the 144,000 Children of Israel	Enormous Group Before the Throne	
Dan 9:24-25	Luk 3:4	Mat 27	Act 1; Rev 4-5	Rev 6:1-11					1 The 4; 1 Cor 15	Daniel 9:27	Rev 7		
Ch. 5		Ch. 1, 6	Ch 10, 11	Ch. 12	Ch. 13			Ch. 14	Ch. 4, 5, 7		Ch. 9, 15, 16		

- CHAPTER FOURTEEN -

THE FIFTH SEAL: THE BLOOD OF THE INNOCENT

This may be the most important chapter of this book. Within the verses that comprise the description of the fifth seal, an important clue is revealed concerning when the future resurrection, transformation, and catching-up event will occur. Rather than a date, it is the completion of a prophesied period of time of persecution against believers. This chapter will also include an extremely important investigation of what the Word of God says about the shedding of innocent blood, and the judgment that ensues as a result. At the conclusion of the chapter, the overriding purpose of the horrific judgments of Daniel's 70th week will be manifest.

14.1 The Martyrs Under the Altar

As discussed in a previous chapter, there is an important transition at the beginning of Revelation 6:9. The first four seals feature the four horses in symbolism, while the fifth seal features more concrete and literal descriptions. No doubt John was still seeing a vision of the "hereafter" or the things that were to happen "after these things", but the vision moved from using strict symbolism to literal persons and places. Note what John saw when the Lamb opened the fifth seal:

Rev 6:9 Now when the Lamb opened the fifth seal, I saw **under the altar** the souls of those who had been **violently killed [esphagmenon]** because of the word of God and because of the testimony they had given.

Rev 6:10 They cried out with a loud voice, "**How long**, Sovereign Master, holy and true, **before you judge those who live on the earth** and <u>avenge our blood</u>?"

Rev 6:11 Each of them was given a long white robe and they were told to rest for a little longer, **until the full number was reached** of both their fellow servants and their brothers **who were going to be killed just as they had been.**

A very evident characteristic separating the first four seals from the fifth seal is that the opening of the fifth seal did not set loose an evil spirit to wreak havoc on the earth. Instead, it was to show John the souls that had been killed for their faith in Jesus Christ, and that their cry would not be answered until the full number of those who were also going to be killed was reached. This is very different from the first four seals.

Note that the individuals John saw under the altar were those who were violently murdered. The same Greek verb that is used to describe the violent death of Jesus Christ in Revelation chapter 5, *sphazo*, is used to describe the death suffered by these believers. A very interesting conclusion can be drawn from this information: when believers die and enter the third heaven paradise, not all of them go to the same place. According to this passage, believers who die violent deaths in their testimony of the Word of God go under the altar, whereas the location of believers who do not die violent deaths is not provided in this passage. Their place under the altar suggests that they have a specific role. Interestingly, the location of that altar under which they are kept is before God's throne:

> Rev 9:13 Then the sixth angel blew his trumpet, and I heard a single voice coming from the horns on **the golden altar that is before God,**

The cry of the innocent blood from these martyrs, violently killed for their Christian testimony, is constantly before God, reminding him of their innocent blood shed on the earth, and the vengeance that must be meted out for their murders.

14.2 How Long?

The cry of those who suffered a violent death on earth was a question. They wanted to know how much more time would pass before their innocent blood is avenged on the earth. This is a strange question if these are martyrs who had been killed during Daniel's 70th week. Why? There are three convincing reasons that point to the likelihood that these martyrs are not asking this question during Daniel's 70th week, in addition to the rest of the evidence to be explored later in this chapter.

First, if these represent martyrs which will be beheaded by the beast for refusing to take the mark of the beast, as the traditional interpretation of these martyrs suggests, then why would they cry out for the avenging of their blood after Daniel's 70th week would have already begun? After the mark of the beast has been implemented, all six trumpet judgments will have been unleashed, and possibly some of the bowl judgments. This view would require that they would be crying out for the Lord's vengeance *after* the Lord's vengeance had already begun. This is an extremely important question that the traditional prophetic models must answer.

Second, if these will be martyrs violently killed during Daniel's 70th week, why would they be asking "How long" if the length of Daniel's 70th week is already known? The final week of Daniel's prophecy lasts one week, or seven years. So, if these martyrs were killed, for example, six years into the seven year time frame, they would know that there was only one year left. So why ask "How long" when they already know the answer?

Third, if these will be martyrs beheaded during the Daniel's 70th week, they are getting impatient very quickly, because they will have only been seeking vengeance for a few short years. Their question gives off the impression that they have been crying out for a great amount of time, does it not? It seems they have been groaning for a long period of time, waiting and waiting for their blood to be avenged. But the view that the martyrs are killed during Daniel's 70th week also requires that these martyrs are crying out for vengeance a very short time after they were beheaded. This, like the other two reasons, makes no logical sense.

On the other hand, if this is the throne room scene from the beginning of the first century persecution and martyrdom until the time before the sixth seal, as this prophetic model holds, then these martyrs have been waiting for hundreds, perhaps thousands, of years for their blood to be avenged. In addition, no harm is done to the chronological flow of Revelation. The traditional interpretation places the events of the fifth seal near the end of the Daniel's 70th week, which would be out of order with regard to the trumpet judgments, the two witnesses, the beast, the mark of the beast, the image of the beast, the false prophet, and the bowl judgments within the chronological flow of Revelation. Not so with this prophetic model.

There will be a group of believers who, during Daniel's 70th week, will be killed in a violent manner for their testimony about Jesus and the Word of God. About this there is no question. These people will be beheaded during the final 42 months of Daniel's 70th week:

> Rev 20:4 . . .I also saw the souls of **those who had been beheaded** because of the testimony about Jesus and because of the word of God. These had not **worshiped the beast or his image and had refused to receive his mark on their forehead or hand**. . .

Therefore, even after the full number of Christian martyrs is reached in the fifth seal, these individuals will also be violently beheaded for their testimony. However, this is a group of saints who are separate from the resurrected and caught-up body of Christ, whom the beast is allowed to conquer:

> Rev 13:7 The beast was permitted to go to war **against the saints and conquer them**. . .

This group of beheaded martyrs during Daniel's 70th week are specifically referred to in Revelation chapter 15 as a separate group from the vast throng of believers which had *already* been resurrected and caught up to heaven:

> Rev 15:2 Then I saw something like a sea of glass mixed with fire, and **those who had conquered the beast and his image and the number of his name**. They were standing by the sea of glass, holding harps given to them by God.

They will be killed during the 42-month reign of the beast after the establishment of the mark of the beast, at a specific time in the future, rather than over the centuries. Because of their separate mention in Revelation chapters 15 and 20, their specified time of persecution and murder during the 42-month reign of the beast, and the additional three reasons stated above, this group of martyrs is not in view in the description of the fifth seal. More regarding this group of Daniel's 70th week martyrs will be explored in the chapters to follow.

14.3 When The "Full Number" is Reached

The answer the martyrs received to their question "How long?" is equally interesting. They were told to wait until a "full number was reached" of other Christians who would be killed using the same violence with which they were killed. The word "until" is key, because it signifies that there will come a point when the cry from underneath the altar becomes so loud that God can no longer bear to allow their blood to go without revenge. At some point, there will come one final martyr who tips the scales of God's wrath, and that "full number" is finally reached. Until that point, these martyrs continue to cry underneath the altar that is before God.

One of the things that God hates more than any other is the shedding of innocent blood:

> Pro 6:16 There are six things that the Lord hates, even seven things that are an abomination to him:
> Pro 6:17 haughty eyes, a lying tongue, and **hands that shed innocent blood,**

Jesus proclaimed the blood of the righteous souls who were violently slain from Abel, the first victim of murder, until the prophet Zechariah who was one of the final prophets slain, was the responsibility of the generation in which he lived:

> Luk 11:50 so that this generation may be **held accountable for the blood of all the prophets that has been shed since the beginning of the world,**
> Luk 11:51 from **the blood of Abel to the blood of Zechariah,** who was killed between the altar and the sanctuary. **Yes, I tell you, it will be charged against this generation.**

Less than 40 years later, the city of Jerusalem was ransacked and the temple of God destroyed by Titus Vespasian and the Roman armies. This was the judgment for the shed blood of Abel through Zechariah, and that judgment was on the land, which is a principle originally established in the law of Moses. The city of Jerusalem laid basically desolate for many years after that event.

After that judgment, a new batch of innocent blood has been collected in the cup of God's wrath for approximately 2,000 years. The responsibility for the shedding of that innocent blood is revealed later in Revelation chapter 18:

> Rev 18:21 Then one powerful angel picked up a stone like a huge millstone, threw it into the sea, and said, "With this kind of sudden violent force **Babylon the great city** will be thrown down and it will never be found again! For your merchants were the tycoons of the world, because all the nations were deceived by your magic spells!
> Rev 18:24 The **blood of the saints and prophets was found in her,** along with **the blood of all those who had been killed on the earth.**"

This judgment on Babylon is meted out during Daniel's 70th week. God is waiting in his mercy for mankind to repent from its sin and turn back to him. For now, his wrath for the shedding of innocent blood is withheld despite the cry of the martyrs under the altar. However, there will come a time when the final martyr is murdered and the full number is finally reached. It's a strange concept: to know that horrible deaths will be died, yet those deaths must be died in order for the completion of the age of God's grace and mercy to come, and for the body of Christ to be united in heaven.

14.4 The Laws Against Shedding Innocent Blood

When God handed down his laws to Moses, he set forth detailed laws on intentional murder, accidental murder, and unsolved homicide. Some of the laws are very strange, and don't seem to make a lot of sense unless it is understood that the land becomes polluted when innocent blood is shed upon it. Remember what God told Cain after he murdered his brother Abel:

Gen 4:10 But the Lord said, "What have you done? **The voice of your brother's blood is <u>crying out to me from the ground</u>!**

Gen 4:11 So now, you are banished from the ground, which has opened its mouth to receive your brother's blood from your hand.

According to Hebrews, the blood of Abel is still speaking:

Heb 11:4 By faith Abel offered God a greater sacrifice than Cain, and through his faith he was commended as righteous, because God commended him for his offerings. **And through his faith he still speaks, though he is dead.**

Heb 12:24 and to Jesus, the mediator of a new covenant, and to **the sprinkled blood that speaks of something better than Abel's does.**

It seems that blood has some sort of voice when it is shed innocently in the earth. Perhaps the lifeblood of all the offspring that would have been born from that murdered man or woman are crying out as well. Although God revealed the laws concerning murder to Moses, he first established his precepts regarding shedding blood to Noah just after the flood:

Gen 9:5 For your lifeblood I will surely exact punishment, from every living creature I will exact punishment. From each person I will exact punishment for the life of the individual since the man was his relative.

Gen 9:6 **"Whoever sheds human blood, by other humans must his blood be shed**; for in God's image God has made mankind."

The shedding of innocent blood was a serious thing to the Lord. Before the children of Israel were to inherit the Promised Land, the Lord instructed Moses to set aside three cities of refuge for someone who accidentally kills another person whom he doesn't hate at the time of the death. Suppose two men are in the woods, and one is chopping wood with an ax. As he swings the ax back to strike the tree, the ax head flies off, strikes the other man in the head, and kills him. This is involuntary manslaughter–an accidental death. The killer could flee to one of the cities of refuge to be kept safe from the avenger of blood of the victim, perhaps a family member, who in the heat of passion may try to retaliate against him. If the Lord expanded their land after they were there, as he promised Abraham, then three additional cities of refuge were to be set up.

However, in the case of an intentional murder, if the murderer were to flee to a city of refuge, the elders of the city in which the murder was committed were to have that man brought back to his city to face the avenger of blood. Then, the murderer was to be killed due to his capital crime:

> Num 35:19 The avenger of blood himself must kill the murderer; when he meets him, he must kill him.

> Num 35:31 Moreover, **you must not accept a ransom** for the life of a murderer who is guilty of death; he must surely be put to death.

This is the law that God established to deter humans from murder–not even a ransom for the life of a murderer could be accepted. But the reasons why the Lord established the law of capital punishment are clear:

> Deu 19:13 You must not pity him [a murderer], but **purge out the blood of the innocent from Israel, so that it may go well with you.**

Innocent blood must be purged from the land by the blood of the guilty. This is a precept set up by the Lord which some may not understand or agree with. But the Lord stated that it will go well in the land for the inhabitants of the land if the blood of the innocent is purged, in addition to being a powerful deterrent to anyone who was contemplating committing intentional murder. If the blood of the innocent is not purged from the land, it would not go well for the inhabitants of the land. Another verse provides illumination on this subject:

> Num 35:33 "You must not **pollute the land where you live, for blood defiles the land,** and the land **cannot be cleansed** of the blood that is shed there, **except** by the blood of the person who shed it.

> Num 35:34 Therefore do not defile the land that you will inhabit, in which I live, for I the Lord live among the Israelites."

What conclusions can be drawn so far?

1. The shedding of innocent blood both pollutes and defiles the land in which it is shed.
2. The blood of the innocent must be purged from the land in which it is shed.
3. In order to purge the innocent blood from the land in which it is shed, the blood of the murderer must also be shed.
4. If the blood of the innocent is not purged from the land, that land remains defiled and it will not go well for the inhabitants of the land.

Combine these conclusions with the picture of the innocent martyrs under the altar before the Lord, crying out for vengeance of their shed blood, and the picture starts to get more vivid. Their innocent blood was not avenged with the blood of their murderers, therefore, the land in which their blood was shed is defiled, and their blood continues to cry out for vengeance.

14.5 Examples of Breaking the Law Against Shedding Innocent Blood

Are there actual examples in the Bible of the repercussions for shedding the blood of innocent people? There is a great example in the life of Manasseh, former king of Israel. In addition to setting up the worship of idols in Israel, he shed the blood of many innocent people:

II Kin 21:16 Furthermore Manasseh **killed so many innocent people**, he **stained Jerusalem with their blood from end to end**, in addition to encouraging Judah to sin by doing evil before the Lord.

II Kin 24:3 Just as the Lord had announced, he rejected Judah because of all the sins which Manasseh committed.
II Kin 24:4 **Because he killed innocent people and stained Jerusalem with their blood**, the Lord was unwilling to forgive them.

The Lord promised to punish this sin by bringing judgment against the land and its inhabitants, not against Manasseh or his family. Because the blood of the innocent killed by King Manasseh was not purged with the blood of the murderers, as God's laws initially established, judgment came on the land. The Psalmist, in recounting the sordid history of the Israelites from their deliverance from the Egyptians until the reign of King David, records the incredible depravity to which they stooped:

Psa 106:37 They sacrificed their sons and daughters to demons.
Psa 106:38 They **shed innocent blood— the blood of their sons and daughters**, whom they sacrificed to the idols of Canaan. <u>**The land**</u> was **polluted by bloodshed**.

The Psalmist here simply applied the laws handed down to Moses and later recorded in Numbers and Deuteronomy. The blood of innocent people was shed, therefore, the land was polluted. Another example of the consequences of the shedding of innocent blood is recorded in Joel:

Joe 3:19 **Egypt** will be **desolate** and **Edom** will be a **desolate wilderness**, because of the violence they did to the people of Judah, **in whose <u>land</u> they shed <u>innocent blood</u>**.

Once again, the judgments for the shedding of innocent blood came on the land. Note that both Egypt and Edom were to become desolate due to the shedding of the innocent blood of the Judeans. In the process of this desolation, the people that were residing in those lands would also feel the effects of the desolation, but the primary reason for the judgment is to make the land desolate so that the land could be purged of its guilt.

14.6 Laws Concerning Unsolved Murders

Another very interesting law was established by the Lord in the case of a victim of a homicide that no one witnessed. Imagine that a victim was found in the land of Israel, and no one knew how that person died. In such a case, the elders and judges of the surrounding cities were to measure from their city to the victim, and the closest city to the victim was to perform a strange ceremony. A heifer that never had a yoke put around its neck to work was to be taken from its herd and brought to a valley which had water flowing through it. Adding to the complexity, the valley in which the heifer was taken, which had water flowing through it, could never have been plowed or sown for crops.

When all these conditions were met, the heifer was to be taken down to the water, and the elders and judges were to break its neck over the water. The Levitical priests were to be present to observe the proceedings. Then, the elders were to wash their hands with the water in the valley over the neck of the heifer that had just been broken. As they were washing their hands:

> Deu 21:7 Then they must proclaim, **"Our hands have not spilled this blood, nor have we witnessed the crime.**
> Deu 21:8 **Do not blame your people Israel whom you redeemed, O Lord, and do not hold them accountable for the bloodshed of an innocent person."** Then atonement will be made for the bloodshed.

This ceremony was to make atonement for the shedding of the innocent blood in the land. As with the other set of laws, the blood is purged from the land. But, instead of the blood of the murderer purging the defilement from the land, the next verse reveals that the blood of the heifer accomplished the purging of the guilt:

> Deu 21:9 In this manner you will **purge out the guilt of innocent blood from among you**, for you must do what is right before the Lord.

There is guilt in the act of intentionally shedding innocent blood. To purge the guilt, either the blood of the murderer when the murderer is known, or the blood of the heifer when the murderer is unknown, was to be shed. It appears that Pilate may have known about the laws established by the Lord for purging the guilt of innocent blood by the washing of the hands. When Jesus stood innocent before his accusers at his arrest and scourging, the Jews called for his crucifixion over and over. Note Pilate's final response:

> Mat 27:24 When Pilate saw that he could do nothing, but that instead a riot was starting, **he took some water, washed his hands before the crowd and said, "I am innocent of this man's blood. You take care of it yourselves!"**

Pilate was attempting to purge the guilt of innocent blood from his hands, just as described in Deuteronomy chapter 21 with the washing of hands over the heifer. He declared himself to be innocent of the blood of Jesus Christ, an innocent man. Just before this, Pilate's own wife told him that Jesus was an innocent man:

Mat 27:19 As he was sitting on the judgment seat, his wife sent a message to him: "Have nothing to do with **that innocent man**; I have suffered greatly as a result of a dream about him today."

The reply of the crowd of Jews is key, a crowd which included scribes and Pharisees who knew the law of Moses, and what Pilate was representing by washing his hands of the innocent blood of Jesus Christ. So what was their response? One would think they would understand what Pilate was doing and come to their senses. Instead, note their reaction:

Matt 27:25 In reply all the people said, "**Let his blood <u>be on us and on our children!</u>**"

As noted above, the blood of the innocents shed from Abel until Zechariah came on that generation when the city of Jerusalem and the temple was destroyed in approximately 70 AD. The shedding of Jesus' blood did not come on them and their children, as they shouted. Instead, his innocent blood provided a cleansing of all the sin of the world:

I Tim 2:5 For there is one God and one intermediary between God and humanity, Christ Jesus, himself human,

I Tim 2:6 who gave himself as **a ransom for all**, revealing God's purpose at his appointed time.

14.7 The Blood of the Martyrs

After the death and resurrection of Jesus Christ, there seemed to be no kind of torture or type of death that could dissuade his disciples from proclaiming the gospel in every part of the populated world. The first martyrdom on record, of course, is the dramatic stoning of Stephen, a man full of faith and the anointing of the Holy Spirit. One of the men who agreed with the stoning of Stephen was Saul of Tarsus:

Act 7:58 When they had driven him out of the city, they began to stone him, and the witnesses laid their cloaks at the feet of a young man named Saul.

Act 7:59 They continued to stone Stephen while he prayed, "Lord Jesus, receive my spirit!"

Act 7:60 Then he fell to his knees and cried out with a loud voice, "Lord, do not hold this sin against them!" When he had said this, he died.

Act 8:1 And Saul agreed completely with killing him.

This death spawned a major persecution against the church in Jerusalem according Acts chapter 8, and Saul was a major part of it:

Act 9:1 Meanwhile Saul, still breathing out **threats to murder the Lord's disciples**, went to the high priest

Act 9:2 and requested letters from him to the synagogues in Damascus, so that if he found any who belonged to the Way, either men or women, he could bring them as prisoners to Jerusalem.

After Saul's dramatic conversion and name change to Paul, he himself was beheaded under the persecution of Nero. The bloody conquest against Christians from the first century until modern times is chronicled in harrowing detail in the classic work <u>Fox's Book of Martyrs</u>. Each of the twelve apostles, other than Judas Iscariot, willingly gave up their lives for their faith in Jesus Christ in spreading the gospel all over the inhabited world. This included John, who miraculously survived being boiled alive in oil.

To recount everything in Fox's work is not the aim of this section, and would not be fruitful. The innocent blood shed under Nero, under Domitian, under Severus, under Diocletian, and under many other leaders of the Roman Empire, is crying out for vengeance from underneath the altar. Reading that book, chapter after chapter, will cause one to appreciate with mind-numbing clarity what the innocent martyrs experienced.

The persecutions didn't stop with the Jews in the first century and the Roman Empire in the centuries to follow. Soon after, papal Rome began the most severe persecution against professing Christians in all of history. That persecution, waged against those who rebelled against their authority, lasted for hundreds of years and can also be explored in the work by Fox. Millions of Christians in Europe felt the crush of the murderous power of the Inquisitions, including the Albigenses, the Waldenses in France, and the Hussites. At the height of irony, Pope Innocent III, anything but innocent himself, shed perhaps the largest amount of innocent blood that the world has ever known in the Spanish Inquisition. Later, the Protestants during the Reformation suffered under the reign of Queen "Bloody" Mary and other royalties in Great Britain. Mention must also be made of the millions of Christians murdered by Adolph Hitler in Europe and Joseph Stalin in Russia in the past century.

The true heroes of faith of the past suffered the most exquisite torture and deaths that man can devise. Yet the shedding of innocent blood continues today, in such places such as China, Sudan, Somalia, Pakistan, India, Indonesia, Iraq, and many other countries. As this is written, the situation in Sudan is so dire that the United Nations and the European Union have all declared recent atrocities in Sudan to be unacceptable and are considering sanctions against the government of Sudan.[1] The United States Congress declared that what is taking place is genocide[2], and Great Britain's Tony Blair is recommending his government send troops into the country to help those suffering.[3] Hundreds of Christians are being slaughtered and millions of Sudanese are suffering from famine and disease due to the oppressive government and living conditions in Sudan.

---

[1] Scotsman.com, "Britain Backs Sanction Moves Against Sudan", http://news.scotsman.com/latest.cfm?id=3255925, accessed July 24, 2004.
[2] Turks.us, "US Congress says Attacks in Darfur 'Genocide'", http://www.turks.us/article.php?story=20040724063658456, accessed July 24, 2004.
[3] Reuters.co.uk, "Britain Able to Send 5,000 Troops to Sudan", http://www.reuters.co.uk/newsPackageArticle.jhtml?type=topNews&storyID=552898&section=news, accessed July 24, 2004.

With millions upon millions of Christians suffering martyrdom throughout the centuries, perhaps the most desperate and heart-wrenching of all innocent blood currently being shed on the earth is that of unborn children. While a deep discussion of this topic would not be fruitful for the purposes of this book, it is incredible that human beings can justify savage murder of their own innocent offspring while they are still in the womb. Millions of lives are severed from existence for such selfish reasons; and can there be any doubt whether this innocent blood is crying out for vengeance against the perpetrators?

While victims of abortion may not be what is in view in the fifth seal, since those under the altar were violently killed for their testimony and witness about Jesus Christ and the gospel, God's laws against the shedding of innocent blood *still apply*. The guilt of the innocent blood must be purged from the land, and if God is a God of justice, he will exact the same judgment on the land that he did in the previous examples. The land encompassing the United States of America is in particular danger given its short, yet bloody history. God stated that vengeance belongs to him, and he will see to it that the land is cleansed of the guilty for shedding the blood of the innocent.

14.8 An End of the Shedding of Innocent Blood

At this point, it would be productive to revisit the answer the martyred souls under the altar received to the question of how long it would be before their innocent blood was purged:

> Rev 6:11 Each of them was given a long white robe and they were told to rest for a little longer, **until the full number was reached** of both their fellow servants and their brothers who were going to be killed just as they had been.

The degradation and hedonistic iniquity in the world paraded on a daily basis continues, yet the Lord has thus far withheld his wrath. How long will the Lord continue to withhold his judgment? One part of the answer to that question is provided in the answer received by the martyrs under the altar. There will come a point in the future when a "full number" of Christians who have been killed for their testimony is reached. In Matthew chapter 24, a second part to the answer of the question is provided:

> Mat 24:14 And this gospel of the kingdom will be preached throughout the whole inhabited earth as a testimony to all the nations, and **then the end will come**.

Jesus said that all nations will receive a witness of the gospel of the kingdom before the end comes. Many Christians will continue to be violently killed as a result. But there is a third part to the answer of the question about how much longer until the Lord comes:

Rom 11:25 For I do not want you to be ignorant of this mystery, brothers and sisters, so that you may not be conceited: A partial hardening has happened to Israel **until the full number of the Gentiles has come in**.

Paul was referring to the Gentiles coming into a new covenant relationship with Jesus Christ, branches from a wild olive tree that are grafted into a cultivated olive tree with its roots in Abraham. At some point in the future, a full number of Gentiles will have been grafted into the olive tree, and then God will turn his attention to restoring Israel, re-grafting their branches back into their own olive tree:

Rom 11:23 And even they—if they do not continue in their unbelief—**will be grafted in**, for God is able **to graft them in again**.

Rom 11:24 For if you were cut off from what is by nature a wild olive tree, and grafted, contrary to nature, into a cultivated olive tree, **how much more will these natural branches be grafted back into their own olive tree**?

The importance of the re-grafting of the olive tree will be further addressed in a later chapter. The three-part answer to the question, therefore, of when the Lord will finally return to both resurrect the dead in Christ and catch away living believers, can be summarized as follows:

1. The gospel of Jesus Christ will be preached throughout the entire inhabited world before the end of the age comes.
2. A full number of Gentile believers will come into a covenant relationship with Jesus Christ as a result of the preaching of the gospel.
3. A full number of Christians will be violently killed as a result of their testimony of the gospel of Jesus Christ.

Only the Lord knows the full number of Gentiles that will be grafted into the covenant through the preaching of the gospel throughout the nations, and how many Christians will be killed for their witness.

14.9 Isaiah 26:19-21 – A Key Passage

After the full number of Christian martyrs is finally reached, the events of the sixth seal will begin, which will accompany the resurrection of the dead in Christ, transformation to immortality, and catching up of all believers, to be followed by the beginning of Daniel's 70th week. At that point, the shedding of the innocent blood of martyrs will come to an end, and the Lord's judgment will begin. This will be declared by those on the earth after the sixth seal events take place:

Rev 6:16 They said to the mountains and to the rocks, "Fall on us and hide us from the face of the one who is seated on the throne and from the wrath of the Lamb,

Rev 6:17 because **the great day of their wrath** has come, and who is able to withstand it?"

This is also declared by Jesus Christ. When answering questions about the end of the age, Jesus declared the days during the abomination of desolation of Daniel's 70th week would be the time when God would pour out his prophesied vengeance:

Luk 21:22 because **these are days of vengeance**, to fulfill all that is written.

His vengeance includes retribution for the shedding of innocent blood. Recall the principles stated earlier in this chapter and realize that the blood of the guilty was the only thing that was able to cleanse the land of the guilt of the innocent blood shed within it. Without that, the land remained in a defiled state. The earth is currently defiled with the blood of the innocent, and because the blood of the guilty did not cleanse it, God will provide a supernatural source of blood. Isaiah prophesied of the time of God's vengeance and anger:

Isa 26:20 Go, my people! Enter your inner rooms! Close your doors behind you! Hide for a little while, **until <u>his angry judgment</u> is over!**

Isa 26:21 For look, the Lord is coming out of the place where he lives, to punish the sin of those who live on the earth. **The earth will <u>display the blood shed on it</u>; it will no longer cover up its slain.**

Those verses, read in connection with the idea of the cleansing of the defiled earth due to the shedding of innocent blood, are extremely important. This passage concisely ties four important concepts of this prophecy model together:

1. There will be a group of persons, the "my people" of the Isaiah passage, who are hidden in the inner rooms when the Lord's anger is unleashed on the earth. This is the catching up of all believers from the earth.
2. The day of the Lord will begin *after* this group of people is hidden away, and *while* this group is hidden away.
3. The purpose of the unleashing of the Lord's judgment is to punish the shedding of innocent blood that is displayed on it. The slain on the earth will finally receive their vengeance.
4. Something will take place on the earth such that the blood shed on it will be on display; no longer will the blood of the innocent be hidden. This is a reference not only to the blood judgments of Revelation chapters 8 and 16, to be explored below, but also to some kind of event that will trigger a time when blood, before hidden, will no longer be hidden. This triggering event is the future resurrection, transformation, and catching-up event, and the earth will respond with a great shaking and the other effects of the sixth seal.

In addition, the preceding verse to the passage above ties in a fifth important concept of this prophetic model:

Isa 26:19 **Your dead will come back to life**; your corpses will rise up. Wake up and shout joyfully, you who live in the ground! For you will grow like plants drenched with the morning dew, and **the earth will bring forth its dead spirits.**

5. There will be a resurrection of the dead in Christ, and that resurrection will precede the catching up of living believers. Note that the dead come to life first, followed by the people being shut up in the inner room in the following verse.

This is a key passage in understanding the pre-70th week of Daniel resurrection, transformation, and catching-up event. Without question, these verses make it clear that the people of God enter an "inner room", with the door closed behind them. How long are they hidden? For a little while, until the judgment on the earth is over, a reference to Daniel's 70th week of seven years. Take special note that the Lord's judgment does not happen until his people are hidden away, and that the judgment happens while they are hidden away.

14.10 The Judgments Involve Blood

Beginning with the first judgment within Daniel's 70th week, blood is involved. The first angel will blow its trumpet, and judgment will follow:

> Rev 8:7 The first angel blew his trumpet, and there was **hail and fire mixed with blood**, and it was thrown at the earth so that a third of the earth was burned up, a third of the trees were burned up, and all the green grass was burned up.

Blood will be mixed into the fire and hail that, believe it or not, burns up one-third of the earth, one-third of all trees, and all of the green grass. The blood mixed in with the fire and hail will be working the Lord's vengeance for the shedding of innocent blood. In the second trumpet judgment, blood will again be involved:

> Rev 8:8 Then the second angel blew his trumpet, and something like a great mountain of burning fire was thrown into the sea. **A third of the sea became blood,**
> Rev 8:9 and a third of the creatures living in the sea died, and a third of the ships were completely destroyed.

A great mountain of burning fire could be a large asteroid. But one result of it crashing into the sea will be one-third of the sea turned into blood. Why blood? Again, blood is purging the land of the guilt that defiles it. Later in Daniel's 70th week, the bowl judgments will take place. They are even more severe than the trumpet judgments. Note what will happen when the second and third angels pour out their bowls:

> Rev 16:3 Next, the second angel poured out his bowl on **the sea and it turned into blood,** like that of a corpse, and every living creature that was in the sea died.
> Rev 16:4 Then the third angel poured out his bowl on the rivers and the springs of water, **and they turned into blood.**

All of the seas, the rivers, and the springs will turn into blood, killing every living sea creature, whereas with the second trumpet judgment, only one-third of the sea turns into blood. If all of the oceans on the earth turn into blood, and all of the living creatures in them perish, this would obviously be a major ecological disaster. Historical precedence is found in Exodus, where only one river turned into blood:

> Exo 7:17 Thus says the Lord: "By this you will know that I am the Lord: I am going to strike the water of the Nile with the rod that is in my hand, and it will be turned into blood.
>
> Exo 7:18 **Fish in the Nile will die, the Nile will stink**, and the Egyptians will be **unable to drink water from the Nile**."

Now, imagine the devastation from all of the seas and rivers on the earth turning to blood. Imagine the stench of the blood mixed with the rotting sea creatures. Could all this be a part of the cleansing process–revenge for the shed blood of the innocent? If there is any doubt, then take special note of the verses which explain the purpose of the second and third bowl judgments:

> Rev 16:5 Now I heard the angel of the waters saying: "**You are just**—the one who is and who was, the Holy One—**because you have passed these judgments,**
>
> Rev 16:6 <u>**because they poured out the blood of your saints and prophets,** so **you have given them blood to drink**</u>. They got what they deserved!"

The reason the Lord is just, not a mean, hateful, or vengeful tyrant, is because the blood of the saints and prophets has defiled the earth without recourse. The justice will therefore be poured out all at once, and the angel even declared that the inhabitants of the earth are getting what they deserve by being given blood to drink. But the next verse is even more revealing:

> Rev 16:7 Then I heard **<u>the altar</u>** reply, "Yes, Lord God, the All-Powerful, your judgments are true and just!"

Notice the origin of this statement? The altar is where the souls of the martyrs were seen by John, gathered underneath and crying out for vengeance. Here, the altar itself declared that the Lord is both true and just in pouring out the blood on the earth. This is an extremely powerful connection between the altar, the blood of the innocent, and God's wrath involving blood.

The majority of trumpet and bowl judgments poured out will have an effect on the land and water on the earth, not human beings, although they will feel the ramifications of it. But the key point to remember is that the land must be purged of the guilt, regardless of whether human beings are affected. It is a sovereign principle of God.

14.11 Spiritual Babylon – Guilty of Shedding Innocent Blood

Further proof that Daniel's 70th week will be the time when God pours out vengeance specifically for the shedding of innocent blood are found within the closing chapters of Revelation. Babylon, a symbol of man's rebellious attempt to justify himself through idolatry and religious orders that have spanned from the times of Nimrod after the flood of Noah until the end of Daniel's 70th week, is held responsible for the innocent blood shed on the earth:

> Rev 17:5 On **her** forehead was written a name, a mystery: "**Babylon the Great**, the Mother of prostitutes and of the detestable things of the earth."
> Rev 17:6 I saw that **the woman** was drunk with **the blood of the saints and the blood of those <u>who testified to Jesus</u>**. I was greatly astounded when I saw her.

John was "astounded" because the woman was called Babylon, not the beast she was riding. The woman symbolized the religious orders throughout history responsible for the blood of the saints, those who testified of Jesus. So the blood of believers who followed the command to take the gospel into all the world at the risk of losing life is in view:

> Mat 24:9 "Then they will hand you over **to be persecuted and will kill you**. You will be hated by all the nations because of my name.

The persecution has been ongoing ever since Jesus Christ ascended to the heavens. Persecution resulted because the natural man's inherent reaction to the preaching of the gospel is to reject it. It is only received by the spiritual man, and the natural man must be killed in the process:

> I Cor 2:14 The unbeliever does not receive the things of the Spirit of God, for they are foolishness to him. And he cannot understand them, because **they are spiritually discerned**.

> Joh 6:63 The Spirit is the one who gives life; **human nature is of no help!** The words that I have spoken to you are spirit and are life.
> Joh 6:64 But there are some of you who do not believe." (For Jesus had already known from the beginning who those were who did not believe, and who it was who would betray him.)
> Joh 6:65 So Jesus added, "Because of this I told you that **no one can come to me unless the Father has allowed him to come**."

Whether it be the Jews of the first century, the idolatrous Roman Empire, or the papal hierarchy for hundreds of years after them, they are all a part of "Babylon", the antithesis of the virgin bride for whom Jesus Christ will return. In attempting to set up ways to get man back to God, the woman shunned God's attempt to reconcile humanity back to God through Jesus Christ, and she murdered those who tried to declare that message:

Rev 18:24 The **blood of the saints and prophets was found in her**, along with **the blood of all those who had been killed on the earth.**"

Rev 19:2 because his judgments are true and just. For he has judged **the great prostitute** who corrupted the earth with her sexual immorality, and has **avenged [exedikesen] the blood [haima]** of his servants poured out <u>**by her own hands!**</u>"

Note that God "avenged the blood" of the servants. This is exactly what the fifth seal martyrs were crying out for over the centuries. Even the Greek words for "avenge" and "blood" are the same in each verse:
Rev 6:10 They cried out with a loud voice, "**How long**, Sovereign Master, holy and true, **before you judge those who live on the earth** and <u>**avenge [ekdikeis] our blood [haima]**</u>?"

The cry of the martyrs was to avenge their blood, and that is exactly what will happen with the judgments poured out in God's wrath upon Babylon. This is the most convincing proof that the fifth seal martyrs are not those killed during Daniel's 70th week, but rather those killed over the centuries since the ascension of Jesus Christ to heaven. Those who hold that the opening of the seals will occur during Daniel's 70th week are forced to interpret the fifth seal as being only martyrs killed during Daniel's 70th week. For the many reasons established in this chapter, as well as reasons that will be established in chapters to follow, that is not a valid interpretation. Instead, these martyrs cry out for vengeance prior to Daniel's 70th week, and their request is answered during that horrific seven-year period of the Lord's vengeance.

14.12 Summary and Conclusion

Why all this talk about blood? The purpose was to firmly establish that the end of the fifth seal, whenever it arrives, marks a major point in history. When the blood of the final martyr has been shed, the day of God's wrath will begin. It does not begin before this. In the chapter to follow, several reasons will be presented to establish more firmly that the first five seals cannot be a part of Daniel's 70th week, but instead are a part of history leading up to the days just before the beginning of Daniel's 70th week.

It was also necessary to understand the Old Testament laws against shedding blood, and why God went to such lengths to set up laws to make sure the guilt of the shedding of innocent blood was purged from the land in which it was shed. This should aid in understanding the cry of the martyrs in the fifth seal, as well as the reason for judgments of blood that will be poured out during Daniel's 70th week.

Some key points to remember from this chapter include:

- There is a transition between the first four seals and the fifth seal, in which John's vision moved from symbolism to literal people and places in heaven and on the earth.
- The fifth seal martyrs are under the altar, which is before God, constantly crying for their blood to be avenged.
- The martyrs of the fifth seal are not those who will be killed during Daniel's 70th week because (1) they would be crying out for the Lord's vengeance to begin after it had already begun, (2) they would be asking "How long" even though the length of time until the end of Daniel's 70th week would be known, and (3) their question of "How long" shows extreme impatience if they had only been killed for one to two years.
- There will come a point in history at which a final Christian will be mercilessly killed for his testimony of the gospel of Jesus Christ. At that point, God's vengeance will begin to be poured out for the shedding of innocent blood on the earth, in response to the cry of vengeance from the martyrs under the altar.
- God established principles against the shedding of innocent blood, and what to do when it is shed, in the law of Moses. Land is polluted when innocent blood is shed upon it, and only the blood of the guilty can purge the guilt from the land.
- Several examples of God's judgment for shedding innocent blood are found in the Old Testament. In the New Testament, Pilate's words and actions indicate that he had knowledge of the principles established by God.
- Isaiah prophesied that the Lord's judgment would be in response to the blood shed on the earth. He also declared that the resurrection of the dead in the earth and the hiding of the people of the Lord will occur just before his judgment, and that those people will be hidden away until his anger passes.
- The dramatic judgments of Daniel's 70th week include four separate judgments in which blood is involved in burning one third of the earth, the trees, and all of the grass, as well as turning all the seas, rivers, and springs into blood and killing the creatures within them.

In the chapter to follow, several key contrasts between the seal judgments and the trumpet and bowl judgments will be presented. Each contrast will bolster the interpretation that the first six seals do not take place during Daniel's 70th week, but are rather a chronicle of history from the first century until the events of the first five seals are completed.

Contrary to the characteristics of a normal quake, the intensity of the aftershocks were actually increasing slightly from the initial wave. Each wave was a little higher than the previous. A new fear was spawned in my mind as the third wave barreled closer: *How long is this going to last? How many of these waves are we going to have to endure? Who is going to help us stop them?*

Earthquake Resurrection Prophetic Model Timeline Progression

Weeks 1-69			Week 69 Ends, GAP Between Week 69 and Week 70							Week 70 Begins		
457BC - 27AD	27AD	31AD	31AD	31AD - PRESENT						FUTURE TIME		
				Opening of the First Five Seals - Birth Pains Begin					Sixth Seal			
				1	2	3	4	5				
Decree of Artaxerxes Longimanus, Weeks 1-69 of Daniel's 70 Weeks Prophecy	Transfer of the Priesthood of Melchizedek at Christ's Baptism	Christ's and the "Many Saints" Earthquake Resurrection	Christ's Ascension to the Right Hand of God	Spirit of Religious Domination in Christ's Name	Spirit of War and Bloodshed	Spirit of Financial Oppression	Spirit of Death, Disease, and Famine	Persecution and Death of Believers	Future Earthquake Resurrection of the Dead in Christ, Transformation and Catching Up	Confirmation / Strengthening of the Covenant	Sealing of the 144,000 Children of Israel	Enormous Group Before the Throne
Dan 9:24-25	Luk 3-4	Mat 27	Act 1; Rev 4-5			Rev 6:1-11			1 The 4; 1 Cor 15	Daniel 9:27		Rev 7
Ch. 8	Ch. 8	Ch. 3, 6	Ch. 10, 11	Ch. 12		Ch. 13	Ch. 14		Ch. 4, 5, 7			Ch. 9, 15, 16

- CHAPTER FIFTEEN -

CONTRASTING THE SEALS AND THE JUDGMENTS

This chapter will provide a review of the reaction on the earth to the events of the sixth seal, followed by several contrasts between the opening of the first six seals and the trumpet and bowl judgments during Daniel's 70th week. These interesting contrasts will augment the information already presented regarding the opening of the first five seals before the resurrection, transformation, and catching-up event.

15.1 Review of the Sixth Seal Events and the Reaction to Them

Recall that after the events of the sixth seal, a reaction of the people on the earth to what just transpired is provided. That reaction is both physical and verbal:

Rev 6:15 Then the kings of the earth, the very important people, the generals, the rich, the powerful, and everyone, slave and free, **hid themselves in the caves and among the rocks of the mountains.**

Rev 6:16 They said to the mountains and to the rocks, **"Fall on us and hide us from the face of the one who is seated on the throne and from the wrath of the Lamb,**

Rev 6:17 **because <u>the great day of their wrath has come,</u> and who is able to withstand it?"**

First the physical reaction. They hid in the caves among the rocks of the mountains. Remember that the events of the sixth seal caused all mountains to be moved, and caused the crust of the earth to shift and produce earthquakes. That activity may have created new mountains and hills, but definitely moved the already existing mountains. With the existing landscape in shambles, perhaps houses and buildings were destroyed or uninhabitable in some places. Also remember that the people will be so extremely frightened by what they just experienced that they will most likely want to hide in order to avoid any more catastrophic events.

But the verbal reaction, which has already been discussed in previous chapters, is most important. The day of God's wrath, prophesied numerous times in the Old Testament, has now come according to their own words. The one seated on the throne is God, and the Lamb is Jesus Christ. There are not two different days of wrath, but one. The people on earth declare "their wrath" has come.

The most important point to remember, however, is that the prophecy of Joel is fulfilled within the events of the sixth seal. Compare again Joel's prophecy to what occurs in the sixth seal:

Joe 2:31 **The sunlight will be turned to darkness and the moon to the color of blood,** before the day of the LORD comes— that great and terrible day!

Rev 6:12 Then I looked when the Lamb opened the sixth seal, and a huge earthquake took place; **the sun became as black as sackcloth made of hair, and the full moon became blood red;**

As has been stated, while there are many Old Testament passages that state the sun will be darkened during the day of the Lord, only the Joel passage contains the caveat that a darkening of the sun will occur *before* the day of the Lord begins. However, there is *no* other Old Testament prophecy stating that the moon turns to a blood-red color, either before, during, or after the day of wrath begins, nor is there any other mention of this occurring in the New Testament (other than Peter quoting Joel's prophecy on the Day of Pentecost). The unique features of Joel 2:31 mandate that, if the sixth seal description in Revelation 6:12 is found to be referring to any Old Testament prophecy, it can only be Joel 2:31. Furthermore, since Joel 2:31 restricts the events to a pre-day of the Lord time frame, the sixth seal must be opened before, not after, the beginning of the day of the Lord's wrath and Daniel's 70th week.

15.2 Contrasts Between the Events of the Seals and the Trumpet/Bowl Judgments

The sixth seal declaration of the people on the earth that the day of the Lord has begun, as well as the fulfillment of Joel's prophecy of a blood-red moon, provide powerful proof that the events of the first six seals take place before Daniel's 70th week. However, further in-depth study of the differences between the seals and the trumpet and bowl judgments will reveal some startling discoveries that serve to strengthen that interpretation. The following seven points will present many interesting contrasts between the opening of the seals and the trumpet and bowl judgments, and will serve to further firmly establish that the events within the first six seals occur prior to the day of God's wrath.

1. Jesus listed events similar to the events of the first five seals and called them "birth pains" before the end, but the events of the trumpets and bowls definitely occur after the day of God's wrath has begun.

Instead of interpreting the advent of false Christs, wars, famines, pestilence, persecution, and death of Christians as events during Daniel's 70th week, Jesus stated that these are things that will take place before the end comes:

Mat 24:8 All these things are the beginning of birth pains.

What "things" was Jesus referring to? The exact things described in the seals:

Mat 24:5 For **many will come in my name, saying, 'I am the Christ,' and they will mislead many.**

Mat 24:6 You will hear of **wars and rumors of wars**. Make sure that you are not alarmed, for this must happen, but <u>the end is still to come</u>.

Mat 24:7 For **nation will rise up in arms against nation, and kingdom against kingdom**. And there will be **famines** and **earthquakes** in various places.

Luk 21:11 There will be **great earthquakes**, and **famines** and **plagues in various places**, and there will be **terrifying sights and great signs from heaven**.

Mat 24:9 "Then they will hand you over to be **persecuted and will kill you**. You will be hated by all the nations because of my name.

Luk 21:16 You will be betrayed even by parents, brothers, relatives, and friends, and they will have **some of you put to death**.

As a review, consider the following table, which compares what Jesus described in Matthew and Luke as signs *before* the end with the events of the first six seals:

Seals One Through Six Events	Matthew 24 & Luke 21 Events
A spirit of false religion in the name of Christ sent to dominate the people (seal one).	Many will come in my name saying "I am the Christ"; many will be misled.
A spirit of violence, torture, and bloodshed is unleashed on the earth, so that people violently butcher one another (seal two).	Nation will rise against nation and kingdom against kingdom; wars and rumors of wars.
A spirit of financial bondage and oppression (seal three).	(no prediction)
A spirit of death, disease, and famine (seal four).	There will be famines and plagues in various places.
The murder of Christians for their testimony of the gospel (seal five).	You will be persecuted, and they will kill you; you'll be hated and put to death.
Earthquakes, movement of mountains and islands, and signs in the heaven (seal six).	There will be earthquakes; there will be terrifying sights and great signs from heaven.

Again, these are all signs before the end, according to Jesus; the beginning of the birth pains of the end. The events of the first six seals must therefore, according to the words of Jesus, occur before Daniel's 70th week. Jesus described them as the beginning of the birth pains. To what do natural birth pains allude?

When a woman is pregnant and nearing the time of the birth, the first thing to happen is the breaking of the water. At that point, she knows that the birth pains will begin to occur in the form of contractions. As time goes by, the contractions begin to come faster and faster. There is less time between the contractions as the time of birth gets closer. Eventually, the child begins to turn and rotate in the womb, preparing for the exit.

In the first century, the birth pains described in the seals and by Jesus began to occur. As time has gone by, the contractions have begun to come faster and faster with more wars, more death, more disease, more famine, and more religious domination and deception. These things must occur, with less and less time between the contractions, before the birth, the end of the age, and before the beginning of the day of the Lord.

In contrast, the events of the trumpet and bowl judgments will take place after the day of wrath has come. After the events of the sixth seal, the people on earth will declare the day of the Lord has begun. After that declaration, the seventh seal is opened, and the seven trumpet judgments begin.

2. The first four seals involve <u>evil spirits</u> going out into the earth who are granted permission to influence and oppress humanity, whereas the trumpet and bowl judgments are carried out at God's command by the <u>holy angels</u> in heaven.

Recall from previous chapters that the spirits symbolized within the first four seals are evil spirits who are granted permission to carry out their assignments. In addition, Ezekiel chapter 22 reveals that the four sore judgments are the Lord's judgments. Reviewing three of the first four seals, it is clear that these symbolic riders are given permission to carry out their assignments:

> Rev 6:2 . . .a white horse! The one who rode it had a bow, and he was **given [edothe]** a crown . . .
> Rev 6:4 . . .the one who rode it was **granted [edothe] permission** to take peace from the earth . . .
> Rev 6:8 . . .They were **given [edothe] authority** over a fourth of the earth . . .

However, when the trumpet and bowl judgments are examined, which definitely take place during Daniel's 70th week, it is clear that God's holy angels pour them out on the earth from heaven. First, the trumpet judgments are revealed in Revelation chapter 8:

> Rev 8:2 Then I saw **the seven angels who stand before God**, and **seven trumpets** were given to them.
> Rev 8:6 Now **the seven angels holding the seven trumpets prepared to blow them**.

Second, the bowl judgments are revealed in Revelation chapters 15 and 16:

Rev 15:1 Then I saw another great and astounding sign **in __heaven__: seven angels who have seven final plagues** (they are final because in them God's anger is completed).

Rev 15:7 Then one of the four living creatures gave **the seven angels seven golden bowls** filled with the wrath of God who lives forever and ever,

Rev 16:1 Then I heard a loud voice from the temple declaring to the seven angels: "Go and pour out on the earth the seven bowls containing God's wrath."

In both cases, seven holy angels in heaven pour out the judgments from heaven. There is no indication that evil spirits have anything to do with these judgments. Instead, an angel either sounds a trumpet or pours out a bowl onto the earth. This is a clear contrast between the seals and the trumpet and bowl judgments.

3. The mysterious activities at the golden altar of incense, __after__ all seven seals will be opened but __before__ the trumpet and bowl judgments will begin, will be necessary for the judgments of the wrath of God to begin.

As reviewed in prior chapters, the Lamb appeared in heaven just after his ascension to take his seat at the right hand of God. At his right hand was a scroll with seven seals. The traditional interpretation is that the seals describe events during Daniel's 70th week, the first seal being the Antichrist coming on a white horse. That interpretation states that wars, famines, plagues, etc. all take place during "the tribulation period", and those souls under the altar crying out for vengeance will be martyrs beheaded by the Antichrist.

In sharp contrast, the model presented in this book holds that the first six seals are opened prior to the beginning of Daniel's 70th week, and that they are not part of the wrath of God on the earth that was prophesied by the Old Testament prophets to occur during the day of the Lord. The events described within the first five seals, as Jesus stated, are part of the birth pains before the end. These seals are being carried out by human beings on earth who are influenced by evil spirits. These evil spirits have been granted permission, or given authority, to influence humanity.

Continuing into Revelation chapter 8, the seventh and final seal on the scroll is opened by the Lamb, which results in one-half hour of silence in heaven. A messenger, or angel, is then seen standing before the altar of sacrifice, the same altar under which the souls of the martyrs were crying out for vengeance during the fifth seal. The scene just after the seventh seal will be opened was described by John as follows:

Rev 8:3 Another angel [aggelos] **holding a golden censer** came and was stationed at **the altar**. A large amount of **incense** was given to him to offer up, with the **prayers of all the saints**, on the **golden altar that is before the throne**.

Those with a background in the Old Testament ceremonial laws of the temple may recognize what is being described in this verse. This verse mirrors the Lord's instruction to Moses in Leviticus chapter 16 for what was to be done once a year on the Day of Atonement. First, the high priest was to wash himself, put on holy garments, and enter the Most Holy Place with the animals of sacrifice for himself and the people of Israel.

According to Hebrews chapter 9, the high priest of the new covenant is Jesus Christ. The Greek *aggelos*, translated as "angel", is a word not restricted only to an "angel" interpretation. In II Corinthians 12:7, aggelos is used to describe the "messenger of Satan" who was constantly harassing Paul. In the context of the passage, the duties being carried out by this *aggelos* clearly match those performed by the high priest of heaven. Therefore, the messenger standing at the altar in verse 3 above is Jesus Christ, the high priest.

Next, John described the offering of incense by the high priest, which is the prayer of all the righteous ones. The incense was offered on the golden altar before the throne of God. Compare John's description in verse 3 above to what was to be done by the high priest on the Day of Atonement:

> Lev 16:12 and take **a censer** full of coals of fire **from the altar before the Lord** and a full double handful of **finely ground fragrant incense**, and bring them inside the veil-canopy.

Notice the similarities between what John saw and the Leviticus account: both had a censer, both were before the altar, and both had incense. But the similarities do not stop there. John next described what took place when the prayers of the righteous were placed on the golden altar before the Lord:

> Rev 8:4 The **smoke coming from the incense**, along with the prayers of the saints, **ascended before God** from the angel's hand.
> Rev 8:5 Then the angel took **the censer**, filled it with **fire from the altar**, and threw it on the earth, and there were crashes of thunder, roaring, flashes of lightning, and an earthquake.

John saw smoke–the prayers of the righteous–ascending from the altar of incense up to the throne of God. Then the angel took fire from the golden altar and threw it onto the earth. Compare this with what was to be done by the high priest on the Day of Atonement:

> Lev 16:13 He must then put **the incense on the fire before the Lord**, and **the cloud of incense will cover the atonement plate** which is above the ark of the testimony, so that he will not die.

There are more similarities between the two passages. Just as the smoke from the incense came before the throne of God in John's description, the cloud of the incense covered the atonement plate. The atonement plate is the Mercy Seat which covers the ark of the covenant, which in the heavenly temple would be the throne of God. Also note that in both passages, fire from the altar was mixed with the incense. The two passages are nearly identical.

The similarities stop there. In Leviticus, the high priest was to next sprinkle the blood on the animals all over the Mercy Seat and the Most Holy Place. There is no blood sprinkled by the heavenly high priest according to John's vision. According to Hebrews, Jesus already entered the heavenly Most Holy Place once, offering his own blood for all time, which explains the absence of the blood in John's vision.

However, it is interesting that the souls of the martyrs had previously been under the altar crying out for vengeance for the shedding of their innocent blood. Now, their cry for vengeance is answered, because the next thing to take place in the description of John's vision is the trumpet judgments. Those judgments, as covered in the previous chapter, involve blood covering great sections of the earth and serve as vengeance for their innocent blood, fulfilling their cry. As Isaiah prophesied in chapter 26, the earth will display the blood shed on it.

The reason for the Revelation chapter 8 activities by the heavenly high priest, Jesus Christ, are not provided in the immediate text surrounding the description. However, by comparing the Revelation chapter 8 passage with the passage in Leviticus chapter 16, it is clear that the trumpet judgments could not be unleashed from heaven *until* the ceremonial rituals at the altar with the incense and fire had been completed. Once the smoke of incense, the prayers of the saints, came up before the throne of God, the wrath of God could be unleashed on the earth for the shedding of innocent blood that had defiled the land. Acclaimed author of several books on Biblical prophecy, Robert H. Mounce, holds to the traditional models of prophecy, but even he admitted in his commentary on Revelation chapter 8, "The prayers of the saints **play an essential part in bringing the judgment of God** upon the earth and its inhabitants."[1] [emphasis added]

However, when one examines what took place prior to the opening of the seals, there is no activity in the heavenly temple, such as offering incense at the altar, or the temple being opened and full of smoke. This is more solid proof that the seals are not part of the wrath of God during Daniel's 70th week, but are part of the progression of history from the first century until the present. This is yet another strong, clear contrast between the opening of the six seals of the scroll prior to the wrath of God, and the trumpet and bowl judgments during the wrath of God. God's wrath could not be poured out on the earth, and therefore Daniel's 70th week could not have begun, before the temple activities as described in Revelation chapter 8.

4. The sixth seal results in a <u>reaction of humility</u> and fear of God by the people on earth, while the judgments of the trumpets and bowls result in a <u>reaction of blasphemy and further rebellion</u> against God.

When the people on earth will see the results of the opening of the sixth seal, their reaction will be one of fear and of desperation that the day of wrath has come:

---

[1] Mounce, Robert H. (1977). *The Book of Revelation*, p. 182, Wm. B. Eerdmans Publishing Co., Grand Rapids, Michigan.

Rev 6:15 Then the kings of the earth, the very important people, the generals, the rich, the powerful, and everyone, slave and free, **hid themselves** in the caves and among the rocks of the mountains.

Rev 6:16 They said to the mountains and to the rocks, "**Fall on** us and **hide us** from the face of the one who is seated on the throne and from the wrath of the Lamb,

Rev 6:17 because the great day of their wrath has come, and **who is able to withstand it?**"

The actions and declarations show fear and humility. To question who is able to withstand the great day of their wrath is rhetorical in nature, the obvious answer being that no one will be able to stand against it. They cry out in fear for the rocks and mountains to fall on them so that they can be hidden from the Lord and the Lamb. They will rather die by having rocks fall on them than to experience the wrath of the day of the Lord.

However, note the contrast between this reaction and the reaction and conclusion of the trumpet and bowl judgments:

Rev 9:20 The rest of humanity, who had not been killed by these plagues, **did not repent of the works of their hands**, so that they did not stop worshiping demons and idols made of gold, silver, bronze, stone, and wood—idols that cannot see or hear or walk about.

Rev 9:21 Furthermore, **they did not repent** of their murders, of their magic spells, of their sexual immorality, or of their stealing.

Rev 16:9 Thus people were scorched by the terrible heat, **yet they blasphemed the name of God**, who has ruling authority over these plagues, and **they would not repent and give him glory**.

Rev 16:11 **They blasphemed the God of heaven** because of their sufferings and because of their sores, but nevertheless **they still refused to repent of their deeds**.

Rev 16:21 And gigantic hailstones, weighing about a hundred pounds each, fell from heaven on people, but **they blasphemed God** because of the plague of hail, since it was so horrendous.

The passage from Revelation chapter 9 is at the conclusion of the sixth trumpet judgment, and the passages from Revelation chapter 16 are during the fourth, fifth, and seventh bowl judgments. Clearly there is a contrast between the reaction of humanity after these judgments, which occur during the day of the wrath of God, and their reaction to the sixth seal events which occur before Daniel's 70th week.

5. The cry of the martyrs for vengeance <u>takes place</u> during the fifth seal, but their request is <u>granted</u> during the trumpet and bowl judgments.

First, the martyrs made a request for vengeance in the form of a question:

Rev 6:10 They cried out with a loud voice, "How long, Sovereign Master, holy and true, before you judge those who live on the earth and **avenge our blood?**"

Later in Revelation, after the trumpet judgments, the avenging of their blood is being accomplished:
Rev 19:2 because his judgments are true and just. For he has judged the great prostitute who corrupted the earth with her sexual immorality, and has **avenged the blood of his servants** poured out by her own hands!"

The avenging of their blood will not yet have taken place at the time of the opening of the fifth seal, even after all the events of the first four seals. How can this be possible, if the traditional interpretation of the seals being during Daniel's 70th week is correct? That traditional interpretation holds that these martyrs are beheaded for not accepting the mark of the beast, which will take place well into the second half of Daniel's 70th week. If these martyrs are truly those beheaded during the reign of the Antichrist, the trumpet judgments will have already been unleashed. This is certain because the second woe will occur just as the two witnesses are killed and resurrected, allowing the beast to come to power in Jerusalem. The second woe is equated with the sixth trumpet judgment when comparing Revelation chapters 9 and 11, which was discussed in chapter nine.

Yet, the first two trumpet judgments include judgments with blood, which is part of the avenging of the blood of the martyrs. So, by the time the martyrs are crying for vengeance, if they are beheaded in the second half of Daniel's 70th week, blood will have been already sent from heaven to avenge their blood. Their cry for vengeance at that point would be after the fact. They will have already received part of their requested vengeance within the first two trumpets, and it is likely that some of the bowl judgments involving blood will have already taken place as well. So, why would "tribulation martyrs" be crying out for vengeance when the vengeance of the Lord has already been unleashed? This is an extremely important question that must be answered if the traditional prophetic model is to be adhered to.

6. The seals result in a <u>natural</u> origin of innocent blood throughout the centuries, whereas the trumpet and bowl judgments involve a <u>supernatural</u> origin of blood.

The events within the first five seals result in much bloodshed. First, the second seal red horse rider causes people on earth to butcher each other. This is the shedding of blood, but in a natural human way, not God sending supernatural blood from heaven. The evil spirit causes men to violently kill each other, so the origin of the bloodshed is on earth:
Rev 6:4 . . . **so that people would butcher <u>one another</u>** . . .

Second, the fifth seal reveals martyrs that were killed on the earth, by other human beings. The source of the guilt for their deaths, according to their own question, was "those who live on the earth":

Rev 6:10 They cried out with a loud voice, "How long, Sovereign Master, holy and true, **before you judge <u>those who live on the earth</u> and avenge our blood?"**

In sharp contrast, the blood from the trumpet and bowl judgments, which have already been analyzed in depth, will be supernatural in origin, being poured out from heaven onto the earth. The first and second trumpet judgments will result from holy angels sounding their trumpets. Blood will come with a hail and fire mixture in the first trumpet, and then with the large, fiery meteor object. There isn't any natural explanation for the presence of blood with these objects from heaven, with water being turned to blood and killing sea creatures. This is supernatural, while the blood during the seal judgments can be explained by natural means: the actions of human beings deceived by evil spirits.

7. The trumpet and bowl judgments are <u>supernatural</u> in nature, whereas the events that take place within the opening of the first five seal judgments are all explained in the <u>natural</u> world and are currently taking place on the earth.

The events that occur within the first five seals can all be explained by natural means. Within the first five seals, there is religious domination and oppression of humans, by humans, in seal one; war and bloodshed between humans in seal two; financial bondage and oppression of humans, by humans, in seal three; death, disease, famine, and beasts of the earth wreaking havoc on one fourth of humanity in seal four; and martyrs suffering at the hand of other humans in seal five. The supernatural element to these five seals is that an evil spirit is granted permission to carry out the oppression, but that oppression is carried out *through* natural means. However, the results can all be explained by natural or human causes, and each and every one of them are manifest in the world every day. These all occur prior to the sixth seal events, and prior to the declaration of the beginning of the day of God's wrath.

This is in sharp contrast to the trumpet and bowl judgments. Consider all the supernatural events that take place in these judgments, which do *not* occur in the world every day, as shown in the following chart:

	Supernatural Event of the Trumpet Judgments	Supernatural Events of the Bowl Judgments
1	One-third of the entire earth will be burned, one-third of all the trees will be burned, and all the green grass will be burned due to hail with a fire and blood mixture.	Ugly and painful sores will appear on those who have the mark of the beast and who worship his image (this may be a natural reaction to the mark).
2	One-third of the sea will be turned to blood, one-third of all sea creatures will die, and one-third of all ships will be destroyed from a massive burning meteor object hitting the sea.	The sea will turn to blood, and all living creatures in the sea will die.
3	One-third of the rivers and springs will be turned bitter from being hit by a burning asteroid named Wormwood.	All the rivers and springs will turn to blood.
4	One-third of the sun, moon, and stars will lose their shining; or, the sun, moon, and stars are present in the skies one-third shorter time than normal.	The sun will become so hot that it will scorch people with fire and terrible heat.
5	Demonic locust-shaped creatures will ascend out of the bottomless pit and torture those who do not have the seal of God on their foreheads for five months. Men will not be able to die from their torment.	Darkness will cover the entire kingdom of the beast, and the darkness will cause pain for those in the kingdom.
6	Four angels will be loosed from the Euphrates River area, followed by two-hundred million beasts that breathe sulfur and will have snake-like tails that inflict injuries. These beasts will kill one-third of humanity with their smoke, their fire, and their sulfur.	The Euphrates River will dry up, and three evil spirits will proceed from the mouth of the dragon, the beast, and the false prophet to deceive the nations.
7	(none)	Earthquakes will cause all the cities of the earth to collapse, mountains to fall, and islands to be covered. In addition, 100 pound hailstones will hit the earth and its inhabitants.

There is a very clear contrast between the events of the first five seals and the trumpet and bowl judgments. The latter are all poured out in the Lord's wrath, and for the avenging of the innocent blood shed on the earth, and are not seen anywhere in the world today, whereas the former are opened prior to the return of Christ for the dead in Christ and the living, and are seen every day in the world.

15.3 Conclusion

The events which will take place after the opening of the sixth seal are the major turning point within the description of history within Revelation. This is because before they take place, the martyrs still cry out for their innocent blood to be avenged, and the events of the first five seals are still occurring simultaneously until the sixth seal is opened. In addition, after the sixth seal events, the people on the earth will be full of extreme anguish, as they experience what takes place during the sixth seal.

Keep the seven important distinctions explored above in mind as the model begins to conclude. The next chapter will feature an exploration of what John is shown on the earth, and in heaven, at the beginning of Daniel's 70th week. Under this prophetic model, the chronological structure from Revelation chapter 1 to chapter 7 remains intact.

- SECTION V -

THE RE-GRAFTING AND THE COVENANTS

There was no way to stop the waves, of course. We were at the mercy of their fury until the underlying cause was quelled. I found myself on the floor again, no longer able to watch what was happening. I was counting the number of waves as their destructive force rolled underneath me. *Four. Five. Six. Seven. Eight...*

Earthquake Resurrection Prophetic Model Timeline Progression

	Weeks 1-69		Week 69 Ends. GAP Between Week 69 and Week 70						Week 70 Begins		
	457BC - 27AD	27AD	31AD	31AD - PRESENT					FUTURE TIME		
				Opening of the First Five Seals - Birth Pains Begin				Sixth Seal			
				1	2	3	4	5			
	Decree of Artaxerxes Longimanus Weeks 1-69 of Daniel's 70 Week's Prophecy	Transfer of the Priesthood of Melchizedek at Christ's Baptism	Christ's and the "Many Saints" Earthquake Resurrection	Christ's Ascension to the Right Hand of God	Spirit of Religious Domination in Christ's Name	Spirit of War and Bloodshed	Spirit of Financial Oppression	Spirit of Death, Disease, and Famine	Persecution and Death of Believers	Future Earthquake Resurrection of the Dead in Christ, Transformation and Catching Up	Confirmation / Strengthening of the Covenant	Sealing of the 144,000 Children of Israel	Enormous Group Before the Throne
	Dan 9:24-25	Luk 3-4	Mat 27	Act 1; Rev 4-5			Rev 6:1-11			1 The 4, 1 Cor 15	Daniel 9:27	Rev 7
	Ch. 8	Ch. 3-4	Ch. 3, 6	Ch. 10, 11	Ch. 12	Ch. 13	Ch. 14			Ch. 4, 5, 7	Ch. 9, 15, 16	

- CHAPTER SIXTEEN -

THE RE-GRAFTING OF THE OLIVE TREE

With the progression through Revelation chapter 4 through 6 now complete, it is time to move into Revelation chapter 7. The following events will have taken place prior to the events described in Revelation chapter 7:

1. The full number of Gentile believers will have been grafted into the new covenant. (Romans 11:25)
2. The full number of martyrs will have just been reached, with the murder of the final pre-sixth seal believers. (Revelation 6:11)
3. The sixth seal events will have all taken place, including the movement of mountains and islands, a massive shaking of the earth, signs in the sun, moon, and sky, and probable magnetic or crustal pole shift. (Revelation 6:12-14)
4. The resurrection of the dead in Christ. (I Thessalonians 4:16-17; Isaiah 26:19-20)
5. The transformation to immortality of the bodies of the resurrected dead in Christ and living believers. (I Corinthians 15:51-53)
6. The sudden catching up of all believers in transformed immortal bodies into the air to meet the Lord. (I Thessalonians 4:16-17; Isaiah 26:19-20)
7. The day of the Lord's wrath will have begun on the earth, according to the declaration of the people on earth after the sixth seal events. (Revelation 6:16-17; Isaiah 26:21)

Revelation chapter 7 has now come, and with it, the beginning of Daniel's 70th week. In this chapter, John is shown two separate visions: what is taking place on the earth, and what is taking place in heaven, at the beginning of the day of the Lord's wrath. In the visions, two different groups of people are seen: on the earth, a group of 144,000 direct descendants of Jacob who are sealed with the seal of the living God (henceforth referred to as "the 144,000"), and in heaven, a massive and innumerable group of people before the throne.

16.1 The View From Earth

First, the view from the earth just after the sixth seal events. An angel declares that, prior to the judgments of the Lord falling on the earth, the 144,000 must be sealed with the "seal of the living God". This seal is extremely important, because, during the fifth trumpet judgment, the 144,000 are protected from the demonic creatures who ascend from the abyss and torment humanity for five months:

> Rev 9:4 They were told not to damage the grass of the earth, or any green plant or tree, but only **those people who did not have the seal of God on their forehead.**

In Revelation chapter 7, the genealogical descent of the 144,000 is revealed: 12,000 of them are chosen from each of twelve different sons of Jacob. The author goes to great pains to list every son of Jacob from which 12,000 different men descend until 144,000 are accounted for.

The traditional literal interpretation of the 144,000 is that they will be a group of men whom God will call out of the tribes of Israel, or perhaps all nations, just after the beginning of Daniel's 70th week. According to this traditional interpretation, they will be a special group of the children of Israel who will have lived a pious life of celibacy and dedication to God, but they will not be a part of the caught-up believers. Instead, they will remain on earth, be sealed by God for protection during the trumpet judgments, and evangelize the rest of the world. As for the tribe of Israel from whom they are said to descend, some reason that the two witnesses will be able to tell them from which tribe they trace their descent.

This interpretation leaves much to be desired when all of the traits of the 144,000 are considered. In Revelation chapters 7 and 14, the following traits of this group of people are provided:

1. They must all be descendants of the different tribes of Israel. (Revelation 7:4-8)
2. They must all be men, because they did not defile themselves with women. (Revelation 14:4)
3. They are all male *parthenoi* in Greek, or sexually pure. This could mean these men had never had sexual relations, had never been sexually immoral, or that in their current state, they were unable to have those type of relations.[1] (Revelation 14:4)
4. They were "redeemed from among humanity", which means they must be human beings. (Revelation 14:3,4)
5. They had never told a lie, and they were "blameless". The Greek word for "blameless" is *amomoi*, which Peter used to describe Jesus when he was presented as a lamb "without blemish":

---

[1] According to Strong's Notes on Greek words used in the New Testament, the primary meaning of *parthenoi* when used for males is a man who has abstained from all sexual uncleanness and whoredom. The secondary meaning is that he has abstained from <u>all</u> sexual intercourse.

I Pet 1:19 but by precious blood like that of **an unblemished [amomou] and spotless lamb,** namely **Christ.**

The 144,000 are in a state of holiness and purity as Jesus Christ was his entire life, which could only be possible if they had been in an immortal state. This is because, in a mortal state, all are born into sin, and no one is righteous. (Revelation 14:5)

6. They followed the Lamb wherever he went, which is a trait shared by those who are part of the resurrected and caught-up believers. (Revelation 14:4):

   I The 4:17 Then we who are alive, who are left, will be suddenly caught up together with them in the clouds to meet the Lord in the air. **And so we will <u>always be with the Lord</u>.**

7. They are "redeemed from humanity as firstfruits to God and to the Lamb". Firstfruits means that they are part of a larger whole, in this case humanity, that is taken out of, or redeemed from, the larger whole. (Revelation 14:4)

8. They seem to possess supernatural qualities, such as:

- They are protected with the seal of God from the fifth trumpet judgment creatures which appear and torture humanity for five months. (Revelation 9:4)
- After being on the earth during Daniel's 70th week, they mysteriously appear on heaven's Mount Zion in Revelation chapter 14 without explanation. (Revelation 14:1-5)

There is one group of individuals described briefly in the New Testament that appear to possess all the traits above, a group thoroughly analyzed earlier in the book. That group is the "many saints" of Matthew chapter 27 that were resurrected to immortality just after Christ's resurrection. The following is a list of reasons why the "many saints who had died" and were resurrected is a possible explanation for the elusive identity of the 144,000. Each numbered point below corresponds with the eight numbered points above:

1. The "many saints" were raised from the dead in and around Jerusalem at the least, so they would be in a territory where the children of Israel had been. Their description as "saints" couldn't mean saints of Christ, because he had just died and been raised. Therefore, these saints must have been righteous members of the tribes of Israel who died prior to Christ's death.

2. There is no restriction in Matthew chapter 27 to the gender of the "many saints", so it is possible that the Lord chose only males to be raised.

3. In a resurrected state, these men would not have the capacity to lead sexually immoral lives. However, it could also be possible that the "many saints" led sexually pure lives prior to their deaths, and for this cause were sexually pure.

4. The "many saints" were redeemed from humanity, just as the 144,000 are described.

5. The "many saints", in their resurrected state, would be "blameless", or in a state of holiness and purity. The Greek word *amomoi*, in addition to being a word used to describe Christ as a lamb without blemish, is also used several times to describe the people of God when they will be presented to him:

> Eph 5:27 so that he may present **the church to himself as glorious**—not having a stain or wrinkle, or any such blemish, but **holy and blameless [amomos]**.

> Jud 1:24 Now to the one who is able to keep you from falling, and to cause you to stand, rejoicing, **without blemish [amomous] before his glorious presence,**

6. The "many saints", in their resurrected and glorified bodies, would be able to be with the Lord wherever he went. The supernatural seal of God and the Lamb on their foreheads during the time they are on the earth in the first part of Daniel's 70th week may be a mechanism for them to stay supernaturally united with the Lamb while he is in heaven and while they are on the earth.
7. The "many saints" would be considered "firstfruits" to both God and the Lamb, just as the 144,000 are described, since they were the first human beings resurrected to immortality after Jesus Christ. They were part of a larger whole taken out of the larger whole as a firstfruits offering to God and the Lamb.
8. The "many saints" would, in their immortal state, possess the supernatural qualities that the 144,000 seemed to possess. These are the same qualities Jesus displayed after his resurrection and described in an earlier chapter.

This is presented only as a possible explanation of the identity of the 144,000. Many prophecy scholars have tried, ever since Revelation was penned, to explain their identity. Many of the problems of interpretation that they noted are alleviated if the 144,000 are a group of individuals who lived in the distant past and are currently in a resurrected and immortal state, including:

- The tendency to symbolize the 144,000 number, as well as many of the qualities they are described as having, which could only be possessed by individuals who were in a resurrected and glorified state.
- The perceived problem of how they will know of which tribe they are a part, since after 70 AD, many believe the twelve tribes were scattered and disappeared. The resurrection of the "many saints" occurred before 70 AD.
- Whether they are really symbolic of individuals, both Jew and Gentile, who will turn back to the Lord during Daniel's 70th week.
- The tendency to symbolize their description of being virgins and being without any blame.

16.2 The Attention Turns Back to the Broken Branches of Israel

What is more important to note about this group of 144,000 direct descendants of Jacob than their identity is that they will appear on the earth just after the sixth seal and the announcement of the beginning of the wrath of God. There are many scriptures which reveal that God will turn his attention back to Israel to save them during Daniel's 70th week. Remember the overall six-fold purpose of all of Daniel's 70 weeks, including this final week:

> Dan 9:24 "Seventy weeks have been determined **concerning your people** and **your holy city** to finish the transgression, to bring sin to completion, to atone for iniquity, to bring in everlasting righteousness, to seal up the prophetic vision, and to anoint a most holy place.

These purposes, as the angel told Daniel, were concerning "your people", which are the Jews, and "your holy city", which is Jerusalem. Daniel's 70th week will be a time when the Lord turns his attention back to the children of Israel and Jerusalem, according to this prophecy. No other New Testament passage could make it more plain than Paul's explanation of the broken and re-grafted branches of the olive tree in Romans chapter 11. First, Paul explained that the unbelieving members of the children of Israel represented branches of a cultivated olive tree which were broken off, a concept he understood from the prophet Jeremiah:

> Jer 11:16 I, the Lord, once called you **a thriving olive tree**, one that produced beautiful fruit. But I will set you on fire that will blaze with a mighty roar. Then **all your branches will be good for nothing**.

The Gentiles who believed represented branches from a wild olive tree which were grafted into an already cultivated olive tree with a solid root, into the spaces left vacant by the Jewish branches which were broken off:

> Rom 11:17 Now if some of **the branches were broken off**, and you, a wild olive shoot, **were grafted in** among them and participated in the richness of the olive root,
> Rom 11:19 Then you will say, "The branches were broken off **so that I could be grafted in**."

Paul indicated, however, that those Jewish branches that were broken off would be re-grafted into the olive tree at a very specific time. Such time will be when the full number of Gentiles had come into the cultivated olive tree:

> Rom 11:24 For if you [Gentiles] were cut off from what is by nature a wild olive tree, and grafted, contrary to nature, into a cultivated olive tree, how much more will **these natural branches be grafted back into their own olive tree**?
> Rom 11:25 For I do not want you to be ignorant of this mystery, brothers and sisters, so that you may not be conceited: **A partial hardening has happened to Israel until the full number of the Gentiles has come in.**
> Rom 11:26 **And so all Israel will be saved**, as it is written: "The Deliverer will come out of Zion; he will remove ungodliness from Jacob.

When Daniel's 70th week begins, the focus of the Lord's attention on the earth shifts to the salvation of the Jews and the protection of Jerusalem, the holy city. Why the shifting from Gentiles to Jews? The passage above indicates it is because the full number of wild olive shoot Gentiles have been grafted into the cultivated olive tree. In line with this, just before the trumpet judgments within Daniel's 70th week begin to be poured out, the first step will involve the Jews: the 144,000 will be sealed for protection during Daniel's 70th week.

16.3 The Holy City

Daniel was also told that the holy city of Jerusalem would be centrally involved in the six-fold purpose of the 70 weeks prophecy. Just think of all the incredible events that have transpired in that relatively small city over history. Abraham took Isaac to be sacrificed on Mount Moriah in Jerusalem, where God showed him a picture of the future sacrifice of Christ. David purchased the threshing floor on Mount Moriah from Ornan the Jebusite, and Solomon built the first temple on the site. Jesus Christ was crucified in Jerusalem. Today, it is central to the three major monotheistic religions: Judaism, Christianity, and Islam. And in the future, Zechariah prophesied it would still be in the center of the attention of the world:

> Zec 12:2 "I am about to **make Jerusalem a cup that brings dizziness to all the surrounding nations**; indeed, Judah will also be included when Jerusalem is besieged.
>
> Zec 12:3 Moreover, on that day I will make **Jerusalem a heavy burden for all the nations**, and all who try to carry it will be seriously injured; yet all the peoples of the earth will be assembled against it.

Jerusalem laid basically desolate for hundreds of years while the Ottoman Turkish Empire ruled the area. This prophecy can now come to pass due to the reestablishment of the nation of Israel and the building up of the capitol, Jerusalem. When Jesus prophesied of the time of the end, he also declared that Jerusalem would see the majority of the important activity:

> Luk 21:24 They will fall by the edge of the sword and be led away as captives among all nations. **Jerusalem will be trampled down by the Gentiles until the times of the Gentiles are fulfilled.**

The times of the Gentiles will come to an end when the nations who assemble with the beast and false prophet are defeated at Armageddon. In Revelation, John was given similar information about the Gentiles and Jerusalem, but more specifically, about a temple:

> Rev 11:1 Then a measuring rod like a staff was given to me, and I was told, "Get up and measure the temple of God, and the altar, and the ones who worship there.

Rev 11:2 But do not measure the outer courtyard of the temple; leave it out, because it has been given to the Gentiles, and **they will trample on the holy city** for forty-two months.

Note the similar language in Revelation 11:2 and Luke 21:24. The holy city of Jerusalem will be trampled down by the Gentiles. Jesus also prophesied that the abomination of desolation would be standing in the holy place, which is a direct reference to the temple in Jerusalem. It will become the center of controversy when the false prophet sets up the abomination of desolation, or the image of the beast, and the beast sits in the temple as God.

There is much prophetic scripture that indicates both the people of Israel and the city of Jerusalem are centrally involved in the activities of Daniel's 70th week. Just as Paul in Romans chapter 11 explained, the full number of Gentiles will be grafted into the new covenant, then the broken branches of Israel will be grafted back into the olive tree. The sealing of the 144,000 is the first step of the re-grafting process for the nation of Israel. Their appearance just after the events of the sixth seal and the beginning of Daniel's 70th week in Revelation chapter 7 is confirmation of Paul's prophecy that God will turn his attention back to the salvation of Israel.

16.4 The View From Heaven

At the same time that the 144,000 are sealed on the earth, John is shown a vision of an enormous and innumerable group of people before the throne of God in heaven:

Rev 7:9 After these things I looked, and here was an **enormous crowd** that **no one could count**, made up of **persons from every nation, tribe, people, and language**, standing before the throne and before the Lamb dressed in long white robes, and with palm branches in their hands.

Just as the souls of the martyrs under the altar, crying out for vengeance, were given long white robes, so the people in this enormous group were wearing long white robes. But unlike the martyrs, this group was not under the altar, but in front of the throne. The long white robes do not represent the immortal bodies of believers, but rather the righteousness of the believer. The elder points out:

Rev 7:14 So I said to him, "My lord, you know the answer." Then he said to me, "These are the ones who have come out of the great tribulation. **They have washed their robes and made them white in the blood of the Lamb!**

The robes are white because they were washed in the blood of the Lamb, which is something that must be done by all persons who desire to enter the new covenant. The people were righteous because of the shed blood of Christ.

In contrast, the souls of the martyrs under the altar were given long white robes while they were still under the altar, waiting for the avenging of their blood. Perhaps this was a reminder to them that they were cleansed and redeemed souls, or perhaps a reward for what they endured on earth. They were told to wait for the full number of Christians to be killed as they were, though they were given their robes while in soul-state because of their testimony and suffering on the earth. As resurrected believers, they will be part of the enormous crowd before the throne, and all will have the long white robes of righteousness. The enormous group before the throne is not described as being in soul-state, but rather, they are described as a "crowd" of "people".

In light of the model being proposed, which is highly focused on earthquake patterns and resurrections, especially around the opening of the sixth seal and the likelihood that the catching-up event will occur at that time, it is almost impossible to deny the probability that this enormous group of people, which appears out of nowhere in Revelation chapter 7 and is not described in any other passage of Revelation, is the resurrected and transformed body of Christ, having just arrived in heaven in Revelation chapter 7 after the catching-up event. Despite efforts by traditional prophetic models, this enormous group cannot be made up solely of martyrs during Daniel's 70th week. According to Revelation chapter 20, those who will be beheaded and will not worship the beast or the image of the beast, nor receive the mark, will not be resurrected until the end of Daniel's 70th week, whereas this first group of living "people" appears at the beginning of it:

> Rev 20:4 Then I saw thrones and seated on them were those who had been given authority to judge. I also saw the souls of those who had been beheaded because of the testimony about Jesus and because of the word of God. These had not worshiped the beast or his image and had refused to receive his mark on their forehead or hand. **They came to life and reigned with Christ for a thousand years.**

It is interesting to note that the "people" of Revelation 7:9 are also associated with nations, tribes, and languages:

> Rev 7:9 an **enormous crowd [ochlos]** that no one could count, made up of persons from every **nation [ethnous]**, tribe **[phulon]**, people **[laon]**, and language **[glosson]** . . .

This same foursome–nation, tribe, people, and language–are found three other times within Revelation. In each case, the author is referring to living people *on the earth*:

> Rev 11:9 . . .those from every **people [laon]**, tribe **[phulon]**, nation **[ethnon]**, and **language [glosson]** will look at their corpses. . .

> Rev 13:7 [The beast] was given ruling authority over every **tribe [phulen]**, **people [laon]**, language **[glossan]**, and **nation [ethnos]**

> Rev 14:6 . . .those who <u>live on the earth</u>—to every **nation [ethnos]**, tribe **[phulen]**, language **[glossan]**, and **people [laon]**.

Take note that the same root Greek words are used in each case above, and that the people to whom the author was referring were on the earth. For this reason, the "people" of Revelation 7:9 must be living, resurrected human beings, not the souls of martyrs who have not yet been resurrected. Furthermore, the specific usage of the Greek noun *ochlos* for "great multitude" is found in 44 other verses in the New Testament, and in each usage is referring to a group of living human beings on the earth.

If the enormous group in front of the throne is indeed the resurrected and caught-up body of believers at the beginning of Daniel's 70th week, the group cannot include any martyrs beheaded during that time. First of all, the beast and the image of the beast, which they refused to worship, have not yet been introduced in the book, so how can they have been beheaded by the beast and false prophet if they haven't yet been introduced? Secondly, the final week martyrs will remain dead, in an unresurrected state, until the end of Daniel's 70th week, when they will be raised to life.

In Revelation chapter 15, John is shown another vision of the sea of glass. Around it were gathered those who had conquered the beast, his image, and his mark:

> Rev 15:2 Then I saw something like a sea of glass mixed with fire, and **those who had conquered the beast and his image and the number of his name**. They were standing by the sea of glass, holding harps given to them by God.

How will they conquer them? By refusing to worship the beast or his image and refusing to take his mark, which will result in their beheadings. So, John saw this group of beast conquerors in the heavenly realm, but later he revealed that they are not to be resurrected from the dead until the end of Daniel's 70th week. Therefore, what John sees in Revelation chapter 15 must be the *souls* of Daniel's 70th week martyrs. Revelation chapter 20 makes it clear that these martyrs will not be resurrected until the end of Daniel's 70th week. When they come to life, they will reign with Christ 1,000 years. This 1,000-year period will begin after Christ and his armies destroy the dragon, the beast, and the false prophet.

Take note of the revealing contrast between the group before the throne in Revelation chapter 7 and the group around the sea of glass in Revelation chapter 15. The group in chapter 7 is called "enormous" and "no one could count" their number. Furthermore, they are described as "people". However, no mention is made of the size of the group in chapter 15, and it is certain they are not resurrected "people", since Revelation chapter 20 reveals they will not be resurrected until the beginning of the 1000-year period.

In addition, why would John be shown the same group of martyrs in two different visions, one before the beast is revealed, and one after the beast is revealed? Why would they be described as enormous and innumerable in one vision, but be devoid of description in the other vision? Why even refer to them twice? The answer to these questions is that two separate groups are in view: the Revelation chapter 7 group is the resurrected and caught-up body of believers who appear before the throne just after the events of the sixth seal, while the Revelation chapter 15 group is the souls of the martyrs who conquered the beast and are beheaded during the latter half of Daniel's 70th week.

The appearance of this massive group of people around the throne in heaven in Revelation chapter 7, just after the events of the sixth seal and while Daniel's 70th week is beginning on the earth, is an absolutely perfect place for them to be introduced within the chronology of the visions of Revelation. If indeed the future resurrection, transformation, and catching-up event will occur within the events of the sixth seal, and Daniel's 70th week will begin just after this, one would expect to see their transformed and immortal bodies with the Lord in heaven at precisely the point at which they appear in Revelation. One would also expect to see people from every corner of the earth.

The enormity of this group is explained in that it includes countless believers throughout history over all the face of the earth, added to the vast number of Christians alive on this planet today. This would result in an "enormous crowd that no one could count", just as John described in the vision. That is indeed what is pictured in this verse. Looking back through Revelation chapters 4 through 7, this is the only reference to an enormous group of people in heaven, made up of all the nations of the earth.

In summary, remember the following reasons why the group before the throne cannot be, nor can it include, those who will be beheaded during Daniel's 70th week:

- The group appears before the throne at the beginning of Daniel's 70th week, before the beast who kills them for refusing to worship and take the mark of the beast has even been introduced.
- The enormous Revelation chapter 7 group is described as resurrected "people", whereas, in Revelation chapter 20, John revealed that those who will be beheaded for not worshipping the beast or his image are not resurrected until the end of Daniel's 70th week, or the beginning of the 1,000-year period when Satan is incarcerated in the abyss and Christ reigns on the earth. Therefore, the Revelation chapter 7 crowd could not be resurrected "people" and the souls of martyrs simultaneously.
- In Revelation chapter 15, John is shown the souls of the group of martyrs who had conquered the beast, standing around the sea of glass. This group is described as neither enormous nor innumerable.
- The chronological flow of Revelation is disrupted mightily if the Revelation chapter 7 group consists of those beheaded during Daniel's 70th week, because the beast will not have been introduced, nor his image, nor his mark, until Revelation chapters 11 through 13. The chronological flow is kept in perfect stead, however, if the Revelation chapter 7 group is interpreted as the resurrected and caught-up body of Christ, the believers who were washed in the blood of the Lamb before Daniel's 70th week began.

Although the traditional prophetic models may be in disagreement with this interpretation, many of the commentators who wrote after the Protestant Reformation agree with the interpretation presented here. Consider what the following commentators wrote about Revelation 7:9 [emphasis added]:

<u>Albert Barnes Notes on the Old and New Testament</u>

> The multitude that John thus saw was not, therefore, I apprehend, the same as the hundred and forty-four thousand, but a far greater number **the whole assembled host of the redeemed in heaven** ... The number was so great that no one could count them, and John, therefore, did not attempt to do it. This is such a statement as one would make who should have **a view of all the redeemed in heaven**.

<u>Adam Clarke's Commentary on the Bible</u>

> A great multitude—This **appears to mean the Church of Christ** among the Gentiles, for it was different from that collected from the twelve tribes; and it is here said to be of all nations, kindreds, people, and tongues.

16.5 They Came Out Of The Great Tribulation?

The reason traditional prophetic models interpret this enormous, innumerable group of people before the throne to be a group of martyrs beheaded during Daniel's 70th week, or "tribulation martyrs", is due to a phrase in Revelation 7:14. In his vision, John was speaking with one of the 24 elders, who was offering him a chance to understand who these people were. When John admitted he did not know who they were, the elder provided the following explanation:

> Rev 7:14 So I said to him, "My lord, you know the answer." Then he said to me, **"These are the ones who have come out of the great tribulation [tes thlipseos tes megale].** They have washed their robes and made them white in the blood of the Lamb!

The traditional idea is that this enormous group is seen in soul-state under the altar during the opening of the fifth seal where each one is given a white robes, then in Revelation chapter 7, the group is seen before the throne. Still with their white robe, which they had to make white by enduring the beast, his image, and his mark, they came out of the great tribulation.

The Greek phrase for "the great tribulation" in Revelation 7:14 is *tes thlipseos tes megales*. The Greek word *thlipsis* is translated a myriad of ways in the KJV. The following is a list of English words in the New Testament translated from the Greek word *thlipsis*, with examples of each use in the KJV:

- Tribulation(s), 21 times, including:

  > Rev 2:22 Behold, I will cast her into a bed, and them that commit adultery with her **into great [megalen] tribulation [thlipsin]**, except they repent of their deeds.

Mat 24:21 For then shall be **great [megale] tribulation [thlipsis]**, such as was not since the beginning of the world to this time, no, nor ever shall be.

- Affliction(s), 17 times, including:
  Act 7:11 Now there came a dearth over all the land of Egypt and Canaan, and **great [megale] affliction [thlipsis]**: and our fathers found no sustenance.

- Trouble, three times, including:
  II Cor 1:8 For we would not, brethren, have you ignorant of our **trouble [thlipseos]** which came to us in Asia, that we were pressed out of measure, above strength, insomuch that we despaired even of life:

- Afflicted, one time:
  Mat 24:9 Then shall they deliver you up to be **afflicted [thlipsin]**, and shall kill you: and ye shall be hated of all nations for my name's sake.

- Anguish, one time:
  Joh 16:21 A woman when she is in travail hath sorrow, because her hour is come: but as soon as she is delivered of the child, she remembereth no more the **anguish [thlipseos]**, for joy that a man is born into the world.

- Burdened, one time:
  II Cor 8:13 For I mean not that other men be eased, and ye **burdened [thlipsis]**:

- Persecution, one time:
  Act 11:19 Now they which were scattered abroad upon the **persecution [thlipseos]** that arose about Stephen traveled as far as Phoenicia, and Cyprus, and Antioch, preaching the word to none but unto the Jews only.

So many English words, yet one Greek word. One should question how the KJV, and several other translations, knew when to use those different words, and when not to. When should "tribulation" be used? When should "anguish" be used? When should "affliction" be used? When should "trouble" be used? Of course, it depends on the context in which the word is used, but scanning over these verses, it seems that these words could be used interchangeably without any harm to the meaning of the text. What if the usage in Matthew 24:21, instead of "great tribulation", was instead translated as "great anguish" or "great affliction"? Would the popular term for Daniel's 70th week be "The Affliction Period" instead of "The Tribulation Period"? What about "The Persecution Period" or "The Anguish Period"? It seems that any of these words could have been used and still kept the same meaning.

One of the verses above, Acts 7:11, has the same Greek phrase, *megale thlipsis*, as Matthew 24:21, and yet it was translated as "great affliction". So, why wasn't this phrase translated as "great tribulation" in the KJV as it was in Matthew 24:21, Revelation 2:22, and Revelation 7:14? What if the elder told John that the enormous group had just come out of "great anguish" or "great affliction"? Interestingly, in Mark's parallel passage to Matthew 24:21, the Greek *thlipsis* is again used, but the KJV translates it using a different word:

Mar 13:19 For in those days shall be **affliction [thlipsis]**, such as was not from the beginning of the creation which God created unto this time, neither shall be.

Why would the KJV translate two parallel passages, Matthew 24:21 and Mark 13:19, with two different English words when the underlying Greek words are identical? Again, these different English words can be used interchangeably to describe the same meaning, and this verse is absolute proof of that.

What did some of the commentators after the Protestant Reformation have to say on this topic? They agree that *tes thlipseos tes megales* probably refers not to a particular time of trouble, but to great trial and anguish experienced during the life, which will be left behind. Consider what the following expert commentators wrote about Revelation 7:9 [emphasis added]:

<u>Albert Barnes Notes on the Old and New Testament</u>
The word rendered "tribulation"–thlipsis–is **a word of general character, meaning "affliction,"** though perhaps there is here an allusion to persecution. The sense, however, **would be better expressed by the phrase great trials**.

<u>Adam Clarke's Commentary on the Bible</u>
Came out of great tribulation – **Persecutions of every kind.**

<u>John Wesley's Explanatory Notes</u>
These are they – **Not martyrs; for these are not such a multitude as no man can number.** But as all the angels appear here, so do **all the souls of the righteous who had lived from the beginning of the world**. Who come – He does not say, who did come; but, who come now also: to whom, likewise, pertain all who will come hereafter. Out of great affliction – **Of various kinds, wisely and graciously allotted by God to all his children.**

16.6 The Narrow Path to Eternal Life

According to both Strong's Lexicon and Thayer's Greek-English Lexicon of the New Testament, the Greek *thlipsis* literally means pressure applied to someone or something. *Thlipsis* comes from the root word *thlibo*, which means to be compressed, pressured, or constricted. One explanation used by Thayer for *thlibo* was how grapes are pressed in order to produce wine. Think also of the way a snake puts pressure upon, constricts, and crushes its prey as it swallows it. Consider the following verses in which this word was used:

Mar 3:9 Because of the crowd, he told his disciples to have a small boat ready for him so the crowd would not **press toward [thlibosin]** him.

According to this verse, if Jesus was not standing in a boat, he felt the crowd would have pressed in on him so much as to push him into the water. Paul used the word *thlibo* a few times as well, including the following:

II Cor 4:8 We are **experiencing trouble [thlibomenoi]** on every side, but are not crushed; we are perplexed, but not driven to despair;

Paul expressed the pressure and constriction that he was experiencing, yet he was not crushed. All around him, the pressure was closing in, but it did not result in crushing, as in a crushed grape. Now consider this famous passage spoken by Jesus Christ:

Mat 7:13 "Enter through the narrow gate, because the gate is wide and the way is spacious that leads to destruction, and there are many who enter through it.

Mat 7:14 But the gate is narrow and the way is **difficult [tethlimmene]** that leads to life, and there are few who find it.

This is the "straight and narrow" verse, the famous passage in which Jesus explained the broad path that leads to destruction and the narrow, constricted path that leads to life. The Greek *tethlimmene*, derived from the base verb *thlibo*, is used to describe the way that leads to life. What Jesus meant was that he was the only way to eternal life, not a broad array of man's imaginations of how to inherit eternal life. The path is narrow and constricted–there is only one way.

Is it possible that this is what the elder meant when he told John that the enormous group before the throne came out of *tes thlipseos tes megales*? That they had made their way down the narrow path the leads to life? That they had come out of the dark world, the present evil age, and made their path down the compressed path that leads to life? Forget for one moment the common and emblazoned English translation of "the great tribulation" and consider the underlying and predominant Greek words as presented above.

In addition, please note that the elder, after telling John that the group before the throne came out of *tes thlipseos tes megales*, did not go on to further elaborate on the topic he had just introduced:

Rev 7:14 . . .They have washed their robes and made them white in the blood of the Lamb!

These are not acts that only beheaded martyrs must perform, but what all Christians must perform. All must confess their sins and have them washed white in the blood of the Lamb, Jesus Christ. This is basic and fundamental doctrine of the Christian faith.

The elder, after informing John that the people had emerged from *tes thlipseos tes megales*, could have gone on to say, "Yes, these people endured the angry judgment of the Lord. They conquered the beast, did not worship him or his image, and did not accept the mark of the beast. They were beheaded for their testimony, and because of this, they stand here redeemed before the throne." But, he did not say these things. As explained above, this is almost exactly the description of the unnamed people standing around the sea of glass in Revelation chapter 15. No doubt, the Revelation chapter 15 group *is* the group of tribulation martyrs in their soul-state:

Rev 15:2 Then I saw something like a sea of glass mixed with fire, and **those who had conquered the beast and his image and the number of his name**. They were standing by the sea of glass, holding harps given to them by God.

Instead, the elder in John's vision of Revelation chapter 7 went on to list several more traits of the enormous group before the throne in verses 16 and 17, and these traits are embodied in promises common to all believers in Christ found throughout the New Testament:

1. They will never hunger or thirst again.
2. They will no longer experience the sun beating down on them.
3. They will be sheep whom the Lamb will shepherd and lead to springs of living water.
4. They will have their tears wiped from their eyes.

These are not things exclusive to beheaded martyrs during Daniel's 70th week. A scan of the final two chapters of Revelation will reveal that these promises are given to all believers. The evidence continues to mount that this innumerable crowd from all the nations of the earth are the resurrected and caught-up believers in Christ.

16.7 The Anguish of Childbirth

Jesus compared the pain and anguish a woman experiences during childbirth to the sorrow that the disciples would experience on the earth. As shown above, the Greek *thlipsis* was used to describe this anguish:

Joh 16:21 When a woman gives birth, she has distress because her time has come, but when her child is born, she no longer remembers the **suffering [thlipseos]** because of her joy that a human being has been born into the world.
Joh 16:22 So also you have sorrow now, but I will see you again, and your hearts will rejoice, and no one will take your joy away from you.

In another prophetic passage, which was also explored previously, Jesus compared the pressure and stress that the world would be experiencing prior to his return for believers to a woman experiencing the pains of birth:

Mat 24:8 All these things are the beginning of **birth pains**.

Mar 13:8 For nation will rise up in arms against nation, and kingdom against kingdom. There will be earthquakes in various places, and there will be famines. These are but the beginning of **birth pains**.

Paul also related the pain and groaning that life in this world brings, but also acknowledged that all of creation groans and suffers:

Rom 8:22 For we know that **the whole creation groans and suffers** together until now.

Rom 8:23 Not only this, but **we ourselves also**, who have the firstfruits of the Spirit, **groan inwardly as we eagerly await our adoption, the <u>redemption of our bodies</u>**.

Note that Paul understood that the groaning would not continue indefinitely, but would have a definite ending. That end comes with the "redemption of our bodies", a direct reference to the resurrection of the dead, when mortal bodies are changed into immortal. So, not only does the whole of creation groan and suffer, but believers in Christ groan in anticipation of the transformation of their bodies. Another prophetic passage penned by the apostle Paul also ties the beginning of the day of the Lord to the pains of childbirth:

I The 5:2 For you know quite well that **the day of the Lord will come** in the same way as a thief in the night.

I The 5:3 Now when they are saying, "There is peace and security," then sudden destruction comes on them, **like labor pains on a pregnant woman**, and they will surely not escape.

The "sudden destruction" of I Thessalonians 5:3 above is related to the destruction embedded within the events of the sixth seal of Revelation chapter 6. The linkage with the day of the Lord fits with all previously drawn conclusions about the sixth seal. In addition, the reference to "a thief in the night" in I Thessalonians 5:2 fits the interpretation of the lightning-quick resurrection and transformation event occurring at the beginning of the sixth seal. Perhaps some future series of events will culminate with cries of "peace with security", followed by the events of the sixth seal. These cries for peace and security may concern peace treaties, world governmental union, martial law, or even police state powers in the wake of future "terrorist" attacks. Only time will tell, but the present world situation seems perilously close to such circumstances.

First Thessalonians 5:2 is yet another passage that compares the time just prior to the day of the Lord to the pains of childbirth. Is it possible that Paul was referring to a passage from the prophet Isaiah? As explored in a previous chapter, Isaiah prophesied that there will be a group he termed "my people" who will be hidden from the angry judgment of the Lord. In order for that group to be hidden from the judgment, they will have to be removed from the anguish on the earth. It is extremely interesting that Isaiah described that anguish out of which they came using, again, the pains of childbirth:

Isa 26:17 As when **a pregnant woman gets ready to deliver and strains and cries out because of her labor pains**, so were we because of you, O Lord.

Isa 26:18 We were pregnant, we strained, we gave birth, as it were, to wind. We cannot produce deliverance on the earth; people to populate the world are not born.

The prophet compared the straining and crying of labor to the affliction of the people on the earth. The people declared that, despite all their straining, and even successful childbirth, they were unable to produce "deliverance on the earth". Although Israel strained to deliver a child, it was outside of their power. Only the Lord could produce that deliverance. Just after the allusion to the pains of childbirth, the prophet described two separate events that occur after the childbirth, but before the unleashing of the angry judgment of the Lord upon the earth, avenging the shed blood on the earth. The first is the resurrection of the dead in Christ:

> Isa 26:19 Your **dead will come back to life**; your corpses will rise up. Wake up and shout joyfully, you who live in the ground! For you will grow like plants drenched with the morning dew, and the **earth will bring forth its dead spirits.**

The second is the catching up and hiding away of all believers before the judgment begins, and until the judgment is over:

> Isa 26:20 **Go, my people! Enter your inner rooms! Close your doors behind you! Hide for a little while, <u>until</u> his angry judgment is over!**
> Isa 26:21 For look, the Lord is coming out of the place where he lives, to punish the sin of those who live on the earth. The earth will display the blood shed on it; it will no longer cover up its slain.

The entire passage, from verse 17 to verse 21, flows perfectly with this prophetic model, and with the enormous and innumerable group in heaven, and with Revelation chapter 7. The passage has been cited several times throughout this book due to its importance. The *megales thlipsis*, or anguish and pain that was being experienced on earth, with increasing frequency of contractions until the delivery, is left behind. The chosen of the Lord leave the great pressures, cares, and persecutions of mortal life behind and are suddenly standing before the throne of God in heaven.

16.8 Summary and Conclusion

The key points to remember from this chapter include:

- The sealing of the 144,000 descendants of the tribes of Israel on the earth will mark the first step in God's promise to turn his attention back to Israel during Daniel's 70th week. The "many saints" who were resurrected according to Matthew chapter 27 are a possible explanation of the identity of the 144,000.
- The unbelieving branches of the cultivated olive tree, comprised of the children of Israel, which were broken off and replaced by wild olive shoot Gentiles, will be re-grafted into their olive tree when the full number of Gentiles has come into the olive tree.
- The introduction of the enormous and innumerable group of people from all nations of the earth before the throne at the beginning of the day of the Lord, and after the future resurrection, transformation, and catching-up event, is exactly

what would be expected to be seen in heaven within the chronological flow of Revelation.

- The martyrs under the altar are differentiated from the enormous crowd of Revelation chapter 7, though both have white robes, because they are in soul-state. The crowd before the throne in Revelation chapter 7, however, is described as a group of "people", not souls.

- Three other times in Revelation, the author refers to people, tribes, nations, and languages, as is found in Revelation 7:9 in describing the crowd before the throne. In each case, the author is referring to living human beings on the earth.

- The enormous group before the throne cannot be the beheaded martyrs because (1) the beast, responsible for their deaths, has not yet been introduced in the visions, (2) Revelation chapter 20 reveals that those beheaded martyrs are not resurrected until the end of Daniel's 70th week, and (3) Revelation chapter 15 contains a description of this group. To describe the same group in two separate chapters, and to provide totally different descriptions of the two different groups, makes no logical sense.

- *Tes thlipseos tes megales* could just as easily be referred to as "the great anguish" or "the great affliction" than as "the great tribulation". *Thlipsis* is translated numerous ways throughout the New Testament.

- *Thlipsis* means pressure or compression, and comes from the root word *thlibo*, which means to press in and crush someone or something. Jesus described the path that leads to life with the verb *thlibo*, a narrow, constricted path that few will find. The cares of the world press in on Christians during their lives and results in *thlipsis*, a narrow path, that must be followed.

- The pains of childbirth are used over and over to describe human life on the earth, and the birth pains of the earth itself, until the delivery of the child. The pains of childbirth are described by Jesus using the Greek noun *thlipsis*, the same Greek word used in Revelation 7:14, which he indicated his disciples would experience in the world.

- Isaiah 26:17-21 is a key prophetic passage that refers to (1) the pain and anguish experienced during life described as the pains of childbirth, (2) the resurrection of the dead, (3) the hiding away of the people of God during his wrath, and until his wrath is complete, and (4) the purpose of the Lord's wrath as avenging the blood shed on the earth. These are all key concepts of this prophetic model.

This chapter marks the end of the prophetic model, a journey which has proceeded through an explanation of the resurrection of the dead, the transformation to immortality, the catching up of all believers into the air, the connection of earthquakes to the resurrection of the dead, and Revelation chapters 4 through 7. The next chapter will explore some interesting passages in the Bible which indicate the timepiece that the Lord has always used in directing the events on the earth. The Lord has established several important covenant relationships with selected individuals and groups throughout history, and they have a surprising importance in the climax of prophecy.

Finally, the waves stopped. One initial quake followed by seven ferocious aftershocks for a total of eight waves. After the final shock, I slowly rose to my feet with a sense of bewilderment. This changed everything in my life. *Did the rest of the world experience this? Did the rest of the world even survive this?* The landscape was a disaster area: broken and cracked earth as far as the eye could see. I wondered what was the cause of this massive earthquake. *Was it due to a large meteor striking the earth? Was it an eruption of the Yellowstone supervolcano? Or was it something else...something supernatural?*

- CHAPTER SEVENTEEN -

COVENANTS: THE LORD'S PROPHETIC TIMEPIECE

The events that will lead up to the resurrection, transformation, and catching-up event have been explored throughout this book. Three specific, interrelated processes within the progression of the prophetic timeline will come to a conclusion at that event:

1. The gospel of the kingdom will be preached as a witness throughout every nation, and then the end will come.
2. The full number of Gentiles will be grafted into the new covenant cultivated olive tree with Jewish roots.
3. The full number of Christians will be violently killed for their witness, and the Lord will hear their cry of vengeance for the shedding of innocent blood.

These are interrelated in that, as the gospel is preached as a witness to all nations, one response is that Gentiles will be grafted into the new covenant. Another response is persecution, some so severe that people will be killed for their witness about Christ. All three of these events have been taking place since the first century, and will continue to take place until the end comes, until the full number of Gentiles are grafted into the new covenant, and until the full number of Christians are martyred.

17.1 The Patience of the Lord

A purpose overlapping these three "untils" is God's desire to have as many souls saved from the fate of eternal damnation and separation as possible. This concept is best embodied in the second epistle of Peter:

> II Pet 3:9 The Lord is not slow concerning his promise, as some regard slowness, but is being patient toward you, because **he does not wish for any to perish but for all to come to repentance**.

James offers an example from nature to explain the reason for God's patience in waiting for souls to come to repentance:

Jam 5:7 So be patient, brothers and sisters, **until the Lord's return.** Think of how the farmer **waits for the precious fruit of the ground** and is patient for it until it receives the early and late rains.

Is there any way for the believer to know how long the patience of the Lord will last? At least one passage makes it relatively clear that believers who are alive prior the Lord's return will not be in the dark about when it will take place:

I The 5:1 Now on the topic of times and seasons, brothers and sisters, **you have no need for anything to be written to you.**

I The 5:2 For **you know quite well** that the day of the Lord will come in the same way as a thief in the night.

I The 5:3 Now when they are saying, "There is peace and security," then sudden destruction comes on them, like labor pains on a pregnant woman, and they will surely not escape.

I The 5:4 **But you,** brothers and sisters, **are not in the darkness for the day to overtake you like a thief would.**

Aside from the signs that are provided throughout the New Testament of the time of the end, such as signs in the heavens and the behavior of people, is there some other scriptural clue that would allow believers to know the time the Lord will act?

17.2 The Lord Remembers His Covenants

The Lord has always acted based on covenants that he established with his chosen people. By studying the scriptures related to these covenants, the believer can be assured that the Lord will act in the future based upon covenants he has established. Indeed, either the establishment of covenants or the breaking of them by his people have been the marker of important prophetic events throughout history.

Throughout scripture, the Lord is described as remembering the covenants he established with his chosen people. The Lord established a covenant with the earth communicated to Noah, that he would never again destroy the earth with a flood. The guarantee of that covenant was a rainbow in the sky:

Gen 9:11 I **confirm my covenant with you:** Never again will all living things be wiped out by the waters of a flood; never again will a flood destroy the earth."

Gen 9:12 And God said, "This is the guarantee of the covenant I am making with you and every living creature with you, **a covenant for all subsequent generations:**

Gen 9:13 I will place my rainbow in the clouds, and it will become **a guarantee of the covenant** between me and the earth.

The Lord has remembered this covenant promise throughout history, as the beautiful rainbows can be seen when the sun shines after a rainstorm. Another example of the Lord's remembrance of a covenant is the deliverance of the children of Israel from Egyptian bondage. Just before their deliverance, the Lord remembered the covenant he established with Abraham:

> Exo 2:23 It happened during that long period of time that the king of Egypt died and the Israelites groaned because of the slave labor. They cried out, and their desperate cry because of their slave labor **went up to God**.
>
> Exo 2:24 And God heard their groaning, and **he remembered his covenant with Abraham, with Isaac, and with Jacob.**

The remembrance of the covenant with Abraham, Isaac, and Jacob is referred to over and over again in the Old Testament. Consider the Lord's faithfulness to the covenant he made with David, even after he had been unfaithful in the adulterous relationship with Bathsheba and the murder of Uriah her husband, during a time when David's descendants behaved treacherously toward the Lord:

> 2 Chr 21:7 Howbeit **the LORD would not destroy the house of David, because of the covenant that he had made with David**, and as he promised to give a light to him and to his sons forever. (KJV)

The covenant promise to David, even after he had been dead for many years, prevented the Lord from acting against David's descendants. In another passage, the Lord stressed the importance of his covenant with David to Jeremiah the prophet:

> Jer 33:20 Thus saith the LORD; **If ye can break** my covenant of the day, and my covenant of the night, and that there should not be day and night in their season;
>
> Jer 33:21 **Then may also my covenant be broken with David my servant, that he should not have a son to reign upon his throne**; and with the Levites the priests, my ministers. (KJV)

According to this passage, the only way the Lord would break his covenant with David would be if the people could alter the rising and falling of the sun, clearly an impossibility. The Lord is bound to the covenant he makes with man, even when man disobeys. The importance of covenants in the plan of God makes a verse tucked within the first chapter of the New Testament very intriguing.

17.3 The Generations of Jesus Christ

The first chapter of Matthew contains a 17-verse passage many may be tempted to quickly read or skip over when reading Matthew, yet it contains a powerful truth about covenants and their relationship to prophetic events. The passage lists the genealogy of Jesus Christ beginning with Abraham until Joseph, his earthly father. The verse that closes the passage is of extreme importance:

> Mat 1:17 So all the generations from **Abraham to David** are fourteen generations, and from **David to the deportation to Babylon**, fourteen generations, and from **the deportation to Babylon to Christ**, fourteen generations.

A pattern emerges in this verse: that of 14 generations separating the persons or events into three divisions. A difficulty arises, however, when trying to divide the people listed in the passage into three distinct divisions of 14 people each. If you count the number people from Abraham to David in the first division, there is no problem:

> First division of 14 generations: (1) Abraham, (2) Isaac, (3) Jacob, (4) Judah, (5) Perez, (6) Hezron, (7) Ram, (8) Aminadab, (9) Nahshon, (10) Salmon, (11) Boaz, (12) Obed, (13) Jesse, and (14) David.

A problem arises when counting the number of people from David until the deportation into Babylon. Some start the counting with David, and some do not:

> Second division of 14 generations: (1) David, (2) Solomon, (3) Rehoboam, (4) Abijah, (5) Asa, (6) Jehosophat, (7) Joram, (8) Uzziah, (9) Jotham, (10) Ahaz, (11) Hezekiah, (12) Manasseh, (13) Amon, (14) Josiah, and (15) Jeconiah about the time of the deportation to Babylon.

If David is not to be counted, then the list starts at Solomon and goes to Jeconiah and there is no problem. But if David is not to be counted as the first generation in the second list, then should Jeconiah not be counted to start the final 14 generations? If not, then the list comes up short:

> Third division of 14 generations: (1) Jeconiah, (2) Shealtiel, (3) Zerubbabel, (4) Abiud, (5) Eliakim, (6) Azor, (7) Zadok, (8) Achim, (9) Eliud, (10) Eleazar, (11) Matthan, (12) Jacob, (13) Joseph, and (14) Jesus Christ.

Another problem embodied in the listing is that the number of years is not uniform within the three divisions. If a biblical generation is to be set at a number, such as 40 years, then how can 14 equal generations be calculated when the number of years is not uniform within each division? Some try to calculate the length of a generation by counting the number of years and dividing the sum by 14, or counting all the years in the three divisions and dividing by 42. Many have tried to do this and come up with strange numbers, such as 51.5 years, which is clearly not the correct length of a generation. A third problem is that at least three generations are skipped within the genealogical listing so that it is not a uniform or chronological listing of generations. Three generations after Uzziah are Joash, Amaziah, and Azariah, according to a similar chronological listing in I Chronicles chapter 3. In addition, one generation between Josiah and Jeconiah is skipped in Matthew's chronology.

Given these problems, therefore, it seems that there was a reason the author choose to exclude certain people and include others. Matthew 1:17 reveals the reason: four principle markers in the listing are singled out in verse 17 as beginning or ending the 14 unequal generations. A common thread will emerge among these four markers:

1. Abraham
2. David
3. The deportation to Babylon
4. Christ

By examining the covenants involving these four markers, it will become clear that covenants the Lord has established with humanity are a harbinger of the commencement and fulfillment of major prophetic events.

17.4 The Lord's Covenant with Abraham

The first covenant participant in the listing of Matthew 1:17 is Abraham, the father of the Hebrew people. Abraham's faith was singled out as the most important reason why the Lord chose to make a covenant with him:

Gen 15:6 Abram believed the Lord, and the Lord considered his response of faith proof of genuine loyalty.

Rom 4:3 For what does the scripture say? "Abraham believed God, and it was credited to him as righteousness."

To what was Genesis 15:6 referring when it speaks of Abraham's "response of faith"? This was before any covenant was made with Abraham, or before Abraham was told to sacrifice his son Isaac. In Genesis chapter 15, Abraham asked the Lord how he was going to bless him, especially since he was childless. When the Lord first revealed himself to Abraham, the Lord made the following promise:

Gen 12:2 Then I will make **you into a great nation**, and I will bless you, and I will make your name great, so that you will exemplify divine blessing.

Abraham told the Lord in Genesis chapter 15 that he had not been blessed with a child. He must have wondered how he was going to make a "great nation" out of him if he had no children. When the Lord heard this, he responded:

Gen 15:4 But look, the word of the Lord came to him: "This man will not be your heir, but instead a son who comes from your own body will be your heir."
Gen 15:5 He took him outside and said, "Gaze into the sky and count the stars—if you are able to count them!" Then he said to him, "**So will your descendants be.**"

It was these promises that Abraham believed, and that response was credited to him as righteousness. After Abraham showed his belief in the Lord's promise to bless him with a child, the Lord established a covenant with him. The Hebrew word for "covenant" is *beriyth*, derived from the Hebrew word *barah*, meaning to make an alliance or agreement with another by a cutting of flesh. This is literally what took place when the Lord initially established his covenant with Abraham:

Gen 15:9 The Lord said to him, "Take for me a heifer, a goat, and a ram, each three years old, along with a dove and a young pigeon."
Gen 15:10 So **Abram took all these for him and then cut them in two** and placed each half opposite the other, but he did not cut the birds in half.

The animals were cut, and when the sun went down and Abraham was asleep, the Lord passed between the two pieces of the flesh in the form of a smoking firepot with a flaming torch. Passing through the pieces of flesh was a symbol of the establishment of the covenant. After the Lord passed between the animal flesh pieces, he established his covenant with Abraham:

Gen 15:18 **That day the Lord made a covenant** with Abram: "**To your descendants I give this land, from the river of Egypt to the great river, the Euphrates River**—

In the initial establishment of the covenant, the Lord promised the descendants of Abraham an area in the Middle East section of the earth. When the Lord later confirmed the covenant with him, he elaborated on the covenant provisions:

Gen 17:4 "As for me, this is my covenant with you: You will be the father of a multitude of nations.
Gen 17:8 I will give the whole land of Canaan—the land where you are residing—to you and your descendants after you as a permanent possession. I will be their God."

The Lord's covenant with Abraham, therefore, was for the land of Canaan: a land that extended from the river of Egypt in the south to the Euphrates River in the north. This is an extremely important covenant, still in place to this day. Abraham marked the beginning of the first division of 14 generations, and the end of the first division was marked by another man with whom the Lord established another extremely important covenant.

17.5 The Lord's Covenant with David

The Lord spoke to Nathan the prophet concerning David in II Samuel chapter 7. According to this passage, the Lord was choosing David and his lineage to begin an eternal kingdom:

II Sam 7:16 Your [David's] house and your kingdom will stand before me permanently; your dynasty will be permanent."

The 89th Psalm, written by Ethan the Ezrachite, contains confirmation of this initial promise made to David through Nathan the prophet:

Psa 89:3 The Lord said, "**I have made a covenant with my chosen one**; I have made a promise on oath **to David, my servant**:
Psa 89:4 'I will give you an eternal dynasty and establish your throne throughout future generations.'" (Selah)

Psa 89:33 But I will not remove my loyal love from him, nor be unfaithful to my promise.
Psa 89:34 **I will not break my covenant** or go back on what I promised.

Note that this passage repeats the initial II Samuel 7:16 promise, but calls it a covenant. The Hebrew word *beriyth* is again used. The Lord established a covenant with David that one of his descendants would occupy an eternal throne in Zion:

Psa 132:11 The Lord made a reliable promise to David; he will not go back on his word. He said, "I will place one of your descendants on your throne.
Psa 132:12 If your sons keep my covenant and the rules I teach them, their sons will also sit on your throne forever."
Psa 132:13 Certainly the Lord has chosen Zion; he decided to make it his home.

During his message to the people on the day the Holy Spirit first filled Jesus Christ's disciples with the evidence of speaking in foreign languages, Peter confirmed that the descendant to whom the Lord was referring in the covenant established with David was Christ:

Act 2:30 So then, because he was a prophet and knew that God had sworn to him with an oath **to seat one of his descendants on his throne,**
Act 2:31 **David by** foreseeing this **spoke about the resurrection of the Christ**, that he was neither abandoned to Hades, nor did his body experience decay.

Therefore, this covenant relationship was a promise to David that the king of Zion would emerge from his lineage, and would be eternally established there. This was absolutely confirmed when the angel Gabriel appeared to Mary to announce the birth of the promised anointed one of God:

Luk 1:32 He will be great, and will be called the Son of the Most High, and the Lord God will give him **the throne of his father David.**

This covenant, though fulfilled with the birth of Jesus Christ, was made with David, the last marker of the first division of 14 generations. The second division of 14 generations ends with the deportation to Babylon, a result of the breaking of the Mosaic covenant.

17.6 Deportation to Babylon: Breaking the Lord's Covenant with Moses and the People

The Lord made a conditional covenant with his chosen people of Israel after their deliverance from Egypt. After crossing the Red Sea, the Lord first revealed this covenant to Moses at Mount Sinai just before giving the Ten Commandments and the rest of the law:

Exo 19:5 And now, if you will diligently obey me and **keep my covenant**, then you will be my special possession out of all the nations, for all the earth is mine.

The people later agreed to its provisions when it was read to them, and the covenant was ratified by the cutting of the flesh of bulls. The blood of the bulls was then used to sprinkle the altar and the people:

Exo 24:7 And he took the Book of the Covenant and read it in the hearing of the people; and they said, "We are willing to do and obey all that the Lord has spoken."

Exo 24:8 So Moses took the blood and splashed it on the people and said, "This is **the blood of the covenant that the Lord has made with you in accordance with all these words.**"

The history of the people of Israel after that point is chronicled throughout the Old Testament. They disobeyed, fell into idolatry, and broke every commandment the Lord gave them in a myriad of ways. The people went through several cycles of disobedience, forgiveness, and reconciliation. The Lord continuously forgave them, but continued to warn them through the prophets to discontinue their idolatry. Finally, the Lord's patience came to an end, and he sent the armies of Babylon against them:

II Chr 36:15 The Lord God of their ancestors **continually warned them through his messengers,** for he felt compassion for his people and his dwelling place.

II Chr 36:16 But they mocked God's messengers, despised his warnings, and ridiculed his prophets. Finally the Lord got angry at his people and **there was no one who could prevent his judgment.**

The Lord kept his solemn word that the consequences of breaking the covenant and disobeying the commandments would come on the people. In approximately 605 BC and several years to follow, the armies of Babylon ransacked Jerusalem, destroyed the temple and the walls, and took many prisoners. Second Chronicles reveals two important facts about why this fate came upon the Jews when it did:

II Chr 36:21 This took place to **fulfill the Lord's message delivered through Jeremiah.** The **land experienced its sabbatical years**; it remained desolate for **seventy years**, as prophesied.

First, the passage reveals it was prophesied that the length of the desolation would be 70 years. This prophecy is found in the writing of Jeremiah the prophet:

Jer 25:11 This whole area will become **a desolate wasteland.** These nations will be subject **to the king of Babylon for seventy years.**'

Second, the passage reveals that the land would experience its sabbatical years. To what is this referring? In communicating the laws of the covenant to Moses and the people, the Lord made it clear that the land must experience one year of rest at the end of each six-year period:

> Lev 25:3 Six years you may sow your field, and six years you may prune your vineyard and gather the produce,
> Lev 25:4 but in the **seventh year <u>the land</u> must have a Sabbath of complete rest**—a Sabbath to the Lord. You must not sow your field or prune your vineyard.

In the next chapter of Leviticus, the Lord revealed exactly what would happen if the people disobeyed by not allowing the land to experience its sabbatical rest:

> Lev 26:34 "'Then **the land will make up for its Sabbaths all the days it lies desolate while you are in the land of your enemies**; then the land will rest and make up its Sabbaths.
> Lev 26:35 All the days of the desolation it will have the rest it did not have on your Sabbaths when you lived on it.

This is exactly what is described in II Chronicles 36:21. While the Jews were in the land of Babylon, the desolation took place and the land experienced 70 years of rest. Remember that these consequences were prophesied hundreds of years before the deportation to Babylon. Several generations of Israelites had come and gone, and the covenant provisions had been forgotten or ignored over time.

If the land was to experience a rest once per seven years, and the desolation lasted 70 years, it computes that the children of Israel were in disobedience of the covenant provisions of the land receiving a year of sabbatical rest every seven years for a period of 490 years.

The deportation to Babylon was a result of the Jewish disobedience of the covenant provisions, clearly communicated to them through Moses after their deliverance from the slavery in Egypt. Although the people felt the effects of the punishment for breaking the covenant provisions, the desolation was brought about so that the land could experience its necessary rest.

The final marker of the second division of 14 generations, and the first marker of the third division of 14 generations of Matthew 1:17, is the deportation to Babylon. Clearly, this marker was used by the author of Matthew because it was a reference to a covenant relationship with the Lord that was broken, resulting in the deportation to Babylon at that time. The final marker of the third division of 14 generations is Jesus Christ, the mediator of the new covenant.

17.7 The Lord's New Covenant Through Jesus Christ

The first reference to the new covenant established through Christ was a prophecy of Jeremiah. This covenant was not going to be like the first covenant established with them after their deliverance from Egypt:

> Jer 31:31 "Indeed, a time is coming," says the Lord, "when I will make **a new agreement** with the people of Israel and Judah.

289

Jer 31:32 It will not be like the old agreement that I made with their ancestors when I took them by the hand and led them out of Egypt. For they violated that agreement, even though I was a faithful husband to them," says the Lord.
Jer 31:33 "But I will make **a new agreement** with the whole nation of Israel after I plant them back in the land," says the Lord. "I will **put my law within them and write it on their hearts and minds. And I will be their God and they will be my people.**

The nation of Israel includes those who put their faith in Christ, including Gentiles who are cut off of a wild olive tree and grafted into an already existing and cultivated olive tree. This concept was examined in a previous chapter, but Paul's discourse in Romans chapters 9 through 11 is summed up well by this verse:
Rom 11:24 For if you were cut off from what is by nature a wild olive tree, and **grafted, contrary to nature, into a cultivated olive tree,** how much more will these natural branches be grafted back into their own olive tree?

Paul made it clear what the prophecy in Jeremiah was referring to in Hebrews chapter 8. He quoted this exact prophecy in contrasting the first covenant with the new covenant established through Christ. Both the Jeremiah and Hebrews passages reveal that this new covenant not only provides a way for all those who come to God through him after his death and resurrection, but also eliminated the sins committed under the first covenant. Throughout the letter to the Hebrews, Paul argued that this second, new covenant was the one established through Jesus Christ. It was a better covenant established on better promises, with Jesus as the high priest after the order of Melchizedek. This new covenant was consecrated with the blood of Jesus:
Heb 9:15 And so he is **the mediator of a new covenant,** so that those who are called may receive the eternal inheritance he has promised, since he died to set them free from the violations committed under **the first covenant.**
Heb 7:22 accordingly Jesus has become **the guarantee of a better covenant**

When a person makes a decision to enter into the new covenant, that person enters into a personal relationship with Jesus Christ. Just as the covenant with Abraham, the cutting of flesh and spilling of blood was an important part of the covenant. Jesus explained to his disciples that his body was going to be broken and his blood shed for their atonement:
I Cor 11:23 For I received from the Lord what I also passed on to you, that **the Lord Jesus on the night in which he was betrayed took bread,**
I Cor 11:24 and after he had given thanks he broke it and said, "**This is my body, which is for you.** Do this in remembrance of me."
I Cor 11:25 In the same way, **he also took the cup after supper,** saying, "**This cup is the <u>new covenant</u> in my blood.** Do this, every time you drink it, in remembrance of me."

Thus the new covenant was consecrated with his body and blood, and remembered through drinking the fruit of the vine and eating bread. This practice was established long ago between Abraham and Melchizedek, another clue to how Jesus and Melchizedek are related, and why Jesus is the high priest after Melchizedek's order:

> Gen 14:18 Melchizedek, king of Salem, **brought out bread and wine**. (Now he was the priest of the Most High God.)

Eating the bread and drinking the wine is the method of remembering the suffering and death Jesus endured until he returns:

> I Cor 11:26 For every time you eat this bread and drink the cup, you proclaim the Lord's death until he comes.

17.8 Entering the New Covenant

Who may enter into this covenant relationship with Jesus Christ? Any person who humbly admits the sin that causes separation from the Lord, and that there is nothing that can be done to provide their own atonement for that sin. Belief that Jesus Christ atoned for the sin by his suffering, death, and resurrection is the key:

> Rom 10:9 because **if you confess with your mouth** that Jesus is Lord and **believe in your heart** that God raised him from the dead, you will be saved.
> Rom 10:10 For **with the heart one believes** and thus has righteousness and **with the mouth one confesses** and thus has salvation.

> Joh 3:16 For this is the way God loved the world: He gave his one and only Son, so that **everyone who believes in him** will not perish but have **eternal life**.

Notice that the covenant is conditional on a person's confession and belief. Jesus' death did not automatically provide salvation for the entire human race, but a person must enter into the covenant relationship. This eternal life is established by washing away the sin from the mortal body, clearing the way for the eternal soul and spirit to be clothed with a new, immortal body at the resurrection of the dead, as studied in prior chapters. It is a mystery, and there is no discernible physical change, but Jesus referred to this as being "born again" of the spirit. Having eternal life means a believer no longer has a fear of death:

> Heb 2:14 Therefore, since the children share in flesh and blood, he likewise **shared in their humanity**, so that through death he could **destroy the one who holds the power of death** (that is, the devil),
> Heb 2:15 and **set free those who were held in slavery all their lives by their fear of death**.

A fear of death permeates humanity; it is a slave to death. The death of Jesus Christ provided freedom from the fear of dying. It is amazing that the primary focus of the news, of movies, and of television, is death, and that it is the end of life. It is the end only of the life of the physical, mortal body. Jesus told his followers not to fear the one who can kill the physical body, but rather to fear the one who can destroy the eternal soul:

> Mat 10:28 **Do not be afraid of those who kill the body** but cannot kill the soul. Instead, fear the one who is able to destroy both soul and body in hell.

Perhaps the defining feature of the new covenant through the body and blood of Jesus Christ is that a person cannot perform works and deeds, or speak good words, and expect to be saved. The new covenant salvation is a free gift, just as a Christmas or birthday present is a free gift. A person that performs works, such as going to church, giving money to preachers or charities, walking for a mile on the knees, or living with the poor and needy, does not *earn* salvation:

> Eph 2:8 For by grace you are saved through faith, and this is **not from yourselves**, it is the **gift of God**;
> Eph 2:9 it is **not from works**, so that **no one can boast.**

Faith in Jesus Christ's redemptive provision is the key. If this were not the case, there would be no way to judge what kind or amount of human works could save the eternal soul. Jesus Christ's sacrificial death was the ultimate display of love and humility, as he bore the burdens of humanity on the cross. His humility is a model for all of humanity:

> Joh 15:13 No one has **greater love** than this—**that one lays down his life for his friends.**

> Php 2:7 but emptied himself by taking on the form of a slave, by looking like other men, and by sharing in human nature.
> Php 2:8 **He humbled himself,** by becoming obedient to the point of death—even death on a cross!

17.9 The Impact of Covenants on Future Prophetic Events

The four markers of the beginning and ending of the three divisions of 14 generations, Abraham, David, the deportation to Babylon, and Jesus Christ, all have a covenant of the Lord God in common. But what is the point of this? Recall the earlier discussion in this chapter of the length of generations, and the many problems scholars have noted about the number of people in the three divisions, the missing people in the lineage, and other problems. The scholars are focusing on the wrong thing.

Some of the hidden nuggets in the lineage are amazing, such as the reference to the Gentile prostitute Rahab, the Gentile Ruth, the inclusion of Solomon who was the result of David's adulterous act with Bathsheba, and several others. While tracing the lineage of Jesus back to Abraham and David is extremely important, there is another truth hidden in this passage. The focus should not be on the people in the list, but on what the Lord is trying to reveal about generations, and how he computes their length. Fourteen generations between the three divisions, but unequal years.

Here is the key: the Lord God counts and keeps prophetic time *based on covenants*. Students of the prophetic scripture have continuously attempted to calculate the date of major prophetic events in the Bible, such as the future three-stage event, based on the number of years after a major event takes place on the earth. An example is the establishment of Israel as a nation again in 1948. Many considered the length of a generation to be 40 years based on certain scriptures, and therefore predicted the coming of the Lord in 1988. In addition to other verses, these predictions were primarily based on Jesus' words in the Mount of Olives discourse about the signs of the end:

Mat 24:34 I tell you the truth, **this generation will not pass away** until all these things take place.

Most believe "this generation" refers to the generation which would see the fig tree, Israel and the Jews, back in the land. As this took place in 1948, the natural prediction was that 1988 was the year. However, Matthew 1:1-17 provides the reason why the length of a generation <u>cannot</u> be calculated in this manner. This is because 14 generations were not equal years and did not consist of an equal amount of persons. In summary, the passage should be a revelation of how the Lord views prophetic time:

1. The number of years within a particular generation or generations is of no concern. This is clear from the fact that the number of years within each division of 14 generations is not equal or uniform in the least. Therefore, the length of a generation for use in studying prophetic scripture is not calculable.
2. The number of persons within the 14 generations is of no concern. This is evident from the omission of several names that should have been included if a true chronological genealogy was presented.
3. By the inclusion of a marker that was not a human being, the deportation to Babylon, the beginning or ending of a generation doesn't even need to be a human being.

Because of these anomalies, it is clear that the Holy Spirit wanted to convey that within the four markers in the final verse of the passage is hidden a mysterious common thread. A study of this thread, presented in this chapter, reveals why these particular markers were used to mark the beginning and ending of the three divisions, even though the divisions did not contain a uniform number of years or persons. The Lord calculates the length of a generation not by years, nor the number of persons, nor even by human beings, but by covenants. Furthermore, understanding that the establishment and breaking of covenants is how the Lord has calculated the length of a generation in the past sheds light on the importance of covenants for future prophetic events.

17.10 Satan's Covenant to Thwart Fulfillment of the Lord's Two Unconditional Covenants

The beginning of Daniel's 70th week, the next major prophetic event on the horizon which will be immediately preceded by the resurrection of the dead in Christ, the transformation of the bodies of all believers, and the catching up of all believers to meet the Lord, will be triggered by the confirmation of a covenant by the coming prince:

> Dan 9:27 He will **confirm a covenant with many for one week**. But in the middle of that week he will bring sacrifices and offerings to a halt. On the wing of abominations will come one who destroys, until the decreed end is poured out on the one who destroys."

Once again, a covenant marks the beginning of a major prophetic event. Can there be any further doubt that covenants are the key to understanding the timing of the fulfillment of prophetic events? It was evident with the covenant with Abraham for the land of Israel, the covenant with David for the anointed one to proceed from his loins and rule in Zion, the breaking of the Mosaic covenant resulting in the deportation to Babylon, and the new covenant established through Christ. Once again, Daniel's 70th week, a time of terrible testing but ultimate salvation for Israel, will begin at the confirmation or strengthening of another covenant.

But what kind of covenant? Certainly not a covenant the Lord has made, but rather a man-made covenant. The confirmation or strengthening of a covenant by the coming prince may be a reference to the division of the land of Israel, which would be an attempt to abolish the covenants the Lord made with Abraham and David, such as the Oslo Accords. If this is the case, then it would be a direct and deliberate hindrance to the prophesied rule of Jesus Christ from Jerusalem during the 1,000-year period in which Satan is bound in the abyss. This reign takes place in the land of Israel according to the covenant established with Abraham, and on a throne from Zion's holy hill in the city of Jerusalem according to the covenant established with David.

The strengthening of a covenant to partition the Lord's holy land or the holy city of Jerusalem would be an attempt by Satan to jeopardize the fulfillment of the unconditional covenants with Abraham and David through Jesus Christ. In order for these two covenants to be kept, the events of Daniel's 70th week must take place, and the covenant made strong by the coming prince must be overturned.

17.11 Summary and Conclusion

There is nothing more reliable than the covenants the Lord has made with man. The Lord must honor the covenants he makes with man, which includes both the positive and negative conditions. With Abraham, there was no provision for what would happen if Abraham disobeyed the Lord. His covenant with Abraham, therefore, was unconditional. The same is true with David, who disobeyed the Lord many times. The covenant with David was unconditional. In the case of the Mosaic covenant with the children of Israel, there were provisions within the covenant for what the Lord would do if the people were either obedient or disobedient.

Following is a list of points to remember from this chapter:

- The Lord wants all humanity to come to repentance and be saved from eternal damnation. This patience is the all-encompassing reason why the Lord has not yet returned to the earth the second time.
- First Thessalonians chapter 5 seems to suggest that believers should not be in darkness regarding the timing of the day of the Lord. What tool does the believer possess within scripture to understand the timing of the Lord regarding the fulfillment of prophetic events?
- The Lord makes covenants with man in order to prove his unchanging character. Throughout scripture, the Lord is described as remembering covenants he made with men such as Noah, Abraham, Isaac, Jacob, and David, even when they, or their descendants, were disobedient.
- The genealogy of Jesus Christ from Abraham to his father Joseph, chronicled in Matthew chapter 1, concludes with an important verse which divides the list of people and events into three groups of 14 generations. These three divisions begin and end with four markers, all of which involve covenants the Lord made with man.
- The Lord's covenant with Abraham, the first marker in the list, was established after he showed faith and belief in the Lord's promise to bless him with many descendants even when he was childless. The covenant was for the land of Israel stretching from the Euphrates River in the north to the River of Egypt in the south.
- The Lord's covenant with David, the second of the four markers, was an unconditional promise that his lineage would produce an eternal dynasty. That promised seed was Jesus Christ, as declared by the angel Gabriel to Mary just before the birth of Jesus.
- The Lord established a covenant with the children of Israel through Moses after their deliverance from Egypt. This covenant was conditioned on the obedience or disobedience of the people to its provisions. Because the people disobeyed, the Lord kept the promised provisions of that covenant that the land would experience rest, and the Jews were deported to Babylon. This deportation was the third of the four markers.
- The fourth and final marker of the 42 generations of Matthew 1:17 was Jesus Christ. The new covenant was established through his sacrifice on the cross, covering the sins of humanity from Adam until the end of the age for those who believe and confess their sins to him.
- The Lord governs prophetic time and the length of generations based not on the number of years that have passed, nor on the number of people in a list of generations, but on covenants. Because covenants are the key to understanding the Lord's prophetic timing, the attempt to calculate the number of years in a generation, and thereby predict a prophetic event, is a fruitless endeavor.

- Because the covenants with Abraham for the land of Israel and the covenant with David for a king to rule from Jerusalem are unconditional covenants, they must be honored by the Lord. The confirmation of a covenant by the coming prince, which marks the beginning of Daniel's 70th week, may be an attempt by Satan to jeopardize these two covenants. This covenant must be overturned in order for the Lord to honor his unconditional covenants with Abraham and David.

The final chapter will chronicle some of the recent headlines involving seismic, volcanic, and tsunamic activity around the earth. It will also include a set of possible scenarios for the future based upon this prophetic model.

At this point, I woke up from the dream with the images still in my mind. I have had several dreams that were so vivid that I was either extremely sad or extremely happy that they were not real. But this dream was different. I was utterly convinced it was real while it was in progress, and when I awoke, a rush of relief engulfed me. But a sense of profound shock and awe accompanied the relief due to its clarity and vividness. It was a dream that I will never forget.

- CHAPTER EIGHTEEN -

CONCLUSION: A CATACLYSMIC FORECAST

This chapter will conclude the book with an exploration of current seismic and volcanic activity, followed by a set of scenarios that could occur on the earth in the near future based on the earthquake resurrection prophetic model.

18.1 Current Seismic and Volcanic Activity

The seismic and volcanic activity on the earth has seen a major upswing during the time of the writing of this book. In fact, there was so much activity that it was very difficult to keep up with it. Scientists who study the seismic activity under Yellowstone National Park have begun to issue warnings. Mount St. Helens has rumbled and its lava dome risen, resulting thus far in only minor eruptions. Elsewhere, several severe earthquakes have taken place in Japan and other spots along the Ring of Fire, and volcanoes have erupted on islands. As explored in previous chapters, the second largest earthquake on the planet in recorded history, of 9.3 magnitude[1], occurred on December 26, 2004 approximately 155 miles off the coast of the Indonesian island of Sumatra in the Indian Ocean, triggering tsunami waves that, at the time of this writing, resulted in the deaths of over 200,000 people, with many still missing. Consider some of the recent stories that, for the most part, do not make newspapers or television newscasts [emphasis added]:

- September 5, 2004. Quake Jolts Japan, Tsunami Waves Hit: An earthquake measuring 7.4 on the Richter scale has shaken western Japan, the second strong quake to hit the area in five hours. Hundreds of people have been evacuated from low-lying areas as **quake-generated tsunami waves approached.**[2]

---

[1] News@nature.com. "Sea Bed Reveals Earthquake Scars",
http://www.nature.com/news/2005/050207/pf/050207-15_pf.html, accessed February 12, 2005.
[2] Go Asia Pacific. "Quake Jolts Japan, Tsunami Waves Hit",
http://www.goasiapacific.com/news/GoAsiaPacificBNA_1192750.htm, accessed December 1, 2004.

- <u>September 13, 2004. Mauna Loa Rumbles Awake</u>: "Unprecedented" activity deep under Mauna Loa this summer could be another sign that **the world's largest volcano is headed toward an eruption**, a scientist says. More than **350 earthquakes have been recorded since July. Such frequent, small earthquakes have never before been measured beneath Mauna Loa's summit caldera.** Data on Mauna Loa's seismic activity started to be collected in the 1930s, and Hawaiian Volcano Observatory scientist-in-charge Donald Swanson said even the instruments of that era would have detected the quakes. "They're unprecedented," he said, "since we started studying Mauna Loa."[3]
- <u>September 27, 2004. Mount St. Helens Quakes Prompt Warning</u>: Scientists issued a rare warning Monday that Mount St. Helens in Washington state could soon erupt following several strong earthquakes during the weekend . . .the "main concern is that this increase in activity and the magnitude of the earthquakes we are seeing, **we have not seen in a long time, not since the end of the last dome eruption in 1986**," said Cynthia Gardner, the acting supervisor in charge at the Cascades Volcano Observatory.[4]
- <u>October 8, 2004. Major Quake Shakes Philippine Capital</u>: An earthquake with a magnitude of 6.4 shook Manila on Friday night, swaying high rises, knocking out power over a wide area and sending frightened residents into the streets. There were no immediate reports of injuries or damage.[5]
- <u>October 24, 2004. Deadly Earthquakes Strike Japan</u>: Sixteen people are dead and more than 900 injured after a series of earthquakes rattled northwestern Japan Saturday . . .The first quake, with a magnitude of 6.8, struck near Ojiya at 5:56 p.m. local time at a depth of 20 kilometres . . .**Officials said the quake was the strongest to hit the region in 70 years.**[6]
- <u>October 24, 2004. Japan Quake Kills 18; Aftershocks Strike Fear</u>: Tens of thousands of fearful residents in the rural Niigata prefecture spent the night in evacuation centers or outdoors after the initial quake with a magnitude of 6.8 hit at 5:56 p.m. on Saturday . . .They are "desperately in need of food, water and blankets for the local residents," said an official in Ojiya, which has a population of 40,000 . . .More than 240 aftershocks that could be felt by humans had struck

[3] Honolulu Star-Bulletin.com. "Mauna Loa Rumbles Awake", http://starbulletin.com/2004/09/13/news/story1.html, accessed December 1, 2004.
[4] Washington Times.com. "Mount St. Helens Quakes Prompt Warning", http://www.washtimes.com/upi-breaking/20040927-085419-9004r.htm, accessed December 1, 2004.
[5] Usatoday.com. "Major Quake Shakes Philippine Capital", http://www.usatoday.com/news/world/2004-10-08-manila_x.htm, accessed December 1, 2004.
[6] CBC News. "Deadly Earthquakes Strike Japan", http://www.cbc.ca/story/world/national/2004/10/23/japan_quake041023.html, accessed December 1, 2004.

since the initial quake, the Meteorological Agency said, and officials warned of further strong tremors.[7]

- October 25, 2004. Japan in Shock After Earthquake Devastation: Thousands of people were spending a second night in emergency shelters or out in the open yesterday after the deadliest earthquakes to strike Japan for nine years killed at least 21 people and injured more than 1,800 . . ."We don't know in detail the extent of the damage because the roads are still blocked in the mountains and telephone lines are still down," Hirokazu Seki, the mayor of Ojiya, told the Kyodo news agency. "**All lifelines - electricity, gas and water - are crippled.**" The prime minister, Junichiro Koizumi, said the earthquake had been "**beyond our imagination in terms of fear and damage.**" The Niigata area last experienced seismic shifts on a similar scale in 1828, when 1,400 people died.[8]

- November 20, 2004. 4 Killed in Strong Costa Rica Earthquake: A strong, early-morning earthquake shook presidents and prime ministers attending a Costa Rican summit from their beds Saturday and killed eight people, including several who were **frightened into having fatal heart attacks.**[9]

- November 29, 2004. Japan Braces for 'Big One' After Major Quake: A powerful earthquake measuring 7.1 on the Richter scale injured 13 people on Monday in northern Japan in a new sign of seismic activity a month after the country's deadliest tremor in a decade . . .The latest tremor followed a quake registering 6.8 on the Richter scale in the central region of Niigata on October 23, which killed a total of 40 people and was followed by hundreds of aftershocks that have kept residents on edge.[10]

- December 15, 2004. Explosive Predictions for Mount St. Helens: The recent "extraordinary" behaviour of one of the world's most notorious volcanoes, Mount St. Helens in the US, may mean it is preparing for a dramatic eruption. "**Something extraordinary is happening at Mount St. Helens. We are scratching our heads about it,**" says Dan Dzurisin of US Geological Survey's Cascades Volcano Observatory (CVO) in Vancouver, Washington, US. The new dome has grown so quickly—almost four cubic metres every second—that it has bulldozed a 180-metres-thick glacier out of its way. If this rapid growth rate continues, there is a growing risk of a dome collapse **which could trigger a**

---

[7] Chinadaily.com. "Japan Quake Kills 18; Aftershocks Strike Fear", http://www.chinadaily.com.cn/english/doc/2004-10/24/content_385139.htm, accessed December 1, 2004.

[8] Guardian Unlimited. "Japan in Shock After Earthquake Devastation", http://www.guardian.co.uk/international/story/0,3604,1335078,00.html, accessed December 2, 2004.

[9] The State.com. "4 Killed in Strong Costa Rica Earthquake", http://www.thestate.com/mld/thestate/news/world/10234377.htm, accessed December 3, 2004.

[10] Independent Online. "Japan Braces for 'Big One' After Major Quake", http://www.iol.co.za/index.php?set_id=1&click_id=126&art_id=qw1101702784147 B215, accessed December 3, 2004.

major eruption, researchers warned at the American Geophysical Union meeting in San Francisco.[11]

- December 24, 2004. World's Biggest Earthquake in 4 Years. The world's biggest earthquake in almost four years, measuring 8.1 on the Richter scale, was registered off the coast of Australia's southern island state of Tasmania, seismological officials said. Seismologist Cvetan Sinadinovski said . . . **"If it happened underneath a population centre in Australia, this would probably have destroyed a whole city"** . . .[12]

- December 26, 2004. Asia's Quake Tsunamis Kill Nearly 10,000. An earthquake of epic power roiled the Indian Ocean on Sunday morning, unleashing **20-foot walls of water** that came crashing down on Asian beaches in six countries across thousands of miles, smashing seaside resorts and villages and leaving nearly 10,000 dead in their wake. **"It's an extraordinary calamity of such colossal proportions that the damage has been unprecedented,"** said Chief Minister Jayaram Jayalalithaa of India's Tamil Nadu . . . **"All the planet is vibrating" from the quake**, said Enzo Boschi, the head of Italy's National Geophysics Institute. Speaking on SKY TG24 TV, **Boschi said the quake even disturbed the Earth's rotation** . . . Michael Dodds, a reporter for The Washington Post. "The speed with which it all happened **seemed like a scene from the Bible**—a natural phenomenon unlike anything I had experienced before," he wrote on the Post's Web site.[13]

- January 19, 2005. Global Tsunami Death Toll Tops 226,000. The global death toll from the Asian tsunami shot above 226,000 Wednesday after Indonesia's Health Ministry confirmed the deaths of tens of thousands of people previously listed as missing. The ministry raised the country's death toll to 166,320. It had previously given a figure of 95,450 while Indonesia's Ministry of Social Affairs had put the death toll at around 115,000 before it stopped counting . . . The new figure lifted the total global death toll from the tsunami disaster to 226,566, although the number continues to rise as more deaths are reported around the region.[14]

These amazing stories, especially the December 26, 2004 magnitude 9.3 earthquake which occurred during the final edit of the book, confirmed much of the description of the events of the sixth seal, but to a smaller scale. Even the earth's

[11] New Scientist.com. "Explosive Predictions for Mount St. Helens", http://www.newscientist.com/article.ns?id=dn6806, accessed December 26, 2004.
[12] Red Nova.com. "World's Biggest Earthquake in 4 Years", http://www.rednova.com/news/display/?id=113940, accessed January 4, 2005.
[13] Yahoo News. "Asia Quake's Tsunamis Kill Nearly 10,000", http://story.news.yahoo.com/news?tmpl=story&e=1&u=/ap/20041226/ap_on_re_as/indonesia_earthquake, accessed December 26, 2004.
[14] Yahoo News. "Global Tsunami Death Toll Tops 226,000", http://news.yahoo.com/news?tmpl=story&cid=574&u=/nm/20050119/wl_nm/quake_dc&printer=1, accessed January 20, 2005.

rotation was disturbed by the December 26 earthquake, and one reporter actually stated that the devastation was of Biblical proportions. As these headlines and stories were compiled, the effects of these earthquakes, volcanoes, and tsunamis were startling. A common thread throughout most of the stories were the hearts that stopped beating because of the shock of the earthquake as it rolled underneath. People were always described as being in shock and extreme fear of aftershocks. In addition, chaos, looting, and disease was rampant, food and water supplies were contaminated, and electricity was always knocked out in the areas struck by quakes.

18.2 Possible Future Devastation

In the wake of the December 26, 2004 earthquake and resulting tsunami waves that devastated millions in Asia, British geologist Simon Day was prompted to remind anyone who would listen of his research regarding Cumbre Vieja, a volcano on the island of La Palma. This island is positioned just off the northwestern tip of the continent of Africa, and the volcano, overdue for an eruption, has not erupted since 1971. According to Dr. Day's research, an eruption would cause a massive mountain to fall into the Atlantic Ocean, generating the largest tsunami waves ever seen on the earth. Dr. Day stated, "It is not a question of if it will happen, only when it will happen."[15] According to Day, the waves would reach 300 feet in height when they hit the African country of Morocco in one hour, and 130-160 feet in height when they struck the North American continent within 8 hours. The waves would devastate the coastlines of South America, North America, Africa and parts of Europe, as well as heavily-populated island nations such as Great Britain and those in the Caribbean. Cities on the eastern United States coastlines, from Miami in the south to New York City in the north, will be inundated by waves up to 5 times higher than those that struck in Asia on December 26, 2004.[16] In August 2004, one of Dr. Day's colleagues, Bill McGuire, confirmed Day's research, warning that, "Eventually, the whole rock will collapse into the water and the collapse will devastate the Atlantic margin."[17]

There is also some very ominous seismic and volcanic activity currently taking place underneath Yellowstone National Park in Wyoming that, for the most part, is going unreported in the major media. One of the world's largest supervolcanoes is the Yellowstone caldera, located in a 30 by 45 mile section of the park. Scientists believe that in the past, this supervolcano erupted and covered most of the North American continent with ash. There are over 2,000 small to medium earthquakes

---

[15] News.telegraph. "Giant Wave Will Hit Britain at 500mph", http://www.telegraph.co.uk/news/main.jhtml?xml=/news/2001/08/29/nwave29.xml, accessed December 27, 2004.
[16] The Australian. "Volcanic Island a Threat to US Coast", http://www.theaustralian.news.com.au/common/story_page/0,5744,11794033%255E30417,00.html, accessed December 27, 2004.
[17] Ibid.

underneath Yellowstone every year as a result of its positioning on top of a large chamber of magma in one of the globe's most geologically active hot spots. Scientists believe the Yellowstone caldera is overdue for a major explosion, and a full-scale eruption could result in millions of deaths and a global catastrophe. Yellowstone is only one of several supervolcanoes located within the geographical United States of America, and there are many others around the world.

This current seismic and volcanic activity doesn't necessarily prove the validity of this prophetic model, nor the notion that the coming of the Lord is any closer than it was hundreds of years ago. Earthquakes have been occurring, and volcanoes erupting, ever since the flood, and they will continue to occur in the future. However, it serves as a warning to all that the earth's crust is full of faultlines, is unstable, and is primed for a disaster of epic proportions when the moment of the ages, that moment with which this book was introduced, finally arrives.

18.3 When That Moment Arrives

As that moment approaches, the signs in the earth, on the earth, and in the sky will continue to occur. But when that day finally arrives, the sixth seal of the scroll will be opened by the Lamb in heaven, and the following events will take place:

1. The dead in Christ throughout history will be resurrected, awakened by the voice of God which will shake the earth.
2. The bodies of all believers, both those resurrected dead in Christ, and the living and remaining believers, will be transformed. Jesus Christ, who created all things and has control over all things, will use that omnipotence to transform the bodies of believers into the likeness of his immortal body.
3. All believers, in transformed immortal bodies, will be suddenly caught up into the air to meet Jesus Christ.

Meanwhile, the earth and its inhabitants will not be able to avoid the *effects* that the resurrection and transformation will have on the natural world, the first two stages of the three-stage event. Those effects will include the following:

1. Massive worldwide earthquakes and movements of the continental and oceanic plates.
2. The shifting and shaking of the earth, causing the mountains and islands to move from their current geographic locations, whether by small or large amounts.
3. Volcanic activity, resulting from the movement of the crust of the earth on top of the underlying magma. This will cause worldwide volcanoes to spew lava and ash into the air. The moon will turn blood red, and the sun will be blackened.
4. The shifting of the oceanic plates, causing massive tsunami waves capable of completely devastating entire coastlines, cities, and island nations.
5. The convergence of supernatural activity with the natural world may cause a polar shift, where a severe shift in the earth's crust causes the poles to move

from their current position. This may cause the stars to appear to be "falling", or moving toward the earth's horizon. There may also be meteors or asteroids associated with this activity that strike the earth's surface, causing even more damage.

Visualize the following scenario: in the briefest of moments, all the dead in Christ are resurrected, and all believers, both those living at the time and those just resurrected, are transformed into immortal bodies as the piercing sound of a reverberating horn-blowing is heard all around the world. People look up in a state of bewilderment wondering what that strange sound could be, then, the supernatural and the natural world converge.

Suddenly, the earth's crust begins to shift on top of energized magma from pole to pole, triggering worldwide seismic, volcanic, and tsunamic activity. The supervolcano in Yellowstone Park begins to explode molten lava and toxic ash across the North American continent; the San Andreas Fault ruptures, splitting California in two; the New Madrid Fault erupts and the Gulf of Mexico floods the Mississippi River as the continental plates shift upward and downward; earthquakes around the oceanic faults cause monstrous tsunami waves to strike the coastlines; similar catastrophic events occur around the globe.

As this activity begins to take place and the crust of the earth begins to react, believers will still be on the earth, yet in newly-transformed, immortal bodies. Just before the devastation and destruction begins to take its full effect, they are suddenly and forcibly snatched up off the earth into the atmosphere. As they rise, they look down to see the planet they just left shifting, quaking, and exploding.

18.4 In the Aftermath of the Catastrophe

As chronicled in the various stories of earthquakes, volcanoes, and tsunamis earlier in this chapter, humanity will suffer deaths not only from the massive seismic, tsunamic, and volcanic activity, but many will die simply from heart attack and shock. The technological infrastructure of cities will be at least severely crippled, if not completely destroyed. Electric power will be unavailable, making communication between other nations very difficult. Communication by radio waves may be the best form of communication at that time, providing both parties attempting to communicate have functioning equipment and the required electricity to transmit the signal.

According to Revelation chapter 11, when the two witnesses are resurrected to immortality in the city of Jerusalem, a local earthquake will occur that levels one-tenth of the city and causes 7,000 deaths. When the future resurrection of the dead and transformation event occurs, the land with the greatest numbers in which the dead in Christ are buried may experience a higher proportionate share of the supernatural power of the resurrection, resulting in more intense destruction. The damage could be due to seismic activity on major fault lines, tsunami waves, or exploding volcanoes, such as the supervolcano in Yellowstone Park, capable of covering much of the North American continent with lava and ash.

As for the whereabouts of caught-up believers missing on the earth after the events of the sixth seal, perhaps, due to the worldwide calamity and devastation, they will be claimed as missing or dead; casualties of the chaos. Their vanishing may be completely overlooked due to the masking characteristic that the associated destruction brings. This was clearly the case on the island of Sumatra after the earthquake and resulting tsunamis on December 26, 2004. The damage was so extensive in some parts that rescue efforts could not be undertaken. Entire cities, one with a population over 100,000, were 80-100% destroyed, and it was impossible to reach them until the water assuaged. Several smaller islands off the coast of Sumatra had simply "disappeared".[18]

Will there be news reports of people missing? Or, will the physical, logistical, and technological infrastructure on the earth be so disrupted and damaged as to prevent this? If satellites that enable worldwide television and cellular phone communications are disabled by the supernatural power of the future three-stage event, then the ability to disseminate news would be severely crippled. At a bare minimum, satellites will likely require repositioning to compensate for the movement of the earth's surface, as well as other natural and supernatural phenomena that may disrupt their proper functioning. In addition, electricity plants may be completely powered down or otherwise damaged by the electromagnetic activity, or by the shifting of the earth's crust and tsunami damage. If the power of the resurrection of Christ caused an image to be photographed on his burial shroud, then a massive wave of power at the moment of the resurrection of the dead could most definitely have this effect.

If these scenarios prove to be correct, flash newscast reports of millions of people disappearing around the earth, suggested in popular movies and books, would probably be impossible. While the news may be slowly spread by word of mouth, confusion and chaos will ultimately rule the day. Perhaps some of the islands and countries that were formerly accessible or inhabitable will be completely covered underwater, or the land so marred by the earthquakes, volcanoes, and tsunamis, that an accounting for the whereabouts of people is simply impossible.

This type of chaos was clearly evident in the aftermath of the December 26, 2004 magnitude 9.3 earthquake near Indonesia. According to some estimates, over 164,000 people were missing, meaning they were not counted among the dead or injured.[19] After a certain amount of time, the missing persons will be considered among the dead. For example, Great Britain announced on January 16, 2005, over two weeks after the event, that the missing would be declared dead if they were not

[18] Bernama.com. "Indonesia Needs Help, Death Toll Expected to Exceed 400,000", http://www.bernama.com/bernama/v3/news_lite.php?id=111574, accessed December 31, 2004.

[19] Wikipedia.com. "Indian Ocean Earthquake", http://en.wikipedia.org/wiki/2004_Indian_Ocean_earthquake, accessed January 15, 2005.

found after one year.[20] On January 19, 2005, when approximately 70,000 Indonesian people who were previously among the missing were declared among the dead, Indonesian President Yudhoyono stated "Perhaps we will never know the exact scale of the human casualties."[21] Indeed, widespread confusion has ruled the day during the entire process of trying to assess the dead. According to one source from Jakarta, Indonesia, "the massive levels of destruction wrought by the tsunami and the sheer numbers of corpses meant that in the early post-disaster stages, many of the victims were buried in mass graves without prior identification."[22]

Imagine the chaos that will occur at the sixth seal when the effects of the Southeast Asia catastrophe are multiplied worldwide. Many millions could be missing, and as such, those believers who were living and remaining prior to the event, but could not be found afterward, would simply be declared dead in the catastrophe. This is a very solid and plausible explanation for the future disappearance of millions of believers on the earth, a question that has perplexed Bible prophecy students for decades.

18.5 Unification Amongst the Chaos

After some time passes, the planet's surviving inhabitants will begin to pick up the pieces. In the wake of catastrophic events, human nature has always been to pull together and become united for a common cause. This was the case in the wake of what happened to the United States on September 11, 2001. Citizens banded together when newscasts showed the planes hitting the buildings and the towers coming down over and over, along with purported celebrations by people in the Middle East over the calamity.[23] Vengeance on the attackers, whoever they were, became the rallying cry. When such a natural disaster occurs on the earth in the future, a spirit of unity would arise to come together for a common cause, and to rise from the ashes and rebuild.

---

[20] News.telegraph. "Tsunami Missing to be Declared Dead after a Year", http://www.telegraph.co.uk/news/main.jhtml?xml=/news/2005/01/16/wtsun16.xml&sSheet=/news/2005/01/16/ixnewstop.html, accessed January 15, 2005.

[21] Yahoo News. "Global Tsunami Death Toll Tops 226,000", http://news.yahoo.com/news?tmpl=story&cid=574&u=/nm/20050119/wl_nm/quake_dc&printer=1, accessed January 20, 2005.

[22] Yahoo News. "Indonesia Drastically Reduces Possible Tsunami Death Toll", http://story.news.yahoo.com/news?tmpl=story&u=/afp/20050407/wl_afp/asiaquakeindonesia_050407150722, accessed April 10, 2005.

[23] Since airing celebrations of anonymous Middle Eastern individuals, including the burning of the flag of the United States, cheering, and laughter, at least one major news network has publicly admitted that pre-September 11, 2001 video clips were used to give the impression that they were celebrating the September 11, 2001 attack.

This was also the case after the December 26, 2004 earthquake in the Indian Ocean that struck without warning and devastated the lives of millions. Consider the initial response of the nations around the world to help the region[24]:

- United Nations Secretary General Kofi Annan announced the UN would send disaster and coordination teams to the region for relief and rescue assistance.
- The Russian government sent a helicopter, tents and equipment to help the relief effort.
- The Chinese government promised to provide emergency humanitarian aid.
- The Canadian government pledged approximately $800,000 in relief aid, as well as other humanitarian assistance on the ground.
- The Philippine government promised a group of humanitarians to help with rescue and cleanup.
- The Australian government sent two Air Force crafts full of medical supplies and blankets, and pledged approximately $7,000,000.
- The United States government pledged an initial $15,000,000 relief package, then later an additional $20,000,000, and stood ready to help in other ways.
- The European Union offered approximately $4,000,000 immediately and said more would be offered in the future.
- The French government sent a plane of 100 doctors to Sri Lanka to help.
- The Israeli government promised to send doctors and experts.
- The Pakistani government launched a humanitarian search and rescue mission, mobilized its Navy to help the search, and dropped emergency food supplies.
- Greece sent a plane with 11 tons of medical supplies and volunteers.
- The governments of Germany, Ireland, Britain, and Kuwait all promised monetary assistance.
- The government of Singapore sent a special emergency consular team to Thailand.

The unification that resulted from this disaster is a preview of what will likely occur after the sixth seal events have taken their toll. While every nation on the planet will be affected by the events, the nations will come together to help each other.

On the coattails of this unification, perhaps the Middle East peace situation, at an impasse for so long, will finally be settled when a man is able to draw the Palestinians and Jews together over the division of Israel's covenant land. Consider these important comments by former United States President Bill Clinton in connection with the devastating December 26, 2004 earthquake and tsunami:

> I am grateful for **the opportunity** that this terrible tragedy gives
> **for religious reconciliation in the world**. . .[in which people
> around the world are] "reaching out for the <u>Muslims</u> of Indonesia,

---

[24] China View. "International Community Rushes Aid to the Tsunami-hit Countries", http://news.xinhuanet.com/english/2004-12/27/content_2386519.htm, accessed December 27, 2004.

for the <u>Hindus</u> and the <u>Buddhists,</u> and the <u>Muslims</u> and the <u>Christians</u> in Sri Lanka **to reconcile**.[25] [emphasis added]

Imagine a worldwide catastrophe that affected all ethnic and religious groups, and the chance for reconciliation. Could not the Jews and the Palestinians also fit in that list if a similar catastrophe thrust them into reconciliation mode? Tensions between the Hindus and Buddhists were very high prior to the event, but after the event, there was a temporary lull in the fighting and hatred. Below is a list of specific examples of peace between bitter enemies not only after the 2004 tsunami disaster, but also after other natural disasters in history:

1. After the December 26, 2004 earthquake and resulting tsunami, Pakistan, a bitter nuclear enemy of India, sent relief teams to India and dispatched their Navy to help with the rescue effort. Conflicts between the Muslim population of Pakistan and the Hindu population of India were temporarily set aside in the face of the disaster.

2. Another temporary reconciliation after the 2004 earthquake and tsunami included a separatist group in Banda Aceh, Indonesia, who announced a unilateral cease-fire in order to help people who were affected by the tragedy. According to Sidney Jones, the Southeast Asia project director for the International Crisis Group, "This is a watershed. . .the tsunami will change the dynamic of the conflict in a number of important ways."[26]

3. Again after the 2004 earthquake and tsunami, the Tamil Tigers were quelled in their resistance against the Sri Lanka central government. According to Hans Brattskar, the Norwegian ambassador to Sri Lanka, "This was definitely one of those events that change history. We are in darkness now, but people are looking for rays of hope."[27]

4. In 2003, the United States provided 68 tons of relief to Bam, Iran after an earthquake devastated the city and killed over 31,000 people. The United States and Iran were not friendly countries, but the United States set aside differences in the face of a humanitarian emergency.[28]

5. In 1999, both Greece and Turkey were rocked by severe earthquakes. Tensions were quelled amongst the bitter enemies when rescue crews were sent from both countries to help each other. According to Soli Ozel, teacher of politics at Bilgi University in Istanbul, Turkey, "Suddenly, the perception of the 'other' as evil

---

[25] Yahoo News Asia. "Tsunami Tragedy to Boost Religious Unity, Reduce Terrorism: Clinton", http://asia.news.yahoo.com/050111/afp/050111230533people.html, accessed January 15, 2005.

[26] The Christian Science Monitor. "From Sparta to Nicaragua, Disasters Alter Political History", http://www.csmonitor.com/2005/0111/p01s04-wogi.htm, accessed January 15, 2005.

[27] Ibid.

[28] Ibid.

changed. The earthquakes provided indispensable public support for the policy of rapprochement."[29]

Humanity has always come together to help in the time of natural disasters, and the events of the sixth seal will be no different. The world will be drawn together in an effort to rebuild what has been toppled, and to salvage what is salvageable. Such an undertaking will require an end to fighting and killing amongst these peoples. The result of the unity could result in the strengthening of a covenant to parcel the land of Israel, triggering the beginning of Daniel's 70th week. In addition, the stressful situation surrounding the Jerusalem temple mount may be temporarily relieved, allowing the Jews to build a temple where two modern Muslim mosques currently sit.

18.6 The Real Suffering Begins

Many will not survive the events that take place, but those who do will not find much solace. They will be thrust into a period about which Jesus said no one would survive unless its time span were shortened: the days of God's vengeance on the earth. It will be a time of great delusion due to the emergence of the prophesied man of sin, who will deceive the surviving humanity:

II The 2:9 The arrival of the lawless one will be by Satan's working with **all kinds of miracles and signs and false wonders,**

II The2:10 and with **every kind of evil deception** directed against those who are perishing, because they found no place in their hearts for the truth so as to be saved.

II The 2:11 Consequently **God sends on them a deluding influence** so that **they will believe what is false.**

II The 2:12 And so all of them who have not believed the truth but have delighted in evil will be condemned.

It will also be a time of great death and horror due to the destructive events within the trumpet and bowl judgments that will come upon the earth during the seven-year period. Revelation chapter 9 states that humanity will experience a five-month torment from creatures who emerge out of the abyss, a torment from which they will not be able to die, despite their desire to do so. That same chapter states that a full one-third of remaining humanity will be killed by the plagues contained in the sixth trumpet. Jesus prophesied that it will be a time of unparalleled suffering:

Mat 24:21 For then there will be great suffering **unlike anything that has happened from the beginning of the world until now, or ever will happen.**

These times will truly be as horrific and desperate as one could ever imagine. The warnings are being heard from pulpits, from the Internet, and from the television and

---

[29] Ibid.

radio airwaves, that the time is short. In the days of Noah, the warnings of future destruction went unheeded, and calamity struck the earth, killing all but eight of its inhabitants. Similarly, the earth's impending cataclysm will strike without warning on a day just like any other. Those who are unprepared beforehand will feel all of its intense force.

18.7 Where is God When Natural Disasters Strike?

Tsunami waves resulting from an earthquake in Southeast Asia devastate the lives of millions. A powerful tornado wipes out a small Kansas town. A deadly hurricane sweeps through the Southeastern United States, causing billions of dollars of damage. An island volcano erupts, killing thousands. These are all horrific natural disasters, and questions sometimes asked by those who see these things happen are "Why did this happen to them, God? Why didn't you protect them? If there is a God, where was he when this happened?"

When Jesus was confronted with a similar type of question, he provided what may at first seem to be a cold-hearted and inadequate answer. Some people came to him asking why God allowed Pilate to mix the blood of a group of Galileans who were killed with animal sacrifices. Note his response:

> Luk 13:2 He answered them, "Do you think these Galileans were **worse sinners** than all the other Galileans, because they suffered these things?
> Luk 13:3 No, I tell you! But unless you repent, **you will all perish as well!**

Jesus then provided another example of disaster, where the victims just happened to be in the wrong place at the wrong time:

> Luk 13:4 Or those eighteen who were killed when the tower in Siloam fell on them, do you think they were **worse offenders** than all the others who live in Jerusalem?
> Luk 13:5 No, I tell you! But unless you repent **you will all perish as well!**"

According to Jesus, there was a tower that fell in the city of Siloam in that day, claiming 18 lives. One could insert any other group of people that have been killed in chance accidents, such as the Southeast Asia tsunami, the recent Hurricane Katrina, or the September 11, 2001 World Trade Center victims, in the place of the Galileans or the Siloam tower victims. He stated that these people were not being punished for being worse sinners than anyone else.

But his answer to these two situations did not address their question about injustice or grief over their loss. Instead, Jesus emphasized that <u>everyone</u> is going to eventually die, meaning <u>eternally</u>, if they did not repent. He de-emphasized temporal, present-life loss and difficulty, and emphasized the inevitable eternal consequences of those still living if they did not repent. According to Solomon in Ecclesiastes, no one knows their appointed time of death, and it can ensnare anyone like a fish caught in a net:

> Ecc 9:11 . . .for **time and chance may overcome them** all.

> Ecc 9:12 Surely, no one knows his appointed time! Like **fish that are caught in a deadly net**, and like **birds that are caught in a snare**—just like them, **all people are ensnared at an unfortunate time that falls upon them suddenly.**

God does not allow natural disasters to punish people for not believing in him. The physical structure of the earth is in a fractured state due to Noah's flood, and Jesus prophesied in Matthew chapter 24 and Luke chapter 21 that earthquakes and other natural disasters would take place. The content of this book has dealt with a time of catastrophe and disaster coming upon the earth that has not been seen since the days of Noah's Flood. As in past disasters, the important question when these things happen will not be "Why, God?", but rather, "Have I repented, asked for forgiveness, and prepared myself if this were to happen to me?"

That is the key question. Will you be prepared before this horrific time comes? Forget about trying to survive it. This preparation is not of the physical body, but of the spiritual. Neither surplus canned goods, nor hoarded silver dollars, stored bottled water, or stockpiled weapons will be able to deliver on that day. The only way to prepare for that *future* day is to ready your eternal soul and spirit on this *present* day.

18.8 A More Important "Moment"?

If the scenario of chaos and destruction that will come on the world as proposed in this model is alarming to you, there is an even more frightening scenario: eternal damnation in the lake of fire:

> Rev 20:15 If anyone's name was not found written in the book of life, **that person was thrown into the lake of fire.**

The lake of fire is reserved for the devil, the beast, the false prophet, those who accept the mark of the beast, and all those whose names are not written in the book of life. Why is it when we read a verse like this, we always think it applies to someone *other* than ourselves? Because we think we are generally good people, and that God's wrath and the lake of fire are reserved for bad people, not good people. However, it is clearly communicated in scripture that those who have broken God's laws and not turned from their sin, or who practice deliberate sin despite hearing the message of truth, will not inherit the kingdom of God, but are rather reserved for judgment and fiery wrath:

> Heb 10:26 For **if we deliberately keep on sinning** after receiving the knowledge of the truth, no further sacrifice for sins is left for us,
> Heb 10:27 but only a certain fearful expectation of judgment and a fury of fire that will consume God's enemies.

Which of us can deny we have broken the law of God, the Ten Commandments? Do not lie to others. Honor your father and mother. Do not commit adultery. Do not steal from others. Do not covet the belongings of others. Do not use the name of God in a vain manner, to name a few. Though we may think of ourselves as "good", against the mirror of God's moral law, we are not good, but rather guilty.

In fact, Christ established even *more stringent* standards than the Ten Commandments during his ministry. The sin of adultery, for example, the actions King David took with Bathsheba, was expanded to include mere thoughts:

Mat 5:27 "You have heard that it was said, '**Do not commit adultery.**'
Mat 5:28 But **I say to you that whoever looks at a woman to desire her has already committed adultery with her in his heart**.

In other passages, Jesus equated anger against another person with murder, and John equated hatred of another person with murder:

Mat 5:21 "You have heard that it was said to an older generation, '**Do not murder,**' and 'whoever murders will be subjected to judgment.'
Mat 5:22 But **I say to you that anyone who is angry with a brother will be subjected to judgment**. . .

I Joh 3:15 **Everyone who hates his fellow Christian [brother] is a murderer [anthropoktonos]**, and you know that no murderer [anthropoktonos] has eternal life residing in him.

The Greek word for murderer, *anthropoktonos*, is found in only one other verse in the New Testament: the one in which Jesus called Satan a "murderer from the beginning" in John chapter 8. Clearly, Jesus set a much more stringent standard for both adultery and murder than the Ten Commandments, so much so that it seems no one would be innocent of even these. So how can we live up to these standards? Is there anyone who can? The Bible states there has never been one person born through Adam who has *not* fallen short of God's perfection:

Rom 3:23 for **all have sinned** and fall short of the glory of God.

So what is the purpose of the moral law, if it can't be obeyed by any person? What is the purpose of equating adultery with looking at a woman with sinful thoughts, or equating murder with hating another person, if not to make the laws of God even more onerous?

There are two main purposes of the moral law of God, the first being that it is a mirror set in front of each of us, reflecting back the grim reality that we have broken his commands:

Rom 7:7 . . . Certainly, **I would not have known sin except <u>through the law</u>**. For indeed I would not have known what it means to desire something belonging to someone else if the law had not said, "Do not covet."

Because God's laws are established, we can know what sin is. Paul said he would have no idea what it meant to sin except for those moral laws: the mirror of the law set in front of him to show him his guilt.

The second main purpose of the moral law is to lead us to the cross of Christ, to an innocent man who gave up his life in a brutal and tortuous Roman crucifixion, so that through faith we can be saved:

> Gal 3:24 Thus **the law** had become our guardian **until** Christ, so that we could be declared righteous by faith.

The law was to be a schoolmaster, showing us that Christ is the only way to justification. There is no possible means of *self*-justification, such as doing all kinds of good works or giving to the poor. To admit this requires conviction and humility, traits that pride-filled individuals fight to keep from manifesting.

Before Christ laid down his life for his friends, the most selfless sacrifice a person can make, he washed the feet of his disciples to show them what humility was all about. Washing another person's feet at this time in history was a true act of shame, usually performed only by the lowly servants of the household. Yet, those disciples who protested Jesus' actions received a sobering rebuke:

> Joh 13:8 Peter said to him, "You will **never** wash my feet!" Jesus replied, "If I do not wash you, **you have no share with me.**"

This book began with discussion of the coming "moment of the ages". But there is another important moment in your life. A personal moment. The moment of death, when it is too late to confess your sin, and from whence it is impossible to return. What if today, this very day, is the day you take your last breath? It happens to thousands of people every day, most of whom have no idea that it would be their dying day. They live their lives just as anyone else would, but unexpectedly, they are ushered into eternity with no chance to return.

When that elusive moment arrives, you will <u>not</u> have another chance to repent and dedicate your life to Christ. Think about that carefully. Do you think you are special: that you can dodge death and keep sinning until you are "ready" to change? The lake of fire burns for eternity, and there is no escape. You can be delivered from the fear of death by coming to the Lord in humility <u>today</u>, laying your faults at the cross once and for all. You can experience the Lord's incredible forgiveness for whatever you have done in your past; for all those skeletons in your closet that you want no one else to know about. You can know your eternal destination for a certainty.

*I Joh 2:1 (My little children, I am writing these things to you so that you may not sin.) But **if** anyone **does sin**, we have **an advocate** with the Father, **Jesus Christ** the righteous One,*
*I Joh 2:2 and he himself is **the atoning sacrifice for our sins**, and not only for our sins but also for the whole world.*

* * *

Joh 8:10 Jesus stood up straight and said to her, "Woman, where are they? Did no one condemn you?"
*Joh 8:11 She replied, "No one, Lord." And Jesus said, "**I do not condemn you either**. Go, and from now on **do not sin any more**."*

* * *

Mat 16:26 For what does it benefit a person if he gains the whole world but forfeits his life? Or what can a person give in exchange for his life?

* * *

*Jam 4:14 You do not know about tomorrow. What is your life like? For <u>you</u> are a puff of smoke that appears for a short time and **then vanishes**.*

- APPENDIX -

DETAILED CHRONOLOGICAL TIMELINE: EARTHQUAKE RESURRECTION PROPHETIC MODEL

Timeline	Event Description	Scripture	Chapter
457-456 BC	The first decree of Artaxerxes I Longimanus in the 7th year of his reign to Ezra; the beginning of Daniel's 70 weeks.	Ezr 7:12-14; Ezr 9:9	8
	DANIEL'S FIRST 69 WEEKS, 483 YEARS		
27-28 AD	Daniel's 69th week ends. Jesus Christ is baptized and anointed in the Jordan River; his three and one-half year public ministry in Israel begins; the priesthood is transferred from the order of Aaron to the order of Melchizedek, with Jesus as the high priest.	Mat 3:16-17; Joh 1:32-33; Mar 1:9-12; Luk 3-4; Dan 9:25	8
31-32 AD	Jesus Christ is crucified, entombed, and resurrected from the dead; the anointed one of Daniel's 70 weeks is cut off.	Mat 27-28; Mar 15-16; Luk 22-24; Joh 19-20; Dan 9:26	8
During 40 days[1]	John's vision of the throne room begins, in which the 24 elders and the four living creatures are present, but the Lamb is absent.	Rev 4 – Rev 5:4	10
40 days after the resurrection	Jesus Christ ascends to heaven from the Mount of Olives to sit at God's right hand.	Luk 24:50-52; Act 1:9-11	11
31-32 AD	The Lamb appears in the middle of the throne room in heaven; moves to the right hand of God and takes the scroll; the "new song" is sung by the 24 elders and the four living creatures.	Rev 5:5-10	11

---

[1] Jesus was with the disciples after his resurrection for 40 days, according to Acts 1:3, before he ascended to heaven.

Timeline	Event Description	Scripture	Chapter
31-32 AD	The Lamb begins to open the seven-sealed scroll; within the first five seals are revealed what at that time was future, but is currently <u>ongoing</u> history.	Rev 6:1	11
31-32 AD TO PRESENT	Seals one, two, three, four, and five are opened. | | | | | | | | | | | | | | | | | | | | | | | | | Seals one, two, three, four, and five continue until the present.	Rev 6:2-11	12 – 15

Events that will trigger the sixth seal events, including the resurrection of the dead in Christ, the transformation of the bodies of believers to immortality, and the catching up of all believers:

1. The gospel is preached as a witness throughout every nation. (Matthew 24:14)
2. The full number of Gentiles will be grafted into the new covenant cultivated olive tree with Jewish roots. (Romans 11:17-25)
3. The full number of Christians are violently killed for their witness, and the Lord hears the cry of vengeance for the shedding of innocent blood. (Revelation 6:9-11)

*****THE GAP BETWEEN THE 69TH AND 70TH WEEK, SO FAR NEARLY 2,000 YEARS*****

Timeline	Event Description	Scripture	Chapter
In the Future…	The three-stage resurrection, transformation, and catching-up event takes place at the opening of the sixth seal: • The sun turns black and the moon turns blood-red • Massive worldwide shaking of the earth • Mountains and islands move as the earth's crust shifts • Stars appear to fall toward the earth as the earth's crust shifts • The sky is split apart	Rev 6:12-14; Joe 2:31	2 – 7
	The people on earth react to the sixth seal events: • Hide in the rocks and caves, which are more abundant due to the massive movement of the earth's crust • Cry for the rocks to fall on them and save them from God and the Lamb • Declare that the day of their wrath, the Lamb and God, has begun at this point.	Rev 6:15-17	7
In the Future…	Daniel's 70th and final week of prophecy begins, and the gap separating the 69th and 70th weeks ends; a pre-existing covenant or agreement is made strong by the coming prince.	Dan 9:27; Rom 11:25	9, 17
	In the heavenly throne room, an innumerable multitude of people is seen by John, comprised of the all transformed and caught-up believers.	Rev 7:9-17	16
	On the earth, the Lord turns his attention back to the salvation of Israel; the two witnesses come to Jerusalem; the 144,000 assemble for their mission.	Rev 7:1-8; 11:1-13	16
	The seven trumpet judgments begin.	Rev 8	15

- SELECTED BIBLIOGRAPHY -

Anderson, Sir Robert (1957, Tenth Edition). *The Coming Prince.* Grand Rapids, Michigan: Kregel Publications.

Goodgame, Peter D. (2005). *Red Moon Rising: The Rapture and the Timeline of the Apocalypse.* Xulon Press, www.xulonpress.com.

Griffin, G. Edward (1998, Third Edition). *The Creature from Jekyll Island: A Second Look at the Federal Reserve.* Westlake Village, California: American Media.

Habermas, Gary R. and J.P. Moreland (1992). *Immortality: The Other Side of Death.* Nashville: Thomas Nelson Publishers.

Hoehner, Harold W. (1977). *Chronological Aspects of the Life of Christ.* Grand Rapids, Michigan: Zondervan Publishing House.

Hunt, Dave (1994). *A Woman Rides the Beast.* Eugene, Oregon: Harvest House Publishers.

Möeller, Dr. Lennart (2002). *The Exodus Case: New Discoveries Confirm the Historical Exodus.* Copenhagen, Denmark: Scandinavia Publishing House.

Moorehead, William G. (1908). *Studies in the Book of Revelation.* Pittsburgh: United Presbyterian Board of Publication.

Mounce, Robert H. (1977). *The New International Commentary on the New Testament: The Book of Revelation.* Grand Rapids, Michigan: William B. Eerdman's Publishing Company.

Patten, Donald W. (1966). *The Biblical Flood and the Ice Epoch.* Seattle: Pacific Meridian Publishing Company.

Patten, Donald W. (1988). *Catastrophism and the Old Testament: The Mars-Earth Conflicts.* Seattle: Pacific Meridian Publishing Company.

Tipler, Frank J. (1994). *The Physics of Immortality.* New York: Doubleday.

Wilson, Ian (1986). *The Mysterious Shroud.* New York: Doubleday.

Wilson, Ian (1998). *The Blood and the Shroud.* New York: The Free Press.

Yancey, Philip (1995). *The Jesus I Never Knew.* Grand Rapids, Michigan: Zondervan Publishing House.

- ABOUT THE AUTHOR -

David W. Lowe was born in 1969 in Wichita, KS. He was dedicated to the Lord as an infant in an Assembly of God church, and was brought up from his youth with the belief that church was an important part of life, and that the Bible is the inspired Word of God. His parents, Jerry and Janice Lowe, were faithful to attend church almost every service that the doors were open.

When Mr. Lowe became a teenager, he was introduced to a program for youth by his brother Steve called Bible Quiz, in which teens from grades seven through twelve study selected books of the Bible in the King James Version. Teams are formed within a church, and a book or set of books is chosen to study during roughly the same time frame as a normal school year. During a season, participants learn the book or books to be able to answer questions in competition against other teams. During his participation in this program, his team made it to the National Finals competition five of the six years of his eligibility, and Mr. Lowe put to verbatim memory every verse of 14 books of the New Testament.

The events of September 11, 2001 provided an awakening for Mr. Lowe, and prompted him into an even deeper study of biblical prophecy and interpretation. As a result of this study, he has written several essays for publication on his personal web site, and developed the prophetic model as presented in this book.

Mr. Lowe works as a tax accountant for an oil refining and marketing company, and currently teaches a 3rd and 4th grade Sunday School class. He and his wife Vivienne of eight years live in Wichita, KS. Questions or comments about the content of this book can be directed to Mr. Lowe at his closely-monitored email address: david@earthquakeresurrection.com.

- NOTES -